9.95

W9-BMI-442

MAKING BUREAUCRACIES WORK

SAGE FOCUS EDITIONS

MAKING BUREAUCRACIES WORK

Edited by
Carol H. Weiss
and
Allen H. Barton

 SAGE PUBLICATIONS   Beverly Hills   London

Chapters 2, 4, 6, 7, 8, 11, 12, and 15 in this book originally appeared in a special issue of AMERICAN BEHAVIORAL SCIENTIST (Volume 22, Number 5, May/June 1979). The Publisher would like to acknowledge the assistance of the special issue editors, Carol H. Weiss and Allen H. Barton.

For information address:

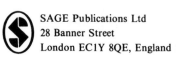

SAGE Publications, Inc.
275 South Beverly Drive
Beverly Hills, California 90212

SAGE Publications Ltd
28 Banner Street
London EC1Y 8QE, England

Printed in the United States of America

Library of Congress Cataloging in Publication Data
Main entry under title:

Making bureaucracies work.

   (Şage focus editions ; 22)
   Bibliography: p.
   Includes index.
   1. Administrative agencies—United States—Addresses, essays, lectures. 2. United States—Politics and government—Addresses, essays, lectures. 3. Bureau-cracy—United States—Addresses, essays, lectures. I. Weiss, Carol H. II. Barton, Allen H., 1924- III. Series.
JK421.M337   353.07   80-12774
ISBN 0-8039-1413-X
ISBN 0-8039-1414-8 (pbk.)

FIRST PRINTING

Chapter 5 is reprinted from *Public Administration Review* © 1977 by the American Society for Public Administration, 1225 Connecticut Avenue, N.W., Washington, D.C. All rights reserved.

Chapter 8 is a revised version of Chapter Four from *USABLE KNOWLEDGE: Social Science and Social Problem Solving,* by Charles E. Lindblom and David K. Cohen, published by Yale University Press.

CONTENTS

To Judith Weiss, who will make bureaucracies
work, if anyone can.

And to Stephen Barton, who will find out how to
democratize them, if they can be.

Efforts at Bureaucratic Reform

What Have We Learned?

CAROL H. WEISS
Harvard University

Bureaucracy is a word with a bad reputation. If you ask people to supply an adjective to go along with the noun, their choices will almost inevitably be pejorative. My recent horseback survey brought forth a list that included "sluggish," "cumbersome," and "byzantine," but the clear leaders in popularity were "swollen" and "inefficient."

Even dictionaries have nasty things to say about bureaucracy. The first meaning listed usually gives the definition we use in this volume: *administrative agencies, staffed predominantly by non-elective officials, that carry on the business of government.* But then comes a slurry of slurs: "government marked by diffusion of authority and adherence to inflexible rules of operation . . . any administration in which the need to follow complex procedures impedes effective action" (American Heritage Dictionary, 1975: 177); "administration characterized by excessive red tape and routine" (Random House Dictionary, 1969: 180); "rigid, formal measures or routine procedure in administration" (Webster's New Collegiate Dictionary, 1961: 111); "a system which has become narrow, rigid, and formal, depends on precedent, and lacks initiative and resourcefulness" (Webster's New International Dictionary, 1949: 358).

Similar—and more far-ranging—complaints abound in the work of scholars. Even Max Weber (1946) who celebrated the efficiency of rational bureaucratic organization lamented the constrictions it imposed on the human spirit. Jacoby (1973), like many others, is concerned about the conflict between bureaucratic organization and democratic values. In operation, bureaucracies are charged not only with rigidity but also with capture by special interests (Herring, 1936; McConnell, 1966), "technocratic power and arrogance" (Suleiman, 1974: 30), "wishy-washy" concern for their clienteles (Metcalf, 1977: 279), expansionist impulses (Parkinson, 1957), and a host of other greater and lesser ills. Crozier (1964: 4), in his study of French bureaucracies, uses the term explicitly to mean "the maladaptations, the inadequacies, or to use Merton's expression, the 'dysfunctions,' which necessarily develop within human organizations."

Complaints about government bureaucracies have probably been commonplace at every period of history and in every country. The United States has a long tradition of suspicion of the agencies that administer the public business. Over the generations, periodic calls have been made to "clean up the mess in Washington," and periodic efforts have been made to reform their organization and performance.

Within the past few decades, as government activities have expanded, public attention has focused largely on the substance of policy. But the growth in activity has led to a proliferation of government agencies—and to increasing impingement of bureaucratic rules and requirements on the daily lives of citizens. In this environment, concern about the shortcomings of bureaucracy rises. A series of reforms have been proposed—and some of them implemented—to cure the ills to which bureaucracy is subject.

The purpose of this book is to take stock of a set of reforms that have been instituted, tried, or advocated to improve agency performance. The authors of the following chapters each examine a particular proposal—its past experience and its prospects for future success. Through this collective effort, we hope to identify strategies that hold promise for making public bureaucracies more effective and collaterally to identify losers—strategies that generate more negative consequences than gains. The aim of the analysis is to give direction to efforts to make government agencies more effective, more efficient, and more responsive to the needs of the citizenry. It is an enterprise that requires all the wisdom and experience we can mobilize.

One of the limitations on past reforms has been that each was based on only partial analysis of "the bureaucracy problem." Contemporary reformers were sensitive to one striking category of failure or abuse— corruption, political patronage, favors to special interests, untidy organization, weak management, discrimination in recruitment—and they introduced changes to deal with that particular problem. But in so doing, they inadvertently generated side effects with untoward consequences. One generation's reform became the next generation's problem and called for new efforts to clean up the mess.

Many reforms are still enacted to cope with one highly visible aspect of a problem, in the expectation that side effects will be minimal. Only after they are implemented do the secondary effects—often unwanted effects—become apparent. The fact that well-meaning reform frequently brings new problems in its wake is largely the result of two-variable thinking: Change in A will lead to (desired) change in B. But what of probable changes in C, D, E, and F? The world is full of multiple effects—and high-order interactions.

Today's sophisticated analysts try to foresee the second- and third-order consequences of the changes under consideration. But even with all our concern, theories, systems language, and gadgetry, we are primitives in foreseeing the unanticipated consequences of planned social change.

But we do what we can. This collection is dedicated to the effort to see public bureaucracies in their multidimensional variety, to assess their shortcomings from a range of perspectives, and to consider the likely effects of a number of proposed remedies.

PUBLIC VIEWS OF BUREAUCRACY

Historically, Americans have been skeptical not only of government bureaucracies, but of government generally. The nation was founded on the doctrine of natural rights and a belief in the self-sufficiency of the individual. In the early years of the republic, overwhelming sentiment supported the Jeffersonian idea that "that government is best that governs least," and the idea of the limited state prevailed in American thought (although it was increasingly contravened in practice) well into the twentieth century (Fine, 1956). Slowly and reluctantly, it yielded to the pressures of a complex industrialized society, with the federal government moving into an active role first on behalf of business and industry, later to take up the cause of farmers, industrial workers, consumers, and eventually the poor. By the mid-twentieth century, views of the proper role of government had expanded to include the gamut of human problems.

But even as Americans accepted the desirability of a positive state, they remained ambivalent toward the civil service to which they had entrusted the tasks of government. Respect, or at least tolerance, has been punctuated with period outbursts of rancor. President Carter's 1976 election campaign was waged in large part against the muddling of "bloated, lazy, and ineffective" (New York *Times*, 1978) government agencies—sentiments that evoked sympathetic resonances in the voting public.

The public, according to recent public opinion polls, shows a splendidly nonpartisan skepticism about government operation and government spending. The Gallup Poll in October 1978 asked: "In your opinion, which of the following do you think will be the biggest threat to the country in the future—big business, big labor or big government?" By far the most common response was "big government." Of all respondents, 47% identified government, as did 52% of Republican respondents, 43% of Democratic respondents, and 51% of independents. (In comparison, 19% of the sample said big business, and another 19% said big labor, with the rest giving no opinion.) When the same question was asked in 1959, only 14% of the respondents had identified big government as the major threat. The October 1978 Gallup Poll asked: "Of every tax dollar that goes to the federal government in Washington, D.C., how many cents of each would you say are wasted?" The median of all responses was 48 cents; for Democrats, it was 49 cents, for Republicans 48 cents, and for independents 48 cents. (See the chapter by Smith, Taylor, and Mathiowetz for detailed analysis of public views.)

People seem to have a pervasive sense that government agencies are not working well. Out of the lavish array of complaints, two themes dominate the public and scholarly literature. One has to do with the ineffectiveness and inefficiency of bureaucracy, and dwells on a series of interlocking malfunctions. Bureaucracies, it is said, are the site of rigidity, red tape, the tyranny of the petty functionary brandishing the rule book. At the operating level, they are staffed by the lazy and the incompetent, people too concerned with their own rights and prerogatives to care about the people whom they are supposed to serve. The staffs of bureaucracies are entangled in petty rules and too timid to go beyond standard procedure to render needed service. A popular image is the staff gathering in clusters around the coffee machine, while clients stand for hours in unmoving lines waiting to be served. When a client finally reaches the desk, he is likely to be told that he failed to fill out some lengthy form in triplicate and must start all over again.

Oddly, the strands of this complaint point in conflicting directions. If the problem with bureaucrats is laziness, arrogance, and incompetence, a logical corrective would seem to be stronger managerial discipline—promotion and pay increases for the able worker and no pay increments, demotion, or dismissal for the nonproductive worker. But if the main problem is timidity and overcautiousness, staff unwillingness to sidestep any paragraph of regulations, no matter how unreasonable, for fear of retribution, then the appropriate remedy would appear to be greater protection from arbitrary action by superiors. Concern with protecting the public from sloth and indolence calls for trade-offs with the effort to encourage initiative and aggressive attention to client needs.

In the upper echelons, the inefficiency argument centers on rigid and stereotypical thinking. Bureaucracies are creatures of routine. They resist innovation, reject new information and new perspectives. The corridors of bureaucratic power are malodorous with musty old ideas, better suited to the needs of the past than the challenges of today. Further, the organization of bureaus is irrational—fragmented, uncoordinated. Authority is dispersed, and overlap, waste, and duplication devour public resources. Moving the cumbersome machinery to effective action requires strong managerial leadership, but leadership is endemically in short supply—because the weight of tradition and the absence of incentives work against its emergence.

The other main theme of contemporary criticism is that government agencies are unaccountable to the public or its elected representatives. In their massiveness and ubiquity, they have become a law unto themselves. No one—not the President, the Congress, appointed political officials, or the public—has the time and resources to move them from their customary channels of operation. Through continuity of tenure, inside knowledge of the ropes, and monopoly on expertise, they can shape the operation of enacted policies and influence the initiation of new legislation to suit the interests of the bureaucracy.

Unresponsiveness to the public has been viewed with alarm from two different perspectives. The lack of effective political control can mean open season for the predations of special interest, or it can allow the bureaucracies themselves to range out of control and pursue whatever purposes engage them. At the policy level, both tendencies have been amply documented.

The incursion of special interests into bureaucratic domains is a subject that engaged a generation of political scientists. In the absence of firm policy direction from political leadership, agencies often become subservient to well-organized pressure groups. They pay respectful attention to the demands of interests that are well financed, attentive, knowledgeable, highly motivated, and continuously represented, while the diffuse public interest is neglected. This type of criticism has historically been leveled from the left at pressure from economic interests, but in recent years, successful lobbying by environmentalists, minority group advocates, and citizen groups of several stripes has brought forth similar complaints from unexpected quarters. Bureaucracies, it is charged, are highly permeable to pressure from special-interest lobbies. (See Rourke's chapter in this volume for a useful discussion of "constituency" and "self-directing" agencies.) When executive agencies and special interest groups find allies in the relevant congressional committees, they form a bloc that is highly resistant to counteracting efforts—whether from the President, the cabinet officers, or the public.

If this argument contends that bureaucracies are unduly responsive to segmented special interests, more recent criticism contends that they are unresponsive to anything beyond their own walls. Uncontrolled by political leaders, bureaucrats have become active players of the game of politics, seeking to effect their own ends. In large part, their ends are the survival of their agencies and programs and the expansion of their own authority. Rather than neutral expert administrators, they have become self-serving self-aggrandizing actors, engaged in maneuvers for advantage within the departments and in negotiations with the Congress for budgets, staff, authority, and extended scope of mission (Downs, 1967; Halperin, 1974). The prevalence of bureaucratic politics, according to this view, means that policies are increasingly molded, from initiation to implementation, to accord with the interests of the bureaus.

Even when bureaucrats are acting from principle rather than from self-serving reasons, the absence of effective political control gives them wide latitude to impose their own values on the political process. Career officials come to their positions with commitments to particular professions and policies. Through training, experience, selective self-recruitment, and philosophy, they have allegiances to particular programmatic strategies for achieving the public good. They believe in nutrition services, vocational rehabilitation, drug enforcement, national parks, occupational safety, environmental regulation, and they press their definitions of need, equity, and right in the public arena. One result is pressure for continued growth of government programs, another is the continual identification of new "evils" or "needs" which only further expansion of bureaucracy can set right (Wilensky, 1975).

A major issue in the contemporary discussion about bureaucratic reform is the restoration of effective political control. The civics-book exposition is that the President, with a mandate from the electorate for his policies, directs the executive agencies. He appoints the heads of the agencies and, through his appointees, guides their activities. In practice, as presidents since Roosevelt's time have publicly bemoaned, presidential power is limited. Departmental secretaries are often coopted or immobilized by the department; bureau heads find ways to circumvent secretarial policy; departments are so large and diverse that no appointee has the time or specialized knowledge to make much impression; appointees stay for such brief periods that the bureaus can often wait them out. Unaccountability, despite repeated attempts at tightening the managerial reins, remains an issue of high concern.

The criticisms of ineffectiveness and of unresponsiveness are rag-bags of complaints. Our aim should be to sort them out and try to understand their origins and their complex interrelationships. Only with deeper insight into the processes that give rise to bureaucratic ills can we fashion appropriate remedies—remedies that do not introduce new iatrogenic maladies in the process. Barton's chapter in this book marks an effort in this direction. In very few pages and deceptively simple prose, he offers a trenchant analysis of the interlocking sources of bureaucratic pathologies. His model (see Figure 1 in his chapter) traces both inefficiency and unresponsiveness through a network of intervening variables to underlying political and technological sources. Still, as Rourke (1969) and others have noted, remedies that appear well designed to enhance the responsiveness of bureaucracy sometimes have perverse consequences on effectiveness, and vice versa. Cross-linkages in the system have to be taken into account.

RECENT TRENDS

Government bureaucracies in the United States do not appear to be in a period of particular crisis. No special episodes or major scandals have recently triggered public alarm. Certainly instances of corruption have come to light, such as the kickbacks and payoffs in the General Services Administration. Charges of mismanagement, inappropriate rule-making, and backlogs of paperwork have been leveled at a number of agencies. But normal processes of review and reform seem to be keeping problems under reasonable control.

Compared to the attacks on bureaucracy of not so long ago, all seems relatively quiet on the bureaucratic front. Yet a low-level discontent persists with the conduct of executive agencies. And some important trends are developing that may well put bureaucratic reform back on the public agenda.

(1) Declining public confidence. Over the past 20 to 25 years, public opinion polls show declining levels of public confidence in the agencies of government. True, public confidence in other institutions—from the medical profession to the corporation—has also fallen, and among branches of government, there is little evidence that executive agencies are in particular disrepute. Nevertheless, there is cause for concern when citizens have little trust in the agencies that transact the daily public business. Continued decline in the legitimacy of public institutions may in the long run have serious consequences.

(2) Economic stringency and taxpayer resistance. Inflation, declining productivity, a leveling-off of the Gross National Product (GNP)—these factors suggest that the nation is reaching a limit on government expenditure. Spending by governments—federal, state, and local—is approaching 40% of the GNP. And beyond their direct expenditures, governments generate requirements on the private sector (ranging from extensive reports to facilities for the handicapped) that call for further large expenses. (See Bok, 1980, for the effects of government rules on university costs.) Taxpayers are showing increasing resistance to the continued growth of the public portion, and the day may come when limits are clamped on government budgets.

Without a bigger pie to accommodate the demands for all the causes and programs that have a claim to public support, more competition will ensue for each slice of the pie—and greater demands will be made for an end to waste and inefficiency. Government agencies cannot expect automatic infusions of "more"; they are called upon for increasing proof of "better."

(3) Density and interdependence of agencies. Not so long ago, when a new social problem became the target of government action,

a new program and a new agency were set up to deal with it. The agency entered a relatively empty field and was able to proceed expeditiously with its tasks. Nowadays, when a new program or agency is established, it confronts a crowded program space—filled with similar or competing programs jostling for influence (May and Wildavsky, 1978). In fact, it is often the inadequacies or negative side effects of earlier government programs that generate the need for a new program. So each agency has to stake out its turf, struggle for its niche, and contend with its predecessors. It has to negotiate issues of duplication and overlap, incompatibilities in eligibility requirements and territorial boundaries of service. Specification of appropriate service becomes conceptually and practically more difficult. Demands escalate for better coordination. The strain on managerial competence increases.

(4) High-complexity high-uncertainty missions. As the government takes on new missions, it deals with progressively more complex problems. The easier problems have been brought under control. Today's issues, such as energy, inflation, and the environment, involve complicated trade-offs. Congress often gives the agency only the most general direction, either because it lacks specialized knowledge or because its members cannot agree on specifics. The agency finds little direction in previous experience; tradition and the rule book are unavailing. The lore of the professions—economics, medicine, engineering, and so on—are only a partial guide. Whereas the strength of bureaucracy has traditionally resided in established procedure, bureaucrats now have to improvise. Without a satisfactory body of expertise, they engage in strategies of trial and error—with erratic results.

(5) Declining public faith in bureaucratic expertise. Because the new sorts of government action have taken the bureaucracies into poorly charted waters, they have often run aground. Rourke, in his chapter, offers in evidence such examples as the military failure in Vietnam, the economists' inability to control inflation and unemployment, and the helplessness of planners in dealing with the decay of cities. Even in many technological areas in which expertise is assumed to flourish, no "accurate" solution exists for questions of nuclear risk, safety of food additives, emission standards (see Majone's chapter).

Given the paucity of relevant knowledge, the lack of consensus among experts, and the heavy emotional loadings on many of the issues, emotions which are often rooted in basic discrepancies in social values, it is small wonder that the public is progressively less impressed with bureaucratic expertise. Bureaucracy derives much of its legitimacy from special knowledge. When the public questions the validity or even the existence of that special knowledge, a primary support of bureaucracy is underminded.

(6) Fragmentation of political parties. Just when bureaucracies are engaged in perilous and uncertain missions with inadequate ballast of knowledge, they find themselves buffeted from another quarter. In a political system with strong and disciplined parties, they could at least count on the support of the party in power. But the American party system, never as organized or orderly as its Western European counterparts, has continued to fragment. Voters evidence less and less party loyalty; ticket-splitting abounds. National party leadership has lost considerable ground even since Lyndon Johnson's day. Campaign laws have tended to encourage candidates for office to go their individual ways with less support from—and less allegiance to— the national party organizations. Changes in congressional rules have limited the authority of party leaders and committee chairmen. Where power in the Congress was once dispersed among a set of major and minor fiefdoms (Seidman, 1970), today the situation approaches one where everyone is in business for himself. In an increasingly un- ruly Congress, 100 Senators and 435 Congressmen are steering their own course.

For the agencies, the effect has been a multiplication of the number of overseers and a proliferation of demands. Agencies have to be sensitive to the interests and predilections not only of the party leaders or the chairman of their oversight subcommittee, but to any member with an interest in their business. In a situation of shifting coalitions, the imperative is to respond to the wishes of any member who can become troublesome and to placate (and if possible, to form alliances with) any member who is paying attention. The recent growth in congressional staffs has multiplied the number of people who make demands and negotiate accommodations.

If a bureau can find allies on Capitol Hill, it not only protects its programs and appropriations from random incursions from Congress- men with special axes to grind. It can also protect itself from control by the departmental secretary and other political appointees in the executive offices. The end run around the head of the department is a common feature of bureaucratic life. When a bureau has established support from the interest groups representing its constituency as well as its cognizant congressional subcommittee, it has formed the famous "iron triangle" that insulates it from presidential and executive control.

In the contemporary case, however, the critical feature of congressional politics for agency survival is the multitude of masters to be accommodated. Unresponsiveness to requests from a member of the Congress can bring down retribution; inability to convince congressional staffers of the wisdom of agency actions may portend cuts in budget, rejection of nominees, or prolonged investigation. The lesson early learned is to pay attention.

(7) Proliferation of single-issue interest groups. Just as the Congress is increasingly fragmented, so too is the other corner of the iron triangle, the interest group. Once upon a time, a canny bureaucrat knew the pressure groups that would follow the agency's actions and lobby on its issues. The interest groups tended to be large, well organized, and concerned with multiple issues. Typical were the big business groups and trade associations, labor unions, farm associations, professional associations, civil service unions, and such special constituency groups as veterans organizations.

Although such large and well-financed pressure groups generated abuses—they were able to press their demands with continuity and specialized skill at the expense of the more diffuse and underrepresented public interest—they provided a stable and well-understood environment. Today they continue to exist and prosper, but they have been joined by a multiplicity of new and competitive lobbies. Hundreds of new groups have been formed to press demands upon the legislative and executive branches (Berry, 1977). Segments of the population that were previously poorly represented now have their own representatives to advance their interests—on behalf of women, Mexican Americans, gays, unborn babies, exprisoners, the elderly, foster children, big cities, clean water, nuclear safety, and so on. Beneficiaries of government programs have organized, so that interest groups now represent directors of community mental health centers, university financial aid administrators, clients of welfare programs. The lobbying process is more democratic, serving a much wider array of interests, but it is also more of a free-for-all.

For the bureaucracies, a consequence of the growing array of specialized single-interest groups is the proliferation of demands. No longer do they deal with a stable set of organizations. They are besieged by a cacophany of advocates, and they are forced to forge a consensus across a broader spectrum of interests.

These, then, are some of the trends that are having repercussions on bureaucracies. All of them make the work of the bureaucracy less sheltered and secure. They expose the bureaus to more difficult tasks, more constraints, and more challenge. In this environment, the need for improvements in bureaucratic performance becomes a matter of increasing salience.

A BRIEF GLANCE AT HISTORY

In the early years of the republic, positions of consequence were staffed by the rich and well-born. (There were 780 civilian employees of the U.S. government in 1792.) Andrew Jackson sought to democratize government employment by a system of rotation, on the grounds that the duties of office were simple enough, or could be made simple enough, so that any intelligent person could quickly master them. In practice, rotation meant the distribution of public office in return for political support, and the spoils system put the political obligations of officeholders ahead of their public obligations. Although the resulting inefficiencies, corruption, and declining prestige of public employment made the system costly, before the Civil War "the extension of the spoils system accompanying the rise of democracy was popular and was even regarded by many as reform" (Hoogenboom, 1968: 7).

After the Civil War, opposition to the spoils system grew. The assassination of President Garfield in 1881 by a disappointed office seeker provided it with emotional support, and in 1883 a reluctant Congress finally passed the Pendleton Act, creating a merit system for employment and promotion. Originally the act applied to fewer than 10% of the approximately 107,000 federal civilian employees, but it laid the ground for an apolitical bureaucracy based on principles of merit and career service.

In subsequent years, measures were enacted to extend civil service protection and to insulate employees from political pressures. Safeguards were instituted against demands for political activity and against arbitrary actions by superiors. The zeal to protect the civil service from politics has continued strong, even into a period when critics claim that civil service regulation is preventing effective management—shielding incompetence, condoning waste, and encouraging inefficiency.

It is a consequence of the difficult history of the civil service movement that reformers have long concentrated on "negative protection" from political intrusion rather than on "positive duties and direction" (Heclo, 1977: 22). Only in recent years has concern about the growing power of an uncontrolled bureaucracy led to attempts to give superiors greater authority over personnel actions. (See Campbell's chapter on the civil service reform act of 1978.) That the need for protection is by no means past was demonstrated during the Nixon presidency. Appointment of political officials to what had been civil service positions was intended in large part to bring the departments under administration direction, but there were sufficient abuses of the process to rekindle the passion of the old conflicts (U.S. House of Representatives, 1976). The historical concern with the safeguard of the civil service from political intrusions continues to influence the course of reform.

But how does one—effectively and responsibly—bring the bureaucracy under political control? Presidents have made efforts to appoint cabinet secretaries with strong managerial competence, to increase the numbers of presidentially appointed officials (in some departments, they are beginning to form a new multitiered layer of bureaucracy), to employ new techniques of control, such as management by objectives, to expand the authority of the Office of Management and Budget, to increase the numbers of White House staff as a means to move certain decisions from the departments to safer home preserves and to oversee activities in the departments. Each of the steps has had mixed success.

Other moves have been taken or proposed to restore public oversight more directly—provisions for public participation in agency deliberations, sunshine laws, freedom of information, decentralization. The Congress has its own claims—and its own interests—in establishing control. The courts, too, have taken an increasingly activist stance in examining the procedures and content of agency decisions.

A challenge that continually faces the federal system is the maintenance of an autonomous civil service—officials appointed on the basis of merit, with secure tenure, and freedom to express their own judgments and use their own expertise—while at the same time making the service responsive to presidential policy direction. It is a difficult balance to strike. Career officials have commitments to policies and programs. Efforts by the President or his appointees to alter these policies often lead to conflict or stalemate—the resolution of which can shift to the committee rooms of the Congress. For those interested in better ways to manage the continuing and probably inevitable tension, it is important to recognize the validity of the conflicting claims—a protected service of competent and dedicated professionals on the one hand and responsiveness to the direction of publicly elected officials on the other.

THE RESIDENT EXPERTS
CONTRIBUTE TO THE DISCUSSION[1]

This book begins with two chapters that set the stage. Barton provides an analysis of the nature of the bureaucracy problem—its manifestations, its causes, and the mechanisms that sustain its continuation. He suggests how structural and political factors interact to reduce efficiency, innovation, and responsiveness to public wants. Smith and Taylor, with Mathiowetz, review public attitudes toward government with data from public opinion surveys. The questions in the major polls ask about "the executive branch of the federal government," without trying to separate attitudes toward the President from those toward the executive departments. As the analysis shows, much of the decline in public confidence in the executive branch is related to attitudes toward the President and presidential policies. This point can be dismissed as an artifact of question wording, but it suggests a matter of considerable substantive significance. People's attitudes toward public bureaucracies may well be affected by the extent of their confidence in, and approval of, the policies that are entrusted to the bureaucracies to administer.

The rest of the chapters in the volume discuss particular proposals for bureaucratic reform. Seven chapters address issues of the effectiveness and efficiency of agency performance. Here the techniques are primarily internal to the bureaucracy. The remedies discussed are: civil service reform (Campbell), competition among bureaus (Niskanen), policy research and analysis (Cohen and Lindblom), think tanks (Dror), stronger procedural requirements in the regulatory process (Majone), and better developed theories of program action (Michelson). The chapter by Mitchell despairs of greater bureaucratic effectiveness and proposes turning over many activities that government has assumed to the private sector which, disciplined by market forces, is inherently more efficient.

Issues that underlie these discussions are: What kinds of inefficiencies does each strategy address? What are the structural and political factors that generate and sustain the inefficiencies, and how effective is the plan for counteracting them? What are the limits on the potency of the plan? How does it affect the balance of other incentives and constraints that keep the bureaucratic system operating?

The other six chapters address proposals explicitly directed at the issue of responsiveness and accountability. They analyze the prospects of a variety of mechanisms to establish control over bureaucracies from outside.

The strategies discussed are: legislative oversight of federal agencies (Aberbach), judicial review (Horowitz), increased political control (Rourke), decentralization of agencies, intended in large part to increase the power of clients of government services or of state and local elective officials (Yin), public participation, specifically in the context of regulatory decision-making (Nelkin and Pollak), and at a more fundamental level, the development of a democratic socialist party (Fainstein and Fainstein).

Another chapter, that by Wildavsky, proposes a mechanism to check the unbridled growth in government expenditure—a constitutional limitation on spending. Although not a strategy to hold individual agencies more accountable for their actions, the proposal represents an "outside" control for subjecting the federal bureaucracy collectively to the spending restraint that the citizenry is increasingly demanding.

The discussion in these chapters focuses on two pivotal issues: What kinds of outside controls can effectively be instituted? How well will they work? For effective reform, we need to be alert to the categories of bureaucratic actions and abuses that each proposal is adept at checking (arbitrary action, bureaucratic self-aggrandizement, inertia) and the unanticipated consequences that each is likely to set off in an intricately interrelated system. The larger question is left to the reader: Where should effective controls properly be lodged? The President, the Congress, the courts, public interest groups and parties, the public directly—they are all contenders and legitimate claimants for certain kinds of bureaucratic oversight. For what behavior, through what kind of control, and most fundamentally, to what interests shall bureaucracies be kept responsive?

Obviously, the book does not consider every facet of organizational performance nor every prescription that has been advanced. Nor do the assembled authors all take a neutral stance; many of them have strong (and controversial) positions. But through the juxtaposition of a variety of complementary and clashing viewpoints, they illuminate large portions of the complex landscape.

All of the chapters focus on American experience. Of course, concern about bureaucracy is not a uniquely American phenomenon. The earliest and some of the most trenchant analyses have come from Europeans, and probably the most radical efforts to prevent bureaucratic rigidification were undertaken in Maoist China.

Nevertheless, American government has sufficiently unique characteristics to justify our parochialism. One is federalism, with checks and balances operating not only across executive, legislative, and judicial agencies but up and down the intergovernmental system. As Bagehot (1867) wrote, "The English constitution . . . is framed on the principle of choosing a single sovereign authority, and making it good: the American, upon the principle of having many sovereign authorities, and hoping that their multitude may atone for their inferiority." Other reasons are the convulsions of recent history. The key episodes are the War on Poverty, Vietnam, and Watergate. Along with their other connotations, the words conjure up images of government agencies (1) failing to make discernible headway against fundamental social problems, (2) failing in a military mission against a small and technologically undeveloped adversary, and (3) being subverted to serve partisan and illegal ends. The current Proposition 13 backlash against government spending is in part a reaction to this history, as is the increasing skepticism about the ability of government to accomplish all the wonders the citizenry (for all its complaints) still wants accomplished. Therefore we limit our attention (except for European examples in the chapter by Nelkin and Pollak) to recent experience in the United States.

TAKING STOCK

Having assembled a set of expert reports on the past experience and/or future promise of various series of reforms, what do we know?

Which of the proposals point the way to valuable change and which are unlikely to improve the performance of federal executive agencies? Can we discern a set of action prescriptions in the composite analysis?

It is with some misgivings that I attempt to draw up a scorecard. No brief summary can begin to do justice to the rich diversity of insight and opinion that the authors have brought to the discussion. Only the heavy mantle of editorial responsibility—and curiosity—prompts me to tot up the lessons learned.

My reading of the chapters suggests that none of the authors believes the reform of which he or she writes will "solve" the bureaucracy problem—or even a major part of it. Those who discuss reforms that have not yet been instituted—or instituted only partially or recently— are more sanguine than those who write about reforms that have been in place for some time. In prospect, the virtues of possible change loom large, whereas in retrospect the benefits appear less great—or are seen to be diminished by adverse consequences.

The authors find that experience with a number of reforms shows some positive consequences. They find reason for at least modest support of decentralization (Yin), judicial review (Horowitz), increased political control (Rourke), policy research and analysis (Cohen and Lindblom), think tanks (Dror), and citizen involvement (Nelkin and Pollak). But they are also sensitive to the frailties, the shortfalls, and the countereffects of such practices for far-reaching bureaucratic renewal. Yin, in reporting some positive effects attendant upon de-centralization, notes that there is little evidence of better outcomes for clients of decentralized agencies. Nelkin and Pollak indicate how procedures for public involvement in regulatory decision-making can not only open the process to a broader range of viewpoints but can also be used to coopt public support or cool out public opposition. Cohen and Lindblom devote most of their report on the use of research and analysis ("professional social inquiry") in government to the puncturing of bloated pretensions and expectations; their acknowledge-ment of the refreshing effects that analysis can have on musty systems of bureaucratic thought is at best implicit. Horowitz recognizes the courts' capacity to correct bureaucratic abuse and ineptitude and in-still a sense of accountability, but he counsels caution in relying heavily on the uncertain and unsystematic process of judicial review. Rourke points to the need to balance increased political control of agencies against the advantages of bureaucratic autonomy.

For some of the reforms discussed, little evidence has yet accumulated. We have relatively little systematic information about the consequences of legislative oversight (Aberbach), competition among bureaus (Niskanen), the recent civil service reform (Campbell), more systematic procedures in regulatory deliberation (Majone), better and clearer program theory to guide bureaucratic activity (Michelson). Yet the authors of these chapters tend to be hopeful about the benefits to be gained.

Their optimism is based on some experience. Niskanen, for example, cites the competition among the armed services in weapons development and the beneficial effects of competition upon the quality and cost of weapons systems. Campbell discusses the advantages that the new Senior Executive Service will provide for motivating top-level managers and rewarding them for superior performance. (For bureaucrats' own more limited expectations, see Lynn and Vaden, 1979.) Majone has complimentary words for the "paper hearing" procedure of the Environmental Protection Agency, which leads to careful and considered deliberation of proposed standards and increases the legitimacy of regulation to the regulated. But it is still early to conclude that these reforms, if elevated to the status of governmentwide principles, would have major impact on the quality of government action.

A few of the more far-reaching innovations proposed in the book are still on the drawing board. Wildavsky offers a set of arguments for a constitutional limitation on government expenditures. While he foresees obstacles to its adoption and notes possible use of spending mechanisms outside the budget to evade its provisions if it is adopted, he has hopes for the budgetary discipline it would provide. Mitchell's proposal for reduction of government activities is a piece of advocacy. How sanguine he is about the feasibility of such moves in a century that has steadfastly faced in the opposite direction can only be surmised.

At the other extreme, the Fainsteins propose a system of democratic socialism to counteract the maladies of bureaucracy—which in their view arise not from bureaucratic unresponsiveness, but from responsiveness to the wrong interests, the interests of corporate capitalism. They are not optimistic about the possibilities. A mass party of the working classes and poor which could change the system is nowhere in evidence.

The sum total of expectations, then, is measured—and mixed. The assembled authors recognize a variety of shortcomings in executive agencies that plague the administration of government activities, and they see some hopeful directions for improvement. But the effects are likely to be incremental rather than massive.

Mechanisms now in place in the American system can deliver incremental reforms. The pressure of public opinion, the concern of elected officials, the efforts of organized groups, all provide motor power to overcome inertia and reistance. University-based professors and researchers and private-sector experts with a professional interest in reform are providing analysis, evaluation, and invention—a body of knowledge and skills that is perhaps one jump ahead of the common-sense prescriptions of the past. In the absence of crisis, there is likely to be gradual improvement in the functioning of government services.

However, if the factors that are increasing demands on government agencies and reducing their capacity to respond continue to escalate, they may outpace this gradual progress. In such a case, more extensive reform of public bureaucracy may be called for, and fundamental questions will have to be asked about the organization of politics, government administration, and the private economy—and the adequacy of existing knowledge for devising solutions. Massive reform would probably require extensive changes in a wide range of political and social institutions—with consequences more far reaching and less easy to foresee than those attendant upon the specific reforms discussed here.

NOTE

1. Eight of the chapters in the book appeared in *American Behavioral Scientist*, Volume 22, Number 5 (May/June), 1979.

REFERENCES

BAGEHOT, W. (1867) English Constitution. London: Chapman & Hall.
BERRY, J. M. (1977) Lobbying for the People. Princeton: Princeton Univ. Press.
BOK, D. C. (1980) "The federal government and the university." Public Interest 58 (Winter): 80-101.
CROZIER, M. (1964) The Bureaucratic Phenomenon. Chicago: Univ. of Chicago Press.
DOWNS, A. (1967) Inside Bureaucracy. Boston: Little, Brown.
FINE, S. (1956) Laissez-Faire and the General-Welfare State: A Study of Conflict in American Thought 1865-1901. Ann Arbor: Univ. of Michigan Press.

HALPERIN, M. (1974) Bureaucratic Politics and Foreign Policy. Washington, DC: Brookings Institution.

HECLO, H. (1977) A Government of Strangers: Executive Politics in Washington. Washington, DC: Brookings Institution.

HERRING, E. P. (1936) Public Administration and the Public Interest. New York: McGraw-Hill.

HOOGENBOOM, A. (1968) Outlawing the Spoils: A History of the Civil Service Reform Movement 1865-1883. Urbana: Univ. of Illinois Press.

JACOBY, H. (1973) The Bureaucratization of the World (E. Kanes, trans.) Berkeley: Univ. of California Press.

LYNN, N. B. and R. E. VADEN (1979) "Bureaucratic responses to civil service reform." Public Administration Review 39, 4: 333-343.

MAY, J. V. and A. B. WILDAVSKY (1978) "Volume editor's introduction," in J. V. May and A. B. Wildavsky (eds.) The Policy Cycle. Beverly Hills, CA: Sage.

METCALF, L. (1977) "Bureaucracy," in J. Brigham (ed.) Making Public Policy. Lexington, MA: D. C. Heath.

McCONNELL, G. (1966) Private Power and American Democracy. New York: Knopf.

New York Times (1978) May 17: A-21.

PARKINSON, C. N. (1957) Parkinson's Law and Other Studies in Administration. Boston: Houghton Mifflin.

ROURKE, F. E. (1969) Bureaucracy, Politics, and Public Policy. Boston: Little, Brown.

SEIDMAN, H. (1970) Politics, Position, and Power. New York: Oxford Univ. Press.

SULEIMAN, E. N. (1974) Politics, Power, and Bureaucracy in France. Princeton: Princeton Univ. Press.

U.S. House of Representatives, Committee on Post Office and Civil Service, Subcommittee on Manpower and Civil Service (1976) Final Reports on Violations and Abuses of Merit Principles in Federal Employment Together with Minority Views. Washington, DC: U.S. Government Printing Office.

WEBER, M. (1946) "Bureaucracy," pp. 196-244 in H. H. Gerth and C. W. Mills (eds.) From Max Weber. New York: Oxford Univ. Press.

WILENSKY, H. L. (1975) The Welfare State and Equality. Berkeley and Los Angeles, CA: Univ. of California Press.

A Diagnosis of
Bureaucratic Maladies

ALLEN H. BARTON
Columbia University

THE "BUREAUCRACY PROBLEM"

In a democratic society, when people want something which they do not think either the free market or voluntary action can provide, they call on the government to act. The public in the nineteenth century demanded regulation of railroads and trusts, and laws were passed and agencies set up to do this. In the 1930s the public demanded that something be done about the Great Depression, and a whole collection of programs and agencies were set up to deal with its mass of problems. In the 1960s there was a public demand for more equality of opportunity, avoiding further degradation of the environment, and reducing the suffering of the poor, the mentally ill, and the handicapped; so the legislature passed laws, and created budgets and agencies, to act on behalf of the public to solve these problems.

But by the 1970s the public, legislators, experts in public affairs, and intellectual social critics were all expressing disappointment with government programs and agencies. The programs were costing too much, interfering too much with the private sector, and were not even working. The goals were said to be Utopian, the social techniques and knowledge inadequate, and the organizations for carrying out the programs were accused of being inefficient, irrational, noninnovative, unresponsive, wasteful, oppressive, and devoted to self-service or the service of narrow pressure groups.

Does this mean that we should give up on government as a means of solving social problems and urge instead voluntary action, utopian communities, or reliance on the profit motive of private enterprise? And if these do not work, should we lower our aspirations and face up to the tragic view of life—or at least of other people's lives? Or can ways be found to get government bureaucracy to work better? It is this possibility that we want to explore in this collection: how promising are a variety of remedies for the problems of public bureaucracy?

CAUSES OF THE PROBLEM

Before looking into the remedies, we should look at the explanations which have been offered for the problems. These focus on three parts of the governmental system: the personal traits of the bureaucrats, the structural arrangements of public bureaucracy, and the political system which has ultimate authority over the bureaucracy.

Public bureaucrats are often described as being lazier, less competent, more power hungry than people in comparable jobs in profit-making or nonprofit organizations. Sometimes it is suggested that public offices attract such people; it is often suggested that the structure and traditions of public bureaucracies turn otherwise decent people into "bureaucratic personalities," characterized by negativism, complacency, rigidity, and arrogance (Merton, 1940). Public bureaucrats are compared unfavorably with members of the professions, who are supposedly selected and trained for a commitment to the welfare of their clients and to standards of craftsmanship, and supported in that commitment by a professional community.

The structure of public bureaucracy is said to make it impossible even for well-motivated people to do a good job. Red tape—rigid rules and lack of managerial discretion—prevents efficient and innovative action by public officials, in contrast to the flexibility of action in the private sector. Civil service rules designed to prevent political purges and patronage make it impossible to fire the incompetent, or to hire and reward the competent and productive. The reward system is heavily biased against the risks of innovation compared with that of profit-making enterprises—the bureaucratic innovator who fails is crucified, while successful innovation has little payoff. Public agencies can only act within legally authorized jurisdictions, and these are fragmented both in terms of subject-matter and geographical area, so that effective problem-solving is impossible. Still worse the incentive system for bureaucrats is perverse: they are rewarded with power and privileges for expanding their budgets and staff, regardless of costs and benefits to the public. The decision processes of administrative agencies are said to be weak and irrational compared with those of market-oriented businesses or the scientific community: the bureaucrat does not weigh costs against benefits, or review the evidence the way a scientist would, or give all sides a hearing the way a judge would.

The political system which gives directives to the bureaucrats is also accused of failing to represent the desires of the public. Unlike the market it has to make all-or-nothing decisions, forcing the minority to "consume" the programs preferred by the majority. It is responsive to narrow, concentrated interests at the expense of the more diffuse interests of the great majority. This tendency is reinforced by the "unholy alliance" of pressure-groups, congressional committees over-representing special interests, and bureaucrats catering to these special interests. Those most in need of government help lack adequate political representation. Another set of problems arises because American parties traditionally emphasize spoils and patronage to support their organization, rather than ideology or policy concerns. The average citizen is said to be too poorly educated and informed to act directly on behalf of particular policies, so he must delegate decisions to legislators. But the all-or-nothing choice of candidates does not provide clear directives on a wide range of issues so the legislator is left under only weak public control, and subject to influence of strong pressure groups.

THE INTERLOCKING OF CAUSES

This collection of maladies is interconnected (Figure 1) so that it is hard to cure by changing any one factor. The interlocking causes can be summarized in a series of propositions (here keyed to the figure):

(a) a patronage-based party system has led reformers to impose rigid rules on personnel policies and contracting;
(b) the lack of either scientifically based or market-based measures of performance likewise causes the political leadership to impose rigid rules of procedure on the bureaucracy (Von Mises, 1944);

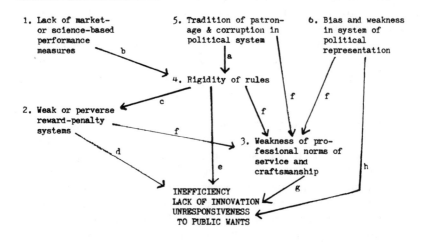

Figure 1: Interrelationship Between Structural and Political Problems of Public Bureaucracy

(c) the rigidity of rules thus created contributes to the weakness of rewards and penalties available to top management;

(d) weak reward systems reduce the motivation to do a good job, and are thus a major source of inefficiency and lack of innovation;

(e) rigid rules themselves are also a direct source of inefficiency, lack of innovation, and unresponsiveness to public needs, even for those who are motivated to do a good job;

(f) development of professional norms of service and craftsmanship, which might motivate doing a good job even in the absence of economic rewards, is discouraged by rigidity of rules, weakness of reward systems, and the political environment of patronage politics and pressure-group representation;

(g) weakness of professional norms of service and craftsmanship contributes to inefficiency, lack of innovation, and unresponsiveness;

(h) the bias in the political representation system toward narrow, highly organized interests makes the bureaucracy unresponsive to public needs.

PUBLIC BUREAUCRACY AND BUSINESS AND PROFESSIONAL ORGANIZATIONS

This diagnosis of the problems of public bureaucracy can be highlighted by comparing that bureaucracy with two other forms of organization for meeting public demands: competitive business firms, and professional service-providing organizations (Figure 2).

Structural characteristics	Competitive enter-prise in a free-market economy	Science-based professional organization	Public Bureaucracy
1. Performance measures (profits, cost-benefit analysis, technical output measures)	STRONG (except for external costs & benefits)	STRONG on benefits, WEAK on costs	WEAK
2. Organizational reward systems (pay, promotion, prestige for good per-formance, penalties for poor performance)	STRONG	STRONG	WEAK (or perverse rewards for cost increases)
3. Professional or ideo-logical socialization and norms emphasizing commitment to clients and craftsmanship	WEAK	STRONG	VARIABLE by agencies and profes-sions
4. Procedural rules flex-ible, permit innovation vs. rigid and hostile to innovation	FLEXIBLE	FLEXIBLE in permitting tech-nical innovation, may be rigid in other matters	RIGID
Political environment			
5. Pressures and opportun-ities for patronage & corruption	LOW in most but not all industries	LOW	HIGH in many localities & fields
6. System of representa-tion of public wants effective and unbiased vs. ineffective or biased	EFFECTIVE rep-resentation of consumer demand but biased by money income	WEAK represen-tation of public wants, priorities set by profes-sionals	BIASED repres-entation of strong narrow interests vs. diffuse, wide

Figure 2: Structural and Environmental Characteristics of Three Types of Organizations

Competitive market organizations are very responsive to effective demand—that is, demand backed by money—and they are very con-cerned with costs—except external costs which they do not have to pay, such as those of pollution or layoffs. (It is precisely the problems of income distribution in relation to human needs, and of external costs imposed on the community by private business, which motivate much government intervention in the economy. But it is clear that the public is highly satisfied with the job the market economy does in providing consumer goods and services.) The market demands of people with varying preferences can be met with little interference from majority and minority tastes—each can get what it wants, although majorities may enjoy lower prices due to economies of scale.

Profits provide business organizations with both a measure of cost-effectiveness in use of resources, and a means of rewarding entrepreneurs, investors, and managers, through increased wealth, income, and organizational expansion. In most areas of business, corruption and patronage are not supposed to be major problems because top management will not tolerate such abuses against profitability. The absence of professional norms of conduct in business is supposed to be compensated for by the profit incentive to respond to public demand, and the competitive penalties on fraud or bad workmanship. The rules and procedures of a business firm are supposed to be flexible and readily adjusted to changes in demand or production methods, and the profitability criterion makes possible a great deal of delegation of authority from corporate headquarters to semiautonomous production units.

Professional service-providing organizations which are based on the "hard sciences," such as those in the fields of medicine and engineering, have good technical measures of performance if they want to use them. Such organizations also offer their members strong incentives to perform well; there are rewards of prestige and power within the professional community for those who are talented, innovative, and productive, as well as incomes which are good, if not as lavish as those in business. They have weaker cost controls—an object of great concern these days—and their responsiveness to public wants is much less direct than that of business organizations: professional norms are supposed to induce a willingness to serve public needs in areas where the public itself cannot judge the quality of the service or even the need for services. Professional norms are supposed to oppose strongly patronage or corruption in the choice of personnel and in purchasing; and procedures are supposed to provide much delegation of decision to the individual professional and responsiveness of rules to technical innovation. (The "housekeeping" operations of large professional-service organizations which do not directly involve professional activities, however—hospital rules for handling patients or university rules for handling students, for instance—may tend to be "bureaucratic" and inflexible.)

It is worth noting that professional service organizations based on weaker scientific knowledge and techniques—such as schools, social work agencies, and mental health services—suffer from weak performance measures and have difficulty in rewarding effective work. Such organizations are often very innovative, but cannot evaluate innovations well, so that they tend to pursue "fads" without improving performance over time.

The comparison of these types of organization suggests that one remedy for bureaucracy problems is to have as many needs as possible met by the market and profit-making businesses, or by science-based professional service providers. One major trend in social reform design has been to emphasize payments to those in need which they can use to buy their own goods and services on the market, subsidies to private enterprise to provide jobs or perform services which they otherwise could not profitably do, and systems of collecting charges for pollution which will lead to the least costly means of reducing it. But as long as some things have to be done directly by the government it will need bureaucracies, and these bureaucracies will have to be made as efficient and responsive as possible.

THE BUREAUCRACY PROBLEM,
CLASS POLITICS, AND IDEOLOGIES

In an oriental despotism, the bureaucracy is part of a largely exploitative state, serving a dynastic family, an aristocratic class, and the bureaucrats themselves at the expense of the great majority. It may be providing some useful services, but its main function is exploitation and oppression. In conservative authoritarian states generally, the bureaucracy performs some mixture of public services and enforcement of ruling-class exploitation of the public. In Leninist-Stalinist party dictatorships, the ruling party and the bureaucracy merge to extract from the masses a large part of their production for investment in heavy industry and arms, with a promise of future abundance and equality. And in the meantime, the reality is a concentration of power and privilege in the party-bureaucratic ruling class.

In all these cases the state bureaucracy is readily identified as an enemy of the majority of the people. In a democracy on the other hand the government is supposed to be the servant of the people. The elected legislators and the chief executive are supposed to prevent the bureaucracy from being exploitative and self-serving. They are also supposed to manage a bureaucracy capable of doing what the public wants done, to provide services which the market cannot provide, redistribute income to the extent that the public feels the market distribution is inequitable, intervene in the business cycle when it fails to be self-regulating, prevent businesses from "externalizing" the costs of pollution, police fraud and exploitative practices against the weak or poorly informed citizens. Those who are regulated or whose income is redistributed may feel that the bureaucracy is their enemy even when it is acting according to the majority demand.

There is thus an interweaving of class interests and ideological issues in discussions of bureaucracy and its problems. To enhance the effectiveness of an exploitative, oppressive bureaucracy is to join the enemies of the people. To be "against bureaucracy" in a democratic capitalist society is to be against the welfare state, the labor movement, the consumer movement, the civil rights movement, and similar groups that want to use the voting power of the majority to counter the economic and social power of wealthy and privileged minorities. At the same time, inefficiency, self-serving or the serving of narrow interest-groups by the bureaucracy constitute serious barriers to achievement of the goals of the majority. The public necessarily has an ambivalent relationship to its "servant."

To the extent that the interests of the majority of the people can be served by methods which minimize the size and power of bureaucracy, they may find better "servants" to work for them—such as means of economic intervention that act through the market rather than requiring centralized planning or detailed enforcement. It is important therefore that attacks on "bureaucracy" be analyzed to see whether they advocate alternative means to serve the goals of the popular majority, or whether they are simply upholding the interests of privileged groups against the efforts of that majority to use its voting power to better its condition. However, the argument is rarely put in terms of simple upper-class interests. Rather, it is argued that existing differences in incomes, wealth, and power are necessary in order to produce a higher national income which will make everyone better off; or that the demands of the popular majority are unreasonable and will make everyone worse off if pursued. There is a correlation between optimism about government interventions and acceptance of egalitarian values, and pessimism about government and attachment to a society with large differences in wealth and income.

In particular the economists who believe most firmly in the virtues of inequality and private profit-making enterprise also are most pessimistic about government. They define politicians and bureaucrats as just as motivated by self-interest as businessmen, but operating without the "hidden hand" of competitive market pressures which turn the businessman's self-interest toward productive activities serving consumer demands. In politics and bureaucracy self-interest results in "vote-maximizing" and "budget-maximizing" actions which are necessarily wasteful and probably perverse in their effects on public welfare (Mitchell, 1978: 9). As a result of this analysis of motives and institutionalized reward-systems of government personnel, these conservative economists argue that the role of government, and of majority rule through politics, should be minimized:

> Majority rule, by its nature, cannot be very efficient. . . . In an age of increasing resource stringency, we must inquire whether a dollar spent in the public sector might be better spent in the private marketplace [Mitchell, 1978: 18].

The question, "better for whom?" is answered by conservative economists by saying essentially, better for the people who are entitled to their money by virtue of their contributions to production. The existing distribution of income and wealth are held to be the just result of the "productivity-income linkage of the market." Political interventions in the market are dismissed as either "the pursuit of private profit by means other than competition in the market," or the efforts of those "'too anxious to do good' who are enabled to dispense goods and social services at the expense of others" (Mitchell, 1978: 7). The assumptions of the justice of the distribution of income, wealth, power, and security resulting from the market economy, and of the selfish motives of politicians and bureaucrats generally combine to support a laissez-faire conservative ideology.

FROM CAUSES TO REMEDIES

For all the class and ideological bias of the conservative critics of "bureaucracy," they do point to serious problems in the expression and implementation of the preferences of the public in a democratic system, which must be considered by liberals who advocate use of the majority's political rights to regulate the economy and redistribute income. The socialist economist Oscar Lange once proposed that a statue of laissez-faire economist Ludwig van Mises be erected in the Ministry of Planning of the future socialist state, in honor of his forcing them to address the problem of the rational allocation of resources under socialism (for which Lange proposed market socialism as a solution). Liberal reformers might similarly want to set up statues of von Mises and other conservative critics in the vast government offices of the welfare state, in tribute to their raising issues of public choice and bureaucratic responsiveness and efficiency, for which the reformers will perhaps have found solutions.

The analysis of the causes of bureaucratic maladies presented here is oversimplified and we have not tried to review the evidence for it. However, it is intended to point to characteristics of the structure of bureaucracy and its surrounding political system, and to interrelationships among these characteristics, which have to be changed in order to cure the maladies. It suggests some approaches, if not any definite solutions: to improve performance measures, to bring bureaucrats into better communication with the people they are supposed to serve, to create means for the elected representatives to oversee performance, to create more market-like conditions to counter the weakness in reward-penalty systems in government, to strengthen control over bureaucracy by representatives of the wants and needs of broader sections of the public.

REFERENCES

MERTON, R. K. (1940) "Bureaucratic structure and personality." Social Forces 18. (Reprinted in Merton, 1968, Social Theory and Social Structure, pp. 249-260. New York: Free Press.)

MITCHELL, W. C. (1978) "The anatomy of public failure: a public choice perspective." Los Angeles, CA: International Institute for Economic Research, Original paper, June 13.

VON MISES, L. (1944) Bureaucracy. New Haven, CT: Yale Univ. Press.

Public Opinion
and Public Regard
for the Federal Government

TOM W. SMITH
D. GARTH TAYLOR
with NANCY A. MATHIOWETZ
University of Chicago

INTRODUCTION

Analyses of public regard for the federal government, trust in government, and confidence in government are in great demand. Compared to other opinion measures, the trust and confidence questions are second only to the polls on presidential popularity in the amount of attention they receive from lawmakers and policy makers. In spite of the publicity and scholarly attention, the trends in public confidence are still enigmatic to the policy maker and the professional opinion researcher alike. No one disagrees that the level of public trust was lower in the middle 1970s than it was in the 1960s or early 1970s. Each of us also has a general sense of why. We locate the cause in the exposure of government deception during the Vietnam war and during Watergate, in the "discovery" of deceptive or unsafe business practices by consumer protection groups, or in the frustrations of an inflation-recession economy. But a refined, statistical understanding of the

Authors' Note: *This research was supported by NSF Grants SOC77-03279 and SOC75-14660. Further support was obtained from the Graduate School of the University of Wisconsin and from the resources of the National Opinion Research Center. We would like to extend special thanks to Toshi Takahashi for timely and capable assistance with manuscript preparation and to Mary Utne and Allen Barton for favoring the manuscript with a thoughtful reading.*

recent trends in confidence and trust has so far eluded us. From the point of view of opinion researchers, loss of trust has been an "across the board" shift. The ethnic and demographic subgroups which have normally differed in their interests and competed for success in the political arena do not differ on the issue of trust and confidence in government (House and Mason, 1975). Because of this, the constituencies on the "trust" issue have been hard to define politically, and the issue has therefore been a difficult one to turn to political advantage. The exception to this rule has been the "fresh faces" who have successfully challenged incumbent officeholders on the ground that the latter have been tainted by their exposure to the federal bureaucracy.

The loss of confidence has been described as "across the board" in at least one other way as well. The decline in trust in major business corporations has been partly explained by the fact that "things are tough all over" (Lipset and Schneider, 1978). By this the authors mean that public confidence in a great many national institutions (e.g., the legislature, the courts, organized religion) is sagging, that the phenomenon is endemic to the social order, and that the causes and/or consequences of the decline cannot be placed uniquely at the door of any particular institution.

Not only have the trends in trust and confidence been hard to explain statistically, but the research has not been done to show the *effect* of a loss of confidence. In other words, we all have a sense that the trends should not be ignored, but we are hard put to say exactly what they mean—what are the consequences of a loss in confidence for the leaders or for the institutions in question. Some say that the confidence questions simply measure a transient national mood (Ladd, 1976-1977) or the popularity of the president (Citrin, 1974). Others write as if fundamental questions of national legitimacy and national purpose were at stake (e.g., Miller, 1974).

In this chapter, our goal is a description of the trends in confidence and an analysis of the causes and consequences of these trends.

TRENDS IN PUBLIC CONFIDENCE
IN GOVERNMENT

According to our search of the General Social Survey (GSS) data archives at the National Opinion Research Center (NORC), there were 25 surveys of the national adult population between 1966 and

March 1977, done either by NORC or the Harris Poll which asked a version of the following question: "I am going to name some institutions in this country. As far as the people running these institutions are concerned, would you say that you have a great deal of confidence, only some confidence, or hardly any confidence at all in them?" Then follows a list which typically includes institutions such as organized religion, banks and financial institutions, organized labor, and the executive branch of the federal government. One of the barriers to a trend analysis of the confidence questions is that no two administrations of the confidence question are exactly alike. Surveys differ in the position of the confidence question in the questionnaire, the introduction to the list of institutions, the number and order of institutions asked about in the list, the timing of the survey (there are only one or two cases where NORC and Harris did surveys during the same field period), and in the mechanics of questionnaire administration (the NORC surveys handed the respondent a card with the response categories printed on it, while the Harris surveys did not).

Turner and Krauss (1978) have raised the question of whether these survey questions are too "fallible" to be analyzed as a time series. The statistical analyses which we report here support our belief in the general validity of the construct of "confidence" and in the comparability between the NORC and Harris data sources.

In this analysis, we concentrate on the trends in confidence between 1972 and March 1977. This was a turbulent period in American political history, and in no way should it be considered a typical time for studying trends in confidence. On the other hand, almost all of the available data points are concentrated in this period. We prefer to concentrate on the detailed pattern of changes corresponding to the sudden emergence of political events rather than on the broader sweep of change since the 1960s, which has been discussed by other authors.

The trends from 1972 to 1977 in the percentage having a great deal of confidence in the executive branch of the federal government are shown in Figure 1. This figure shows the results from the Harris and the GSS surveys separately, with the Harris results in the solid line and the GSS results in the dotted line. The general pattern of change is a decline in confidence between 1972 and March 1974; a leveling-off (except for some fluctuations), and then an increase in confidence after June 1976.

To aid in the interpretation of Figure 1, we have constructed a time line showing the political events occurring during the field period or

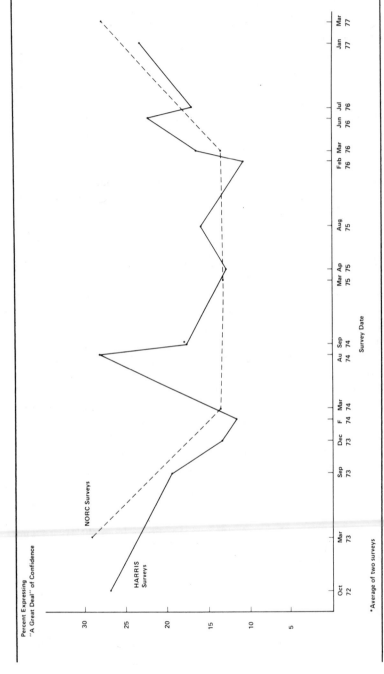

Figure 1: Recent Trends in Confidence in the Executive Branch of the Federal Government

shortly before the field period for each survey. This chart, along with the percentage reporting a great deal of confidence in each survey are shown in Table 1.

Figure 1 and Table 1 are well worth a detailed reading. They document several of the characteristics of public opinion (and of the confidence items in particular) which we often believe are true but which we are sometimes uneasy assuming because we are afraid of projecting too much of our own rationality into speculations about the public philosophy.

The changes in confidence are best understood by dividing Figure 1 into three historical periods. The first period—October 1972 to March 1974—shows a steady decline in confidence and corresponds to the erosion of Nixon's hold on the presidency after his landslide victory over McGovern in November 1972. In August 1974, the level of confidence is suddenly quite high again; this point corresponds to the inauguration of Gerald Ford as Nixon's successor in the White House.

During the period of Ford's presidency—from August 1974 to July 1976 on our graph—the level of public confidence shows a sudden drop, corresponding to his pardon of Nixon, and then a slower decline, with fluctuations which might be attributed to other national political events (such as the rise in confidence during the weeks preceding the bicentennial). The third period, the Carter presidency—January 1977 to March 1977 on our graph—begins with a level of confidence about as high as any other time measured since 1972.

It is clear from Figure 1 and Table 1 that there are meaningful short-term changes in confidence. The percentages are influenced by changes in the political environment, or to put it another way, confidence is at least partly episodic. The political environment and the level of confidence can change greatly within a brief span of time, which means that surveys of public confidence taken even a month or two apart should not necessarily be considered to be exact replications of the same procedures on the same population.

The fact that the confidence questions are susceptible to short-term influences places them in the category of "volatile" social indicators. In interpreting shifts in confidence, the question naturally arises—how important are the short-term changes? We attempt to answer this question in various ways in this report. First, we examine what people mean when they say they are confident in the executive branch, and we compare trends in confidence with trends for other indicators of attitudes toward the government and toward office-holders.

TABLE 1

Events Taking Place During or Immediately Preceding the Field Period for Surveys Measuring Confidence in the Executive Branch of the Federal Government

Survey Date	Events	Percentage with "Great Deal" of Confidence[2]	Survey[3]
Jan 67[1]		37.2	H1702
Oct 72	Final month of Nixon-McGovern contest	27.2	H2236
Mar 73	Last American troops leave Saigon	29.3	GSS73
Sep 73	Agnew investigation announced, Watergate hearings, Nixon accepts blame for Watergate but refuses to resign	19.4	H2343
Dec 73	18½ minute tape gap testimony	13.4	H2354
Feb 74		11.7	H7482
Mar 74	Mitchell, Haldeman, and Erlichman indicted	14.6	GSS74
Aug 74	Ford inaugurated	28.3	H7487
Sep 74	Ford pardons Nixon	20.0	H2430
Sep 74		17.7	H2434
Mar 75	Ford institutes antirecession policies	13.3	GSS75
Apr 75	Communist victory in Vietnam	16.5	H7581
Aug 75	Helsinki agreement, government announces largest peacetime fiscal deficit	16.0	H7585
Feb 76	Primaries begin	10.8	H2521
Mar 76		13.5	GSS76
Jun 76	Preparation for bicentennial, primaries end	22.3	H7684
Jul 76	Ford vetoes Humphrey-Hawkins, Carter nominated	14.5	H2630
Jan 77	Carter inaugurated	23.3	H7690
Mar 77		27.9	GSS77

1. There is one earlier Harris survey measuring confidence, done in 1966. The data for this study have disappeared, so results cannot be replicated or analyzed. Therefore, we do not use this study in our report.
2. Percentages calculated on a case base which includes "don't knows" and excludes missing data, no answer, and so on.
3. "H" denotes a Harris survey, "G" denotes the General Social Survey by the National Opinion Research Center. All surveys are quota samples of the national population with a few exceptions. In some cases, Harris screens people out of the sample if they are not politically active, which changes the percentages slightly. The 1977 GSS was a full probability sample.

THE MEANING OF "CONFIDENCE"

On the 1978 General Social Survey, a random subsample participated in a postinterview debriefing on the confidence questions. They were asked two questions about the meaning of the concept of confidence:

- When we ask about "confidence" in these questions, what does that word mean to you?
- Is there a word of phrase that would be more clear than "confidence" but would describe the same idea?

The object of these questions was to see if respondents understood the word confidence and to see how they defined it. In Table 2 their responses are grouped into twelve major categories. Approximately 95% of the respondents gave a reasonable definition of confidence. Only 2.2% declined to offer a definition—close to the level who give a "don't know" reply to a typical attitude item. Another 3% gave a response that could not be considered a reasonable definition, most commonly consisting of attempts to define confidentiality. Of the 95% giving appropriate definitions, the overall favorite choice was that confidence in the people running institutions means trusting them. Almost 35% mentioned the word "trust" in their response. In addition, the closely related terms "having faith" or "believing in" the leaders were selected by 10% and 12%, respectively. Also closely related to the idea of "trust" were 4% mentioning "honesty," "truthfulness," or some related term, and the 2% replying that it meant you could be "sure" or "certain" of the leaders.

Another major emphasis in the definitions was on capability. Almost 16% stated that having confidence in the people running institutions meant thinking that the leaders were competent and had the intellectual and practical abilities needed to carry out their duties. Related to this notion, as well as to trust, were those definitions emphasizing dependability. This 3% tended to blend together the trust and capability dimensions and considered these two features to be part of dependability.

A third major distinction was made by the 3% who mentioned the common good. They stated that having confidence meant knowing the leaders were acting in the best interest of the country, that they were doing what the common welfare required rather than following either the wishes of special interests or their own personal inclinations.

TABLE 2

RESULTS FROM AN OPEN-ENDED QUESTION
ASKING PEOPLE TO SAY WHAT THEY MEAN
BY THE WORD "CONFIDENCE"

Key Word or Concept	Proportion of Responses in Each Category
Trust	34.5
Capability	15.9
Believe in	12.4
Faith	10.0
Miscellaneous	5.4
Honesty	4.3
Common Good	3.7
Dependability	3.4
Approval	3.0
Incorrect Response	3.0
Sure	2.2
Don't Know, Nothing	2.2
	100.0

N = 830 responses from 738 cases

Data are from the 1978 NORC General Social Survey.

The final major distinction was in sharp contrast to the common good concept. This 3% stated that having confidence in leadership meant that the leadership was doing things that the respondent approved of, carrying out policies that the respondent personally favored.

These different emphases were not always mutually exclusive. About 12.5% of respondents gave multiple responses. For all categories except miscellaneous and dependability, trust was the category most commonly accompanying other choices. For example, of the people mentioning capability, 30% also mentioned some other concept, with 10% of them also using the word "trust." Similarly, of those choosing the common good, 42% also included another category, with "trust" again leading. Of the four major dimensions, only the common good and personal approval did not overlap at all.

When asked for a substitute term for confidence, the majority (58%) replied that there was no preferable word and that confidence was fully satisfactory. Those who offered alternatives gave the same list of terms they had mentioned previously, with 20% naming trust

(48% of those mentioning an alternative), 4% faith, 3.5% believing in, 3% dependability, 3% honesty, 2% capability, 1% respect, 1% approval, and 5% miscellaneous and incorrect. Compared to the high percentage of people giving an acceptable definition of confidence (95%), the low level of people giving an alternative (42%) indicates that confidence is a meaningful and perhaps even preferred term for the evaluation of institutional leadership.

As with other inquiries into the meaning of public opinion, this discussion of the confidence question may raise more questions than it answers. In reviewing this chapter, Allen Barton suggests that the CSS respondents provided synonyms for confidence rather than responses reflecting the bases of confidence. He suggests that meaningful answers would have required probing and that the proportion of respondents who gave their bases or reasons for confidence is too small to draw conclusions about the relative importance of honesty and competence, for instance, or the extent to which government is perceived as devoted to special interests rather than the common good. While we agree with much of this criticism, we believe that the results reported here are an important first step in assessing the meaning of the confidence items.

CONFIDENCE AND TRUST:
THE CHANGING NATIONAL MOOD

Following from our understanding of the public's conception of "confidence," we interpret the trends in Figure 1 to mean the national mood has changed so that people are less trusting of the objectives and leaders of the executive branch of the federal government. We are less likely to believe that the executive branch (and other national institutions) will govern themselves in a way which is mindful of the common weal, and there are even questions as to whether institutions can administer themselves competently.

There are several other time series which are parallel to the trends we have observed in confidence in the executive branch. These are the Michigan (SRC) questions on political cynicism, the Michigan questions on political efficacy, and the Harris alienation items.

The longest series on political cynicism comes from the election surveys conducted by the Center for Political Studies, Survey Research

Center, University of Michigan. Since 1958, these surveys have included a political cynicism scale comprised of the following questions:

(1) Would you say the government is pretty much run by a few big interests looking out for themselves or that it is run for the benefit of all the people?
(2) Do you think that people in the government waste a lot of the money we pay in taxes, waste some of it, or don't waste very much of it?
(3) Do you feel that almost all of the people running the government are smart people who usually know what they are doing, or do you think that quite a few of them don't seem to know what they are doing?
(4) How much of the time do you think you can trust the government in Washington to do what is right—just about always, most of the time, or only some of the time?
(5) Do you think that quite a few of the people running the government are a little crooked, not very many are, or do you think hardly any of them are crooked at all?

The wordings vary slightly some years. Except for the change in the crookedness item (question 5) between 1972 and 1974, none of the variations is notable. In 1974 and 1976, the crookedness item dropped the phrases "a little" and "at all," thereby making it harder to give a cynical response.

In Table 3, the proportion giving the cynical or mistrusting responses to each of these items is shown. Looking at the individual items in the scale, we see that from 1964 to 1976 the proportion believing that special interests rule more than doubled, from 31% to 73%. The proportion believing that taxes are being wasted climbed from 45% in 1958 to 76% in 1976. Those thinking that leaders are not smart rose from 39% to 53%; mistrust went from 24% in 1958 to 66% in 1976; and suspicions of crookedness climbed from 26% in 1958 to 38% in 1972. The revised version of the question hit 47% in 1974 before it tapered off to 44% in 1976.

Personal political efficacy (a person's sense that he or she can influence the political system and governmental decision-making) follows a trend distinct from political cynicism and alienation. Michigan's three-point scale asks:

(1) People like me don't have any say about what the government does.
(2) Sometimes politics and government seem so complicated that a person like me can't really understand what's going on.
(3) Voting is the only way that people like me can have any say about how the government runs things.

In general, this scale shows a slight rise in efficacy in the 1952-1960 period, stability in the 1968-1976 period, but with a major drop in

TABLE 3
TRENDS IN POLITICAL TRUST, POLITICAL EFFICACY, AND OTHER MEASURES OF PUBLIC ATTITUDES TOWARD THE FEDERAL GOVERNMENT, 1952-1976

Survey Questions	Percentage Agreeing With Each Statement, Year										
	1952	1956	1958	1960	1964	1966	1968	1970	1972	1974	1976
Political Trust											
1 Special interests rule					30.9	38.5	43.6	55.1	58.6	72.9	73.4
2 Taxes wasted			45.1		48.1		60.6	69.7	67.0	75.8	76.4
3 Leaders not smart			39.3		27.8		39.2	46.2	42.2	48.0	53.0
4 Untrustworthy			24.3		22.3		37.3	45.3	45.9	63.1	65.5
5 Crooked			25.6		30.0		26.3	32.7	37.7	46.8	44.1*
Political Efficacy											
1 Have no say	31.5	28.3		27.4	29.6		41.2	35.8	40.5	41.3	42.2
2 Politics too complicated	71.3	63.8		58.8	67.9		71.3	73.8	73.9	73.3	72.7
3 Voting is only recourse	82.7	74.5		74.3	74.0		57.4	60.6	62.3	61.5	56.5
Other Measures											
1 Government does not listen a good deal of the time					66.0		75.4	75.5	82.2	90.6	89.2
2 Government doesn't care	35.8	27.0		25.0	37.0		43.7	48.7	50.1	52.2	53.7

For question wordings and data sources, see text.
*See discussion in text of change in wording of the Michigan "crooked" question in 1976.

between. The story line is complicated, however, by the likelihood that the meaning of the vote-only question changed between 1964 and 1968. The upsurge in civil rights demonstrations, antiwar protests, and other acts of civil disobedience empirically disproved the idea that voting was the only way to influence the government. This may account for the rise in inefficacy shown by the other measures in the mid-1960s at the same time as there is a decline in inefficacy on the vote item. For further discussion of the problems with this item, see Converse (1972), House and Mason (1975), and Wright (1976).

In sum, it appears that even though both political cynicism and inefficacy have increased, the pattern and magnitude of the changes have been different. Cynicism has increased dramatically since 1958 with large increases in 1964-1968 due to Vietnam and in 1972-1974 due to Watergate. Inefficacy on the other hand has increased moderately, with most of the rise in the mid-1960s and *no* Watergate effect in the early 1970s.

The trends of the political cynicism scale are mirrored by changes in the Michigan questions on governmental responsiveness ("Over the years, how much attention do you feel the government pays to what the people think when it decides what to do: a good deal, some, or not much?") and concern ("I don't think public officials care much what people like me think.") Both show increases in alienation since the mid- or early-1960s.

Table 4 indicates that the rise in cynicism was paralleled in the 1970s by Louis Harris's index of alienation. This five-item scale asks people to agree or disagree with the following statements:

(1) The people running the country don't really care what happens to you.
(2) The rich get richer and the poor get poorer.
(3) What you think doesn't count very much anymore.
(4) You're left out of things going on around you.
(5) Most people with power try to take advantage of people like yourself.

As Watergate unraveled between 1972 and late 1973, the alienation index (the average of responses to the five items) went up fifteen percentage points. A slight drop appeared in August 1974 when Gerald Ford assumed office, but by September, after Nixon's pardon, alienation moved up again. (Gallup's measure of presidential popularity or approval also fell sharply during this period.) Alienation continued to rise into 1976, but some time between then and 1978 recovered to some extent, since the 1978 General Social Survey showed a decline

TABLE 4

TRENDS IN THE HARRIS ALIENATION INDEX, 1972-1978

Survey Questions	Percentage Agreeing, Survey, Date						
	H2236 10/72	H2343 9/73	H7487 8/74	H2430 9/74	H2434 9/74	H2521 2/76	GSS78 3/78
1 Public officials don't care	38.6	54.9	47.7	55.2	55.3	61.2	51.3
2 Rich get richer	60.3	75.4	77.0	77.6	77.4	77.3	73.8
3 Your thoughts don't count	45.1	61.0	53.6	58.2	57.0	64.0	55.1
4 Feel left out of things	17.8	28.1	31.6	39.2	39.9	42.1	28.3
5 Powerful take advantage	36.6	54.1	55.9	60.4	59.3	63.1	55.6

For question wordings, see text. For a discussion of data sources, see the notes for Table 1.

in all measures of alienation. In brief, the alienation index shows the same upward growth in mistrust as the political cynicism scale and likewise shows a large Watergate upsurge.

Each of these trends supports the interpretation we have offered of the meaning and sensitivity of the confidence in government question. When we look at these trends together, we can see that the recent decline in confidence in government is not only registered by the confidence question: Other measures of the national mood show similar changes beginning much earlier than 1972.

On difference between the items reported in this section and the confidence items is in the volatility of the trends. There is little evidence that the trust or alienation items change as rapidly as the confidence items. (On the other hand, they are not asked as often, and so we cannot be completely sure of this statement.) We believe that the trust and alienation items are less sensitive to short-term political influences than the confidence questions. The question which remains is: How volatile are the confidence questions? Are they short-term reflections of the popularity of the incumbent, or are they somewhere between the presidential popularity questions and the trust/alienation questions in their sensitivity to short-term influences? To answer this question, we take a more detailed look at the causes of confidence in government.

WHAT CAUSES CONFIDENCE
IN THE EXECUTIVE BRANCH OF GOVERNMENT?

The work published to date has not really explained the causes of change in the level of public confidence. We do not have a well-developed picture of the particular stimuli people respond to in gauging their sense of confidence in those running the executive branch of the federal government or other institutions. Miller (1974) has suggested that confidence is related to policy position, those who disagree with the policies of the incumbent will be less confident in the executive branch. Citrin (1974) puts the issue more simply. He argues that confidence is an alternative measure of presidential popularity.

Citrin, and others who minimize the importance of the confidence questions, base part of their argument on the "party in power" effect—the finding that those who identify with the party in power are more confident. Figure 2 shows the differences in confidence in the executive by political party affiliation. During the Nixon era, there are large differences, with Republicans 15% to 25% more likely to have a great deal of confidence. During the Ford era, the differences are in the same direction but smaller. And during the Carter era, the differences are still smaller, but they are in the opposite direction—Democrats are more confident in the executive branch. It is interesting to note, from this perspective, that self-designated independents are like a party that is continually out of power as far as confidence in the executive is concerned. During the Republican eras, they are about as confident as Democrats, and during the Democratic eras, they are about as confident as Republicans.

The "party in power" effect also applies to voting behavior. People who voted for the victor are more likely than people who did not to have confidence in the executive branch. The data are shown in Table 5.

Both of these demonstrations of the "party in power" effect support the argument that confidence is a transient mood which responds to the popularity of the President and other momentary frustrations or "issue" dissatisfactions. If this interpretation of confidence is correct, democratic theorists should take heart because it suggests that citizens who are disaffected will be brought back into the system if and when their candidate is elected. On the other hand, the most striking feature of Figure 2—and one which contradicts Citrin's argument—is that the tremendous swings in confidence occur within each political group. Most of the changes from 1972 to 1977 are not due to changes in which

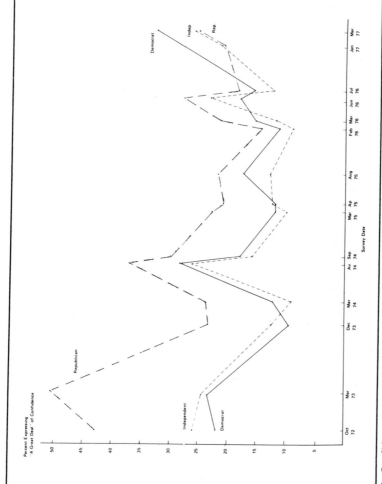

Figure 2: Trends in Confidence in the Executive Branch of the Federal Government, by Political Party Identification

TABLE 5

CONFIDENCE IN THE EXECUTIVE BRANCH OF THE
FEDERAL GOVERNMENT BY VOTING PREFERENCE
IN PREVIOUS PRESIDENTIAL ELECTIONS

Election	Voted for . . .	Percentage expressing a great deal of confidence
1968[1]	Humphrey	15.0
	Nixon	47.1
	Wallace	26.8
	Did not vote	26.9
1972[2]	McGovern	14.1
	Nixon	43.5
	Did not vote	27.4
1976[3]	Carter	34.8
	Ford	22.6
	Did not vote	28.3

1. Data are from the 1972 NORC General Social Survey.
2. Data are from the 1973 NORC General Social Survey.
3. Data are from the 1977 NORC General Social Survey.

party is in party, but to factors—transient or permanent—influencing
all citizens.

We do agree with Citrin's general observation that the confidence
trends are better analyzed if we control for some of the transient
factors affecting opinion. One issue which must be studied is the extent
to which replies to the confidence question are measures of an incumbent's popularity as an individual. Fortunately, there are data
available addressing this point directly. Between 1972 and 1976, there
are six Harris surveys that contain the confidence in government
question and also a question about the respondent's confidence in
the particular person holding office at the time. The wording of the
latter question is: "Let me ask you about some specific things [INCUM-
BENT] has done. In inspiring confidence personally in the White House
would you rate him excellent, pretty good, only fair or poor?" Table 6
shows the percentage responding in each of the four categories. The
trends in this item closely parallel the trends in the item measuring
confidence in the executive branch (see Table 1).

If confidence in the executive branch is really a measure of the
appeal of the incumbent, then the rating of the incumbent's personal
ability to inspire confidence should be highly correlated with one's

TABLE 6

TRENDS IN THE EVALUATION OF THE PRESIDENT'S PERSONAL EFFORTS TO INSPIRE CONFIDENCE IN THE WHITE HOUSE

Evaluation	Percentage, Harris Survey Number, Date					
	2236 10/72	2354 12/73	7487 8/74	2430 9/74	2521 2/76	7684 6/76
Excellent	13.6	3.4	31.2	10.6	3.5	5.9
Pretty Good	34.4	12.4	44.2	41.6	25.4	29.8
Fair	26.8	17.9	12.0	26.5	35.8	34.3
Poor	16.3	61.7	2.3	12.6	27.0	21.8

For question wording, see text.

level of confidence in the executive branch. The Pearson correlation between these measures is usually about .35. This is a high enough correlation so that we cannot deny it is difficult to disentangle the personal appeal of an incumbent from one's sense of trust in the executive branch of government. There is, however, a great deal of variation in confidence which is not explained by the personal appeal of the officeholder. We can gain some sense of the source of this unexplained variation by examining the crosstabulation of the two confidence measures at each of the six points in time. These data are displayed in Table 7.

First, we note again that trends in confidence are only partly explained by trends in the popularity of the incumbent. Second, the correlations between personal appeal and confidence are higher for Nixon than for Ford. This could be due to the particular nature of the Nixon presidency, or it could be explained by the fact that the Nixon correlations were taken at the end of a long incumbency, and the lower Ford correlations represent the effect of a shorter period of acquaintance with the officeholder. The latter interpretation is supported by the observation that the lowest correlation in the table is the one for August 1974, the month of Ford's inauguration. This suggests that office and institutions become personalized during the incumbent's tenure. It also supports the more general argument that issues and personalities become clarified during the course of an incumbency.

In addition to rating the incumbent's personal ability to inspire confidence in the White House, respondents used the same categories

TABLE 7
PERCENTAGE REPORTING "A GREAT DEAL" AND "ONLY SOME" CONFIDENCE IN THE EXECUTIVE BRANCH FOR THOSE WITH DIFFERENT EVALUATIONS OF THE PRESIDENT'S PERSONAL EFFORTS TO INSPIRE CONFIDENCE IN THE WHITE HOUSE

Personal Evaluation of President	2236 10/72		2354 12/73		7487 8/74		2430 9/74		2521 2/76		7684 6/76	
	Great Deal	Only Some	Great Deal	Only Some	Great Deal	Only Some	Great Deal	Only Some	Great Deal	Only Some	Great Deal	Only Some
Excellent	51.6	38.1	56.0	26.0	40.9	47.4	43.1	46.2	29.4	52.9	45.2	45.2
Pretty Good	36.5	47.7	30.6	48.3	26.2	55.9	25.2	60.2	19.3	64.4	31.1	53.7
Fair	18.4	57.6	18.9	63.0	15.5	60.8	13.0	58.6	7.6	64.8	19.5	57.3
Poor	8.1	40.5	5.9	35.7	20.0	34.3	3.9	48.1	4.5	40.2	10.9	39.4
Pearson Correlation Between Evaluation and Confidence	.44		.42		.21		.37		.37		.33	

Percentage with a "Great Deal" and "Only Some," Harris Survey Number, Date

to rate the incumbent's accomplishments in several different areas, including working for peace, handling Russia, handling Congress, managing the economy, controlling inflation, and cutting government spending. Each of these ratings showed the same pattern of correlation with confidence in the executive as did the rating of Ford's ability personally to inspire confidence. The correlations were all low in August 1974 (i.e., all were around .20) and then all rose quickly during Ford's incumbency, with the economic issues rising further (.35-.40) than the foreign policy issues (.25-.30). It is interesting to note that the correlations rose *faster* for Democrats and independents than for Republicans. The increase between August 1974 and September 1974 in the correlations between the evaluation of Ford's efforts and confidence in the executive branch took place only for those who considered themselves Democrats or independents. The increase in the correlation between evaluation and confidence for Republicans took place between September 1974 and February 1976.

We can summarize this set of findings by saying that public opinion during Ford's reign was generally favorable, confident, and loosely structured at the beginning of his incumbency. His reception was uncritical in the sense that a favorable (or unfavorable) sense of confidence in the executive was only slightly related to evaluation of his efforts in particular issue areas. This could be due to a general glow which surrounds incumbents during the early months of their term (Mueller, 1970, 1973; Stimson, 1976) or to the fact that very few people knew much about Ford when he took office. Then issues become defined, and the standards are set by which people will judge the success of an incumbency and their confidence in the office. This process is set in motion faster for those who are "out of power" (or for people who are Democrats and independents) than for those who identify with the party in power. In time, however, all adopt the same criteria for evaluation, regardless of political affiliation.

Confidence in the incumbent is clearly tied to the confidence people express in the executive branch. It is one of the things people take into account when they arrive at their overall assessment. There are other criteria for confidence, however. In particular, the office will be assessed on the basis of the incumbent's ability to deal successfully with the salient issues of the day. (Smith, 1978, shows that in Ford's day the salient issues were mostly economic.) An incumbent who is sensitive to public opinion would try to manage the image of his administration in such a way that the issues which are strongly correlated with confidence and approval are the ones which he is seen as most successful in handling.

We believe that Table 7 shows that although the two concepts are related, there is a significant difference between confidence in the President personally and confidence in the executive branch. In addition to the observations in the previous paragraphs, we note that half of those who rate the President as doing a "poor" job in personally inspiring confidence still say that they have at least "some" confidence in the executive branch.

What are some of the other factors, besides popularity of the incumbent and issue dissatisfaction, to which people might respond in determining their level of confidence in the executive? There is the possibility that political eras are characterized by different levels of confidence in government and possibly by different levels of confidence in most major national institutions. The extreme of this argument is that the confidence in government question is actually an *insensitive* measure, because it merely reflects the national "mood" of confidence toward a great many institutions. Let us consider some of the evidence on this point.

A GENERAL MOOD OR DIFFERENT RESPONSES TO DIFFERENT INSTITUTIONS?

The simplest way to answer this question is to study the level of confidence in several different institutions simultaneously. Table 8 examines trends in confidence in the nine institutions which are most often included in the Harris and NORC lists. For each institution, we show the average level of confidence within five different historical periods. Sometimes the average is based on one or two surveys, sometimes on several. Not all of the institutions are named in all of the surveys so it is necessary to pool the results in this way to make maximum use of the data.

By calculating change scores between each historical period, we can determine how each institution was affected by the events which occurred. Our general observation is that when one institution goes down, they all tend to be in decline, and when one goes up, they are all going up. In this sense, there is a general mood of confidence which affects all institutions.

TABLE 8

PERCENTAGE WITH A GREAT DEAL OF CONFIDENCE IN NINE SELECTED INSTITUTIONS DURING RECENT HISTORICAL PERIODS

Institutions	Percentage, Period, Dates Included[1]						
	Early Vietnam 1/67	Pre-Watergate 5/72-3/73	Fall of Nixon 6/73-6/74	Ford & Recession 6/75-7/76	Early Carter 3/77	Total Change 1967-1977
Medicine	60.5	55.1	57.6	50.0	51.5	− 9
Military	55.5	33.9	40.1	31.7	36.3	−19
Major Companies	46.6	30.0	28.2	19.8	27.2	−19
Congress	40.9	22.3	17.1	13.1	19.1	−21
Organized Religion	39.6	32.5	36.3	30.0	40.0	0
U.S. Supreme Court	39.5	30.0	33.3	30.9	35.7	− 4
Executive Branch	37.2	28.3	14.5	15.6	27.9	− 9
Press	26.5	22.2	28.0	24.5	25.1	− 1
Organized Labor	19.6	17.9	18.1	13.2	14.8	− 5

1. Data are pooled from all available sources during each historical period. Each percentage shows the combined results of at least two surveys—one Harris and one NORC. Some percentages are based on between three and six surveys, depending on the number of surveys done during each period and whether or not the list in any particular survey included the institution in question.

To end the analysis here, however, obscures several important findings. Within the general trends, institutions change at different rates, and it is not always the same institutions which change the fastest. During 1967 to 1973, which corresponds to the ascendancy of Nixon and the worst years of the Vietnam war, the military, big business, and the Congress showed particularly notable declines. During the next era, 1973 to 1974 (Watergate), the Congress and the executive branch lead the decline. Interestingly, the military and the press gained in confidence during this period. During the latter part of Ford's presidency, a period characterized by recession and economic worries, medicine, business, and the military showed the greatest losses.

It can be argued that during each of these three periods, the institutions showing the greatest declines were the ones most nearly responsible for the crisis shaping that period—the "military-industrial complex" in the 1960s, the crooks during Watergate, and the institutions which cost a lot to maintain during the recession. The reasoning here is admittedly ad hoc, but the analysis in the last section provides some further ground for our conclusion. There we found that issues vary in the extent to which they predict confidence in the executive, depending on the salience of the issue. Now we find that institutions vary in the extent to whicy they are affected by particular changes occurring in the society, depending on the extent to which an institution is seen as responsible for causing or solving a crisis. The picture of public opinion which is probably the most accurate is that there is a general climate of confidence in each period, but that institutions play different roles in leading or being led by the general trend.

Furthermore, institutions which are seen as helping to solve the predominant crisis at any point in time can actually gain in their level of public confidence. It is not difficult to extend our ad hoc reasoning to explain the greater regard for the press during Watergate. The military presents a greater difficulty. Perhaps it was the military alerts or the visibility of military officials (e.g., General Haig) in the waning moments of the Nixon administration which account for this increase in confidence. We note that during this period the GSS shows an increase in support for military spending. During the early months of the Carter administration, there is the "new incumbent" effect, which raises support for the executive branch (the early months of the Ford administration are not shown in Table 8).

The final comment to be made on Table 8 is that not only are institutions differentially sensitive to social changes, but the rank order of institutions in terms of public confidence is substantially different in 1977 from what it was ten years earlier. The military, big business, and the Congress have suffered substantial declines in trust *relative to* the other institutions on the list. To summarize this section, Lipset and Schneider are only partly right when they say things have been "bad all over." The explanation of the trends in support for the executive branch (or any single institution) is actually more complex.

The evidence on the determinants of the level of confidence in the executive branch suggests that this measure is of intermediate volatility. It is not as responsive to short-term changes as the Gallup and Harris measures of presidential popularity (Kernell, 1978a, 1978b; Brody and Page, 1975; Monroe, 1978; Kensi, 1977). On the other hand, it is not as steady or unambiguous in its movement in recent years as the various trust and alienation measures which we have considered. The explanation at which we have arrived is that there are general levels or "plateaus" of confidence which characterize different historical or political periods. Within each period, there are fluctuations in the level of confidence in the executive which depend on the "party in power effect," issue satisfaction, personal appeal of the incumbent, and the other causes we have discussed (for further discussion, see especially Santi, 1978). In terms of importance to the society, it is probably the long-term changes, the shifts from one plateau to another, which are of the greatest concern. And, within this perspective, it is not so much the fact of moving to a lower (or higher) plateau which is of direct importance to us as citizens or as social theorists. Rather, we are most interested in observing what changes in social institutions occur when the level of confidence is at a relatively low (or at a relatively high) level. We consider this argument in more detail in our next, concluding section.

THE IMPORTANCE
OF CHANGES IN CONFIDENCE

The ultimate test of the significance of the trends in confidence lies in the implication for other changes in the political system. There are two ways that changes in public confidence could cause changes in the political system. Changes in confidence have a *direct* effect on the political system if people behave differently *because* they have changed their level of confidence: for example, changes in electoral participation and political party identification (e.g., Converse, 1972). Another direct effect would be people withdrawing visible kinds of support because they no longer trusted the decisions and/or decision makers in particular national institutions. An example is the current tax revolt. To what extent are people less willing to be taxed because they no longer trust the government? Table 9 shows that people who are less confidence in the executive branch are more likely to say that they are paying too much in taxes. We recognize the thorny issues in causal direction which are inherent in this analysis. Nevertheless, the issues of confidence and orientation to levels of taxation are related.

Changes in confidence might also have *indirect* effects on the political system. Public opinion creates a climate within which certain types of appeals and certain types of proposals have more or less legitimacy and more or less likelihood of support if the issues are ever defined in such a way that a referendum or some other public display is in order. A decline in confidence creates a situation where the public sees a greater need for the candidates, leaders, and interest groups which act to insure that the institutions in question behave in a trustworthy manner.

Some of the institutional changes which we believe are related to the decline in trust in the executive branch are: a greater public reliance on fact-finding and overseeing commissions such as congressional committees, a more critical tone in public media and public news reporting, and the fact that it is no longer considered un-American to expose and criticize government actions which might have been considered secrets essential to national security even a few years ago.

These changes are sometimes described as elements of the post-Watergate morality. We believe that this observation does not go far enough in placing the Watergate investigations within the context of the changes in public trust which occurred before 1973.

The Watergate prosecutions and congressional committees certainly had their impact on the public trust—particularly on the governmental agencies and incumbents most directly involved in the scandal. But the overseeing and investigating activities of the Congress, the press, and citizen action groups such as Common Cause would have

TABLE 9

Percentage Who Consider the Amount of Federal Income Tax
They Pay "Too High" by Levels of Confidence in the
Executive Branch of the Federal Government

Confidence	Percentage "Too High"	(N)
Great Deal	59.7	(578)
Only Some	67.0	(1593)
Hardly Any	72.5	(552)

Data are from the pooled 1976 and 1977 NORC General Social Surveys. The wording of the tax question was: "Do you consider the amount of federal income tax which you have to pay as too high, about right, or too low?"

been pursued with much less vigor (and funding) if the credibility and legitimacy of these groups had not already been established by changes in public trust before the early 1970s. A falling rate of confidence was both a cause and an effect of the Watergate era. In a social structural sense, a decline in confidence, such as the changes which occurred before the Watergate era, creates a need for social institutions (i.e., investigative bodies, congressional commissions) which monitor and "expose" the workings of government, business, or whatever institutions are losing credibility. One of the consequences of monitoring and exposure, however, is a continued fueling of the lack of trust in institutions. An indirect effect of a decline in confidence, then, is the creation of new institutions which because of their investigative roles, act so as to insure a continued lower level of confidence.

In spite of this gloomy prognosis, the data show that institutions can improve their level of public trust. The institutions which are hardest hit by a loss of confidence during any period of time are those which are seen as most directly responsible for causing or failing to solve the greatest social problems of that period. We find that there *is* an aura of public trust which influences most institutions during any period, but a decline in support is not equally felt by all. Some institutions, in fact, rise while others fall. At the present time, we are in a period of low trust in government. Furthermore, in the past few years, the society has legitimized investigative groups, overseeing groups, and political appeals which are based on the premise that government, business, and other social institutions cannot be trusted. These groups will surely act so as to achieve their purposes and provide us with daily reminders of the need for their continued existence. Because of this, trends in the near future should show a fluctuating level of confidence in the executive branch which will be generally lower than it was in the 1950s and 1960s.

REFERENCES

BRODY, R. A. and B. I. PAGE (1975) "The impact of events on presidential popularity: the Johnson and Nixon administrations," in A. Wildavsky (ed.) Perspectives on the Presidency. Boston: Little, Brown.

CITRIN, J. (1974) "Comment: the political relevance of trust in government." Amer. Pol. Sci. Rev. 68: 973-988.

CONVERSE, P. E. (1972) "Change in the American electorate," in A. Campbell and P. E. Converse (eds.) The Human Meaning of Social Change. New York: Russell Sage.

HOUSE, J. S. and W. H. MASON (1975) "Political alienation in America, 1952-1968." Amer. Soc. Rev. 40 (April).

KENSI, H. C. (1977) "The impact of economic conditions on presidential popularity." J. of Politics 39.

KERNELL, S. A. (1978a) "A disaggregated model of trends in presidential popularity, 1952-1974." Presented to the annual meeting of the American Statistical Association, San Diego.

——— (1978b) "Explaining presidential popularity . . . " Amer. Pol. Sci. Rev. 54.

KERNELL, S., P. W. SPERLICH, and A. WILDAVSKY (1975) "Public support for presidents," in A. Wildavsky (ed.) Perspectives on the Presidency. Boston: Little, Brown.

LADD, E. C. (1976-1977) "The polls: the question of confidence." Public Opinion Q. 40.

LIPSET, S. M. and W. SCHNEIDER (1978) "How's business?: what the public thinks." Public Opinion Q. 1, 3: 41-47.

MILLER, A. H. (1974) "Political issues and trust in government, 1964-1970." Amer. Pol. Sci. Rev. 48.

MONROE, K. R. (1978) "Economic influences on presidential popularity." Public Opinion Q. 42.

MUELLER, J. E. (1973) War, Presidents, and Public Opinion. New York: John Wiley.

——— (1970) "Presidential popularity from Truman to Johnson." Amer. Pol. Sci. Rev. 44.

SANTI, L. (1977) "Confidence in the executive branch of the federal government, 1973-1976." M.A. thesis, University of Arizona.

SMITH, T. W. (1978) "America's most important problem: a trend analysis, 1946-1976." Presented to the Midwest Association for Public Opinion Research, October.

STIMSON, J. A. (1976) "Public support for American presidents: a cyclical model." Public Opinion Q. 40.

TURNER, C. F. and E. KRAUSS (1978) "Fallible indicators of the subjective state of the nation." Amer. Psychologist 33.

WRIGHT, J. D. (1976) The Dissent of the Governed: Alienation and Democracy in America. New York: Academic.

Changes in Congressional Oversight

JOEL D. ABERBACH
University of Michigan, and
Brookings Institution

VARIETIES OF CONGRESSIONAL OVERSIGHT

Congress has shown increasing concern about oversight as the federal bureaucracy has expanded in size and program initiation has passed to the executive branch. In 1946, following the New Deal and World War II, a provision of the Legislative Reorganization Act prescribed "continuous watchfulness" over the actions of the executive agencies in carrying out the laws. In the 1970 Amendments to the Act, Congress required most committees to issue periodic reports on their oversight endeavors. This was an obvious attempt to spur them to action. Data gathered on congressional oversight in 1973 for the Bolling Committee staff and comments by congressmen before the Committee indicated that this requirement had not produced the desired effect and the House

Author's Note: *This is a revised version of papers originally prepared for the Commission on the Operation of the Senate and the 1977 Annual Meeting of the American Political Science Association. Generous support from the institute of Public Policy Studies and the Rackham Faculty Development Fund at the University of Michigan and from the Brookings Institution allowed me to recheck the original data analyzed in the Commission and Association papers. Most of the corrections from the rechecking process were entered on the data tape in time for inclusion in this chapter. The chapter, therefore, contains some modifications in the data reported in earlier papers, although none substantial enough to change any conclusions. Final data reflecting all corrections will be reported as part of my Brookings volume on oversight. I wish to express my thanks to the graduate students at Michigan who assisted so ably in the arduous task of coding, preparing, and analyzing the data used here, particularly Celinda Lake and Susan Van Alstyne, and to Cynthia Enquist who did much of the checkcoding while a summer intern at Brookings. Thanks also to Doug Neal of the Bureau of Social Science Research who produced the graphic in Figure 1.*

amended its rules in an attempt to stimulate more activity and provide some coordination. There is sentiment in the Senate for similar action as indicated by the *Interim Report of the Commission on the Operation of the Senate* (U.S. Congress, 1976) and by Senate support for "Sunset" legislation in 1978.

When it comes to performance Bibby's (1968) comment that oversight is "Congress' neglected function" is still the standard introductory observation in papers on the subject. The second definition of oversight found in *Webster's New Collegiate Dictionary* may be unintendedly appropriate: "an overlooking or something overlooked; (an) omission or error due to inadvertence." However, the first meaning, "watchful care or supervision" is surely what we have in mind when we speak about congressional oversight.

There is a debate within the scholarly literature about how to define oversight. Harris proposes a relatively narrow definition. For him, oversight "strictly speaking, refers to review after the fact. It includes inquiries about policies that are or have been in effect, investigations of past administrative actions, and the calling of executive officers to account for their financial transactions" (Harris, 1964). Ogul takes a much broader approach and defines legislative oversight as "behavior by legislators and their staffs, individually or collectively, which results in an impact, intended or not, on bureaucratic behavior," (Ogul, 1976). The Ogul definition is useful in that it directs attention to the fact that oversight is a latent as well as a manifest function of Congress and that many of the things done by Members and Senators contribute to oversight. It is so broad, however, that it is hard to exclude very many congressional activities from inclusion under the oversight rubric. I define oversight as congressional review of the actions of the federal departments, agencies, and commissions and of the programs and policies they administer. This includes review that takes place *during* program and policy implementation as well as afterwards, but excludes much of what Congress now does when it considers proposals for new programs or even for the expansion of current programs.

As noted above, it is often asserted that Congress neglects oversight. What does occur, with a few exceptions, is said to be neither continuing, comprehensive, nor systematic (Bibby, 1968). Agencies or programs are rarely overseen persistently, the focus of the oversight effort is often very narrow, and it is certainly the case that systematic oversight efforts (those involving a methodical approach governed by some rational principle which orders and gives unity to the elements of the effort) are just about impossible to uncover.

A basic assumption underlying much of the normative discussion in this chapter is that, simply stated, oversight of administration is desirable because it provides one mechanism by which those who administer the public policies which singly or cumulatively affect us in fundamental ways can be held accountable and their programs evaluated. I also assume that more oversight is usually better than less.[1] The idea behind this is quite simple: even oversight performed sporadically, focused on fairly narrow subjects, and utilizing an unsystematic approach should at least hold down flagrant abuses of power by administrators, make them more responsive to the wishes of Congress, and provide Members and Senators with better knowledge and use in making judgments about the effectiveness of programs. Persistent oversight of programs or agencies is, I assume, more likely to yield these benefits than random reviews, but the benefits of regular efforts in an area may not be commensurate with the high costs in time and effort involved unless the quality of the oversight is improved.[2] And quality can only be significantly improved through efforts to evaluate programs in a comprehensive and systematic manner. Great difficulties are suggested by the latter point because our political system diffuses authority and promotes legislation which often enumerates unclear and even contradictory goals for programs.

The issue, then, is how to promote more and better oversight. Separating the elements of quantity and quality is, of course, a simplifying device. If one accepts it, a futher simplification will aid us in the analysis. This involves a division of the factors often thought to promote oversight into those whose effect is mainly to increase the quantity (incidence) of oversight and those which are very likely also to increase the quality of oversight. A further distinction, given our interest in change, will be drawn between those factors which are subject to planned manipulation (i.e., can be affected through policy changes) and those which are basically beyond our control.

FACTORS MAINLY PROMOTING A GREATER INCIDENCE OF OVERSIGHT

The literature is filled with propositions about factors which promote oversight.[3] A good number seem mainly to affect the quantity of oversight done. The following is a brief enumeration of some of these factors plus some commentary where appropriate:

(1) *Split partisan control of the presidency and Congress.* If different parties control the presidency and Congress, the majority in Congress

has an incentive to harass and embarrass the executive for partisan gain. This is not a factor which is conducive to persistent oversight of a policy or agency and it is not something which we can control. However, there is one reform which has been suggested which would produce much the same stimulus to oversight and would always be as effective as split control; that is to give the minority party in Congress (if it does not also control the presidency) control of the Government Operations Committees and of oversight subcommittees of the authorization committees.

(2) *Casework problems.* If the bureaucracy is unresponsive to requests for assistance for the constituents of a strategically placed Senator or Representative (i.e., a committee or subcommittee chairman or ranking members, and the like), the oversight may be used as a means to set things aright. One would not expect this to happen very often or to require persistent oversight to correct the situation.

Casework problems are not something we can manipulate in the interest of increased oversight, but there might be a way to use casework information to stimulate oversight and perhaps improve its quality as well. Congress could establish a central office to collect and analyze information on casework requests and responses to them. A periodic report which highlighted recurrent problems might create pressure for (and information to be used in) a review of the agencies or programs involved.

(3) *Attempts to satisfy group interests important to the Senator or Congressman.* This is a broader category than two, but shares much in common with it. Most established interests are well represented in the bureaucracy; program administrators wish to provide them with services, and administrators are especially responsive to those groups of concern to important people in Congress. Every once in a while, however, vocal dissatisfied groups stimulate spurts of oversight as in the case of OSHA (Occupational Safety and Health Administration).

(4) *Desire to protect favored agencies.* This factor is related to (3), only here the Senators and Congressmen are mobilized by bureaucrats as well as interest groups to protect a program which is threatened by the administration or which needs a boost for some other reason. The purpose of the oversight effort is to show how marvelous or essential

the program is and to demonstrate the depth of its support. Such efforts, I believe, are especially common when there is split partisan control of the Congress and the presidency, but probably occur at all times. "Sunset" laws of the type now under consideration in Congress would unintentionally stimulate this type of oversight on a regular schedule. While protective oversight is likely to be very superficial, every once in a while it will expose flaws in a program which even its most ardent supporter will want to see corrected.

(4a) *Efforts to preempt opponents.* Preemptive oversight is really a special case of protective oversight. As Scher says, some oversight (which he terms preventive) "results from an unenthusiastic determination that a limited examination of an agency by its friends may cost less than an uncontrolled one by its enemies" (Scher, 1963). Such oversight is likely to be superficial and brief, but the incentive to perform it is subject to some manipulation. A restructuring of committee jurisdictions which encouraged "unfriendly" committees to take a look at the program or agency in question would encourage this type of oversight. The new budget process may be a particularly important stimulus to preemptive oversight since authorization committees will want to present what looks like a strong case to the Budget Committees. I will return to this point later in describing factors leading to higher quality oversight (because should the budget process really work it is likely that superficial evaluations will be at a disadvantage in competition with more systematic efforts).

(5) *Committee structure.* We now turn to a factor which is very much subject to planned manipulation: committee structure. The more decentralized the committee, the greater the likelihood of oversight. As Ogul (1976) notes, "a decentralized committee—one in which power over money, staff, and program is largely in the hands of subcommittee chairmen and others—enhances the opportunity for oversight simply because decision-making is dispersed."

An additional factor which ought to lead to a greater incidence of oversight is the establishment of oversight subcommittees. Once established, many members of these subcommittees and their staffs should want to make something of their assignments and greater oversight activity is a likely result.

(6) *Increasing staff resources.* The latter point raises the general issue of staff resources. One would expect that increases in the number of staff members on committees and subcommittees and increases in staff assigned to individuals both in their offices and through their committee assignments would lead to more oversight activity. There would probably not be a one to one relationship between the number of staff and oversight, but one would expect some impact if only because of the greater number of people available to do things. However, when authority over staff is dispersed, increases in the number of staff are more likely to lead to increases in the level of oversight activity than to increases in systematic oversight. The problems of lack of coordination and lack of an orderly, methodical approach to oversight are, in fact, probably exacerbated by mere increases in the numbers of staff aides.

(7) *Corruption, crisis, and publicity.* Evidence of corruption, the breakdown of a program, or the subversion of accepted governmental processes as revealed by Watergate make oversight attractive because the overseer is almost sure to make a favorable public impression. Most such oversight is not planned for in advance and is likely to be short-lived and somewhat superficial. But Watergate and the feeling that the Great Society programs of the 1960s were ineffective may well have had a profound impact on both the attentive public and the people in Congress themselves, alerting them to the need for "continuous watchfulness."

A related factor which may bring Congressmen who oversee the executive branch publicity previously unavailable is the rise of citizens' lobbies with wide memberships or favorable public recognition. These groups place oversight of target agencies and programs on their agendas and publicize congressional response. They also are sources of information previously unavailable. They seem to be a stimulus to more oversight, but whether they will sustain themselves through time or maintain a steady enough interest in an area to reward persistent congressional attention is not yet clear.

FACTORS LIKELY TO INCREASE THE QUALITY OF OVERSIGHT

The analysis in the preceding section was inspired by recent academic work (especially Scher, 1963; Ogul, 1976) that approaches oversight from the perspective of the incentives of the Senators and Representatives. While more traditional scholars spend much time examining the techniques of oversight (hearings, investigations, and so on) and the resources available (staff, money, and so on), Scher and Ogul ask what net gains accrue to Senators and Representatives from performing oversight. Investigations, to take one example, can yield great publicity dividends if they expose corruption or harass unpopular agencies, but they may prove politically useless or even damaging if they turn up nothing newsworthy or threaten powerful interests. Persistent oversight of an agency or program is even more time-consuming than a one-shot investigation and the publicity rewards are likely to be much lower. In brief, when the disadvantages outweigh the advantages one assumes that Congressmen and Senators shy away from oversight, even though they may believe that it ought to be done.

When one looks at oversight in this way it is not surprising that performance has usually been spotty at best, with persistent oversight a rarity and really thorough systematic jobs almost nonexistent. However, over the last few years there have been changes in the environment which ought to make improvement in the quality of oversight more attractive to many in Congress. This certainly does not guarantee that such improvements will occur, but it does make it more than an academic exercise to discuss factors likely to increase the quality of oversight.

(1) *Relative resource scarcity.* Many of us are accustomed to thinking about an ever-growing economy with rapidly increasing resources available to government for the expansion of old programs and the establishment of new ones. This environment discourages the careful oversight of ongoing programs which usually have the support of entrenched constituencies. There is no pressing reason to worry much about efficiency or effectiveness in such an environment and, therefore, little oversight should be expected, let alone systematic oversight.

We are now in a period of relative resource scarcity. In addition to the strains brought on by the recent recession, many of the programs of the 1960s proved much more expensive than originally estimated. Together with the belief that many government programs are not working very well, these factors have created a growing interest in the attentive public in efforts to determine the effectiveness of programs and to weigh them against possible alternate uses of the resources they consume. There is a growing constituency which supports such efforts and public acclaim to be gained by backing them. In addition, if hard choices must be made, the political costs may be reduced by transferring responsibility for unpopular decisions, i.e., fixing the blame on the outcome of carefully conducted, technically respectable analyses. In short, relative resource scarcity has created a political climate which makes high quality, systematic oversight more attractive than it was before.

(2) *Influx of skeptical Senators and Representatives.* Contributing to this climate is the influx into Congress of Democrats described by Representative Bob Carr as "skeptical of government intervention and solutions." (Singer, 1978) Their electoral success reinforces the belief that a skeptical view is popular with the public and may advance the notion that thorough, systematic oversight can yield some political payoff.

(3) *Widespread program evaluation.* In part as a consequence of the relative scarcity of resources described above, in part as a reflection of the spread of new analytic techniques, and in part as a function of new mandates given to the executive agencies, congressional support agencies, and congressional committees themselves, program evaluation is being done all over the government. It is not always well done and it is often self-serving, but it does put pressure on Congress to examine the findings and at least to consider the results.

A major problem is that low quality evaluations are encouraged by the types of programs Congress typically passes. In order to build a coalition large enough to pass a bill and in an effort to offend as few people as possible, Congress often establishes programs which lack clear, noncontradictory goals for the agencies to accomplish.

Schick (1976), however, notes that

> when Congress muddles through without a clear specification of purpose, the process of evaluation is not aborted. Rather, it must begin with executive implementation rather than with textbook clarity about objectives. Congress, in fact, has two legitimate tasks to get the Executive to produce relevant evaluations. First, Congress can write into law a mandate for the agency to evaluate its program; second, Congress can demand that the evaluative measures used by the agency reflect congressional interest and perspectives, not merely the orientation of the implementing agency. . . . What is required is the prescription in law of a process that agencies must adhere to in evaluating their activities, including milestones for the crucial events in the process, and a reporting schedule.

Schick's proposals are realistic and would improve the prospects for the intelligent utilization of program evaluations by Congress. They suggest a general point which is that congressional committees should work closely with any agency (for example, GAO) doing evaluations for them—or the products are unlikely to have much impact. The process Schick proposes will *not* eliminate all muddled program objectives and the problems they create (it does, after all, involve continuous bargaining between Congress and the agencies) and it will not result in high quality program evaluations as measured by a set of absolute professional standards, but it *will* increase the usefulness and impact of the evaluations done.

Effective congressional utilization of evaluation requires the active interest of Senators and Representatives, staff members who can skillfully direct the work of technical experts, and a congressional willingness to bite the bullet at times when evaluation results cause some political difficulties. No one can mandate such things, but changes in the political climate and in the composition of Congress give some encouragement that this might be possible.

It would be helpful, in this regard, to develop courses in evaluation for politically skilled but analytically untrained staff. This would help facilitate fruitful communication between Congress and evaluators from the congressional support agencies or the executive departments.

(4) *Reforms in the budget process.* The most important *potential* stimulus to systematic oversight by the Congress is the new budget process established by the 1974 Budget Act. As Schick notes (1976):

> there is some possibility that the new congressional budget process might bolster the incentives for evaluation at [the authorization and appropriations] stages, if only because of the pressure to consider particular spending demands in the light of overall national priorities and other claims on the budget. Moreover, the new congressional process might contribute to a narrowing of the authorizations-appropriations gap, the proclivity to authorize one level of expenditure but to appropriate at a much lower level. More realistic authorizations might encourage committees to take more careful looks at the programs subject to their oversight.

A possible scenario is that some presentations to the Budget Committees by the authorization committees of their views and recommendations on matters to be covered in the budget resolutions (as required in Section 301(c) of the Act) will be based on evaluations designed to make favored agencies and programs look good. ("Preemptive oversight" may also take hold here—a desire to evaluate programs before CBO or the Budget Committee staffs get to them.) With any luck, some authorization committees will seek to influence the Budget Committee by presenting more systematic evaluation than those of the competition in order to back up their claims to the available funds. The Budget Committees, if they reward such efforts, can thereby stimulate a continuing improvement in the quality of oversight.

(5) *Rotation of committee memberships.* A final factor which might increase the quality of oversight would be the regular rotation of committee assignments. Such a procedure could have several benefits. First, it would loosen the ties which Senators and Representatives develop with the agencies whose programs their committees authorize or fund. This, in itself, would be a stimulus to more objective perspectives on programs and the agencies which administer them. Second, by moving from committee to committee, each individual might develop a better view of the overall situation. Third, because of the need to develop a quick comprehension of the agencies and programs involved, the Senators and Representatives might be more interested in seeing thorough studies of relevant policies, especially studies which compared benefits across programs or agencies.

The difficulties with this proposal are many, but two (leaving aside resistance to change) stand out. First, unless the staff attached to the committees had low turnover, committees would be even more reliant on the executive for information and expertise than they are now. Second, if the staffs remained in place, the perspectives of program clientele groups and the agencies might still dominate the process. Reserving some staff positions for people whose professional training is in policy analysis might help here.

AN ANALYSIS OF TRENDS IN CONGRESSIONAL COMMITTEE OVERSIGHT BEHAVIOR

As I indicated earlier, the notion that oversight is Congress's neglected function is widespread, shared alike by scholars and legislators. The survey of oversight activity by House Committees done by the Congressional Research Service for the Bolling Committee (1974), for example, showed that 11% of all hearing and meeting days in the first eight months of the Ninety-Third Congress (January 1 to September 5, 1973) were devoted to oversight.[4] The prevailing inference drawn from these data was that 11% was too low a number. Thus, the Committee's report expressed a firm belief that "the oversight responsibilities of the

House Committees are important and too often shunted aside by the press of other business" and endorsed the view "that oversight of programs and agencies should be a principal function of the Congress." The significance of the 11% figure will be considered below in my examination of oversight activity over the last four Congresses.

This part of my article documents and provides some preliminary analysis of trends in congressional oversight behavior. The analysis is longitudinal, covering the Ninety-First, Ninety-Second, Ninety-Third, and Ninety-Fourth Congresses, and comparative, contrasting the House and the Senate. The analysis has two major purposes:

(1) to document the amount of oversight behavior in committee hearings and meetings for each of the last four Congresses;
(2) to perform a preliminary analysis of the impact of some of the factors identified earlier as likely to promote a greater incidence of oversight.

The nature of the data I employ here requires me to place my major emphasis on the quantity of oversight, but I will also briefly consider the implications of the evidence for the quality of the oversight being done.

My data source is the Daily Digest which is appended to the *Congressional Record.* The Daily Digest lists and summarizes the meetings and hearings held by congressional committees. The time period coded for each Congress is January 1 to July 4 of the first year of each session, i.e., 1969, 1971, 1973, and 1975. The unit of analysis is a hearing and/or meeting series dealing with what I call a "matter," defined as a subject, theme, or topic. The coders were instructed to code as a unit a series of hearings and/or meetings on one subject, topic, or theme. The number of days of hearings and/or meetings per matter was also recorded so that the total amount of time spent on each matter can be recovered from the data where that is desirable.

All hearings or meetings listed in the Daily Digest were coded so that effort spent on oversight as measured from this source could be compared to activities devoted to other purposes such as authorizations, nominations, and so on. Oversight is defined here conceptually as congressional review of the actions of the executive branch and operationally as hearings or meetings held for any of the following purposes, either singly or in combination: (1) to review and/or control unacceptable forms of bureaucratic behavior; (2) to ensure that the bureaucracy implements the policy objectives of Congress; and (3) to determine the effectiveness of programs and policies. In addition committee hearings or meetings described in less precise terms than those above simply as efforts to review or oversee the activities of an agency were coded as oversight. The numbered elements of the operational definition were drawn from the CRS study for the Bolling Committee (U.S. Congress, 1974: 267). The difference between their study and mine is that I did not code as oversight hearings or meetings designed, in their words, "to analyze national (and international) problems requiring Federal action" unless they were part of an effort to review government actions in the area.

Before proceeding, I should note some of the shortcomings of the data set. First of all, it understates the amount of committee activity to some extent because the descriptions in the Daily Digest are inserted by the Committees themselves. If for any reason they fail to submit copy to the *Record*, there is no entry for any hearings or meetings they may have held. Second, the descriptions submitted are not always as clear as one might hope. We guarded against error by double-coding any questionable entries in the Digest. Third, the data are records of hearings and meetings, not other activities of the committees. They, therefore, do not necessarily include such efforts as staff investigations and the like which can be important aspects of oversight, unless those efforts are reflected in hearings and meetings. Finally, oversight may occur as a by-product of hearings and meetings held by congressional committees for other purposes. Accordingly, the data analyzed in this article under-estimate the amount of oversight because they consider only the primary purpose of each hearing or meeting as described in the Daily Digest.

CHANGES IN COMMITTEE OVERSIGHT ACTIVITY

Most congressional committees are quite busy and the evidence indicates that the number of hearings and meetings held by them has increased significantly since 1969, the first year coded in our data set. Table 1 presents the number of hearings and/or meetings series coded in each of the four Congresses, the total number of days spent in hearings and meetings, and the mean days per series for all House and Senate committees except Appropriations, Rules, and Administration.[5] The committees dealing with rules and administration were excluded from the analysis because of their preoccupation with internal chamber business. The appropriations committees were excluded for reasons of

TABLE 1

**Frequency of Committee or Subcommittee Hearings and
Meetings in the House and Senate, by Congress[a]**

		Total number of series[b]	Total number days[c]	Mean days per series
Congress				
House	91	340	1087	3.20
	92	398	1184	2.97
	93	467	1448	3.10
	94	593	1641	2.77
	Percent change from 91 to 94	+74.4	+51.0	−13.4
Senate	91	278	717	2.58
	92	326	877	2.69
	93	406	1063	2.62
	94	431	943	2.19
	Percent change from 91 to 94	+55.0	+31.5	−15.1

NOTE: Entries are for the January 1 to July 4 period of the first year of each session of the Ninety-First to Ninety-Fourth Congresses.
a. Hearings and meetings held by the Appropriations, Rules, and Administration committees in each chamber have been excluded.
b. A series is defined as a set of hearings and/or meetings on one subject, topic, or theme.
c. The total number of days is derived by adding the number of days of hearings and/or meetings in each series.

comparability since the House Committee followed its unique tradition until the Ninety-Third Congress of reporting very few of its hearings or meetings for inclusion in the Daily Digest.

The total number of hearings and meetings series increased rapidly in both the House and the Senate in this period. The Senate workload shows some signs of leveling off in the Ninety-Fourth Congress (there was a dip in the total days column from the Ninety-Third), perhaps indicating a rough saturation point in the area of 1,000 hearings or meetings in a six-month period for the Senate committees coded here. What is clear is that committees in both bodies meet even more often than they did just a few years ago and that more and more matters are taken up in each session.[6]

Table 2, which displays data on oversight hearings and meetings, shows a fairly consistent pattern of increases both in the number of series and in the total days devoted to oversight. The one exception is found in the House where the number of oversight series decreased slightly from the Ninety-First to the Ninety-Second Congress while the total number of oversight days dropped rather precipitously. This relatively steep drop in the number of days devoted to oversight is a function of a drop in the mean number of days spent on oversight per series. As the change from a standard deviation of 5.55 in the House in the Ninety-First Congress to 2.40 indicates, there were fewer extreme cases in the Ninety-Second Congress. In fact, one oversight series of 33 days of hearings and meetings in the Ninety-First Congress is the culprit. This was the largest series by far, the next longest oversight series recorded in the period covered by the data being 16 days long. At any rate, with the one exception described, oversight not only increased in absolute terms from Congress to Congress, but it held its own as a percentage of a rapidly increasing committee workload. It began to rise in the House in the Ninety-Third Congress as a percentage of total series of hearings and meetings and in the Ninety-Fourth Congress exploded into prominence in both chambers as a major percentage both of series and of hearings and meeting days.

How does one explain this change in congressional oversight behavior? Earlier, I outlined a group of factors which have been identified as promoting a greater incidence of oversight. Split partisan control of the presidency and Congress has been a constant factor in the period covered by the analysis and unfortunately, therefore, its direct impact on oversight activity cannot be assessed using these data.[7] In addition, the data, because of limited information in the Daily Digest, are not appropriate to answer questions about the relationship between oversight activity and such factors as casework problems, attempts to satisfy group interests important to the Senator or Congressman, or the desire to protect favored agencies. Additional analytic work could be done in these areas by evaluating hearings transcripts and interviewing participants. However, the data collection problem will be a difficult one since the investigator would ideally like to know not only what motivated a given instance of oversight activity, but when similar conditions (casework problems and the like) existed and no oversight resulted.

Fortunately, there are some data presently available which can help to probe the relationships between the remainder of the factors identified earlier and oversight activity. Turning first to staff resources, it

TABLE 2

Oversight Hearings and Meetings by House and
Senate Committees or Subcommittees, by Congress[a]

Congress		Number of oversight series	Oversight series as percentage of total series[b]	Number of days of oversight hearings and meetings	Number of days over- sight as a percent of total number of days[c]	Mean days oversight	Standard deviation days oversight
House	91	35	10.3	128	11.8	3.66	5.55
	92	32	8.0	87	7.3	2.72	2.40
	93	69	14.8	169	11.7	2.45	2.30
	94	118	19.9	285	17.4	2.42	2.17
Senate	91	27	9.7	82	11.4	3.04	2.69
	92	34	10.4	100	11.4	2.94	3.23
	93	39	9.6	112	10.5	2.87	2.75
	94	67	15.5	173	18.3	2.58	2.39

NOTE: Entries are for the January 1 to July 4 period of the first year of each session of the Ninety-First to Ninety-Fourth Congresses.
a. Hearings and meetings held by the Appropriations, Rules, and Administration Committees in each chamber have been excluded.
b. See Table 1 for a count of the total number of series.
c. See Table 1 for a count of the total number of days.

was hypothesized that oversight would increase as a function of the number of staff available to committees and subcommittees. Information collected by the Temporary Select Committee to Study the Senate Committee System on numbers of staff members available to House and Senate Committees is the basis of the rather remarkable plot found in Figure 1. The horizontal axis is the total number of permanent, inquiries and investigation staff available in 1969, 1971, 1973, and 1975 to all Senate Committees as reported by the Temporary Select Committee (1976) and the vertical axis is the total number of days Senate Committees spent on oversight in those years. The total number of days Senate Committees spent on oversight during this period appears to bear an almost linear relationship to the total staff available.

Before declaring increases in staff the definitive factor promoting more oversight, a few cautions are in order. First of all, Figure 1 covers a very short time span and chance may be at work here. The data might not be quite so neat if a longer series could be examined.[8] Second, while complete data on staff growth for the House are not available, the data for 1969 and 1971 which are presented by the Temporary Select Committee present a problem. Staff in the House grew from 688 to 799 in this period, while a look at Table 2 will show that total days of oversight in the House fell during this same time span. Perhaps the relationship between staff and oversight only exists in the Senate, but one would want to see more data on both chambers before reaching that conclusion. Third, correlation does not indicate causation and in the case of these variables the direction of causality is not absolutely clear. More staff may be promoting oversight, but the reverse may also be true and the desire of Senators to oversee the bureaucracy may be leading them to hire more staff. If the latter is correct, when and if the desire abates, staff increases may well be associated with constant or even decreasing levels of oversight.[9] My own feeling on this point is that the system is a complex one in which additional people are slack resources some of whom find their way into oversight activity regardless of the priorities of their employers, but the key point for now is that one should be cautious in interpreting these data.

Next, let us examine the committee structure factor. This factor is an extremely important one for those interested in reform because, like the staff factor, it is very much subject to planned manipulation.

Two propositions were outlined earlier. The first is that the more decentralized the committee, the greater the likelihood of oversight. In order to make a satisfactory test of this proposition one would want to develop good measures of the dispersal of power over money, staff, and the agenda in each committee and then relate them to the level of oversight activity. Such measures are not currently available, but one crude indicator of decentralization—the number of subcommittees on the full committee[10]—does not show very promising results. The average correlation between the number of subcommittees and the amount of oversight conducted (the oversight indicator was coded here as a dummy variable, i.e., 1 = oversight and 0 = other) is .05 in the House and .01 in the Senate for the four Congresses in the data set. In addition, the correlations in the House for the Ninety-Third and Ninety-Fourth Congresses, those after the passage of the so-called "Subcommittee Bill of Rights" (Ornstein, 1975), were -.02 and .05, respectively.

The second proposition on committee structure outlined above, namely that the establishment of oversight committees or subcommittees is likely to lead to an increase in oversight activity, seems very promising. These units would have oversight as a major mandate and the assumption is that if they are active at all they will be more likely than other units to devote their efforts to overseeing the executive. Fortunately, it is fairly easy to identify existing oversight committees and subcommittees (which we will call oversight units) and to compare their behavior to that of nonoversight units.

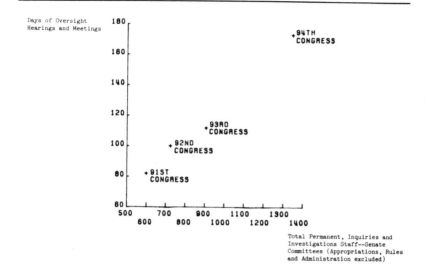

NOTE: Oversight entries are for the January 1 to July 4 period of the first year of each session of the Ninety-First to Ninety-Fourth Congresses.

Figure 1: Staff Size Versus Days of Oversight Hearings and Meetings, Senate

In Table 3 the percentages of hearings and meetings series devoted to oversight are presented both for oversight units and for the remainder of the committees and subcommittees. The data are further divided by chamber and Congress. Oversight units are defined as the Government Operations Committees in both chambers and subcommittees of other committees which have such identifying labels as oversight and department operations in their titles.

A look at the table will show some very clear findings in the House. Oversight units do indeed devote more series of hearings and meetings to oversight than other committee units. The differences are quite pronounced. Indeed, the average correlation (r) between dummy variables for the oversight and committee units indicators is .28.[11]

Both oversight and nonoversight units have increased their oversight percentages since the Ninety-First Congress. However, the House oversight units' share of the total oversight series, i.e., the percentage of the total oversight series in each Congress which they conducted, has dropped from 37.1% in the January 1 to July 4 period of 1969 (the Ninety-First Congress) to 30.5% in the comparable period of 1975 (the Ninety-Fourth Congress).[12] This drop resulted from the fact that the percentages of series devoted to oversight rose more steeply for the nonoversight than for the oversight units. The difference in oversight percentage growth rates was enough to overcome the greater percentage increase in the number of series held by the oversight units.

In the end, then, one must conclude both that the oversight units on the House committees do spend a higher proportion of their time on oversight series than the nonoversight units *and* that the large increase in oversight found in the House cannot be accounted for simply by the increase in activities of the oversight units. What has happened is that most everyone is now getting into the act in a bigger way than before. Before discussing a factor which may have contributed to this substantial increase in oversight effort, let me say a few words about the data on oversight units in the Senate.

The Senate data on the percentages of series devoted to oversight by oversight committee units resembles that found in the House (i.e., much higher percentages) only in the Ninety-Fourth Congress. One wonders why there are virtually no differences for any of the other Congresses. The main reason is that in the Ninety-First, Ninety-Second, and Ninety-Third Congresses the Senate Government Operations Committee was the *only* oversight unit which held any hearings or meetings at all. (In fact, it was the only one in existence in the Senate.) This is important because the Government Operations Committee, unlike most of the oversight subcommittee units, has a firm legislative mandate and, therefore, is likely to be occupied with tasks other than oversight.[13] The committee, for instance, was very busy during much of the period before the Ninety-Fourth Congress shaping complex legislation such as the Budget and Impoundment Control Act. Only in the Ninety-Fourth Congress do oversight units from Senate committees other than Government Operations begin to appear in the data. I am reluctant, therefore, to reach any firm conclusions about the effectiveness or ineffectiveness of Senate oversight units in producing actual oversight activity. Before reaching such conclusions, I would wait until there are a few more oversight subcommittees on regular Senate authorization committees and then examine their behavior.

There is one final factor discussed above which is said to make oversight more attractive to legislators. The relationship between that factor, labeled "corruption, crisis and publicity," and increases in oversight is not the easiest to establish, but Watergate, which was a mixture of all three, seems to have had a clear impact. As Table 2 demonstrated,

TABLE 3

Percentages of House and Senate Hearings and Meetings Series Devoted to Oversight, by Committee Unit and Congress

		Oversight series as a percentage of total series held by oversight units[a]	Oversight series as a percentage of total series held by non-oversight units
Congress			
House	91	41.9 (31)[b]	7.1 (309)
	92	28.2 (39)	5.8 (359)
	93	41.7 (48)	11.7 (419)
	94	52.2 (69)	15.6 (524)
Senate	91	6.7 (15)	9.9 (263)
	92	14.3 (14)	10.3 (312)
	93	5.3 (19)	9.8 (387)
	94	34.3 (35)	13.9 (396)

NOTE: Entries are for the January 1 to July 4 period of the first year of each session of the Ninety-First to Ninety-Fourth Congresses.
a. Oversight committee units are defined as the Government Operations Committees in both chambers and subcommittees of other committees which have such identifying labels as oversight and department operations in their titles. Hearings and meetings held by the Appropriations, Rules, and Administration Committees in each chamber have been excluded.
b. Ns in parentheses are the bases upon which percentages are calculated.

the absolute number of oversight series and days generally increased during the period of the Ninety-First to Ninety-Fourth Congresses, but oversight really jumped into prominence as a major percentage of the daily activities of House and Senate committees in the post-Watergate (Ninety-Fourth) Congress. While other factors are surely important, it is highly unlikely that the juxtaposition of the Watergate crisis and the literal explosion of oversight is mere coincidence.

CONCLUDING COMMENTS

The very rapid recent growth in oversight may well be a temporary phenomenon—a fad inspired by the political currents flowing from Watergate. There is certainly a faddish element to it at the moment and the level of oversight activity may well fade soon. However, there are reasons to think that a fairly solid foundation for substantial oversight activity does exist (although not necessarily at the very high levels found in the Ninety-Fourth Congress) and the data developed in this study indicate some factors which can be manipulated in an effort to maintain a high incidence of oversight activity by congressional committees.

The whole Nixon period brought into focus a growing imbalance of power between the executive and legislative branches. As the data show, congressional activity increased rather dramatically from the Ninety-First to the Ninety-Third Congress. Yet during this time oversight held its own as a percentage of this growing activity, dipping only in the House in the Ninety-Second Congress and recovering quickly in the Ninety-Third Congress, a time when oversight reforms were an important item on the Bolling Committee agenda. Watergate may well have been the chief factor leading to the dramatic increase in oversight recorded in the Ninety-Fourth Congress, but there was already a substantial and growing base of oversight activity prior to that time. I suspect that the pre-Watergate increase in oversight activity derived from the suspicion of presidential power which developed in the Johnson Administration mainly as a result of the Vietnam war and a widespread disillusionment with many of the programs of the 1960s. Even during Nixon's first term Congress attempted to place limits on presidential war and spending powers and initiated serious debate on program priorities. Oversight tended to increase as a natural concomitant of these efforts (and related changes in congressional rules and resources), and as a response to a growing attentive public which showed an interest in congressional efforts to control the executive branch. My argument, in essence, is that Watergate stimulated oversight activity, but that it occurred in a context of related stimuli and reinforced them. If this is so, one would expect the observed increases in oversight activity to persist—although perhaps not at quite such high levels—even as memories of Watergate per se recede.

Turning now to factors which the data suggest might be manipulated to encourage oversight, two stand out: increased committee staffs and the establishment of more oversight units. On the first, some cautions against too simple an interpretation of the data are expressed in the article, but the evidence does at least suggest that increasing committee staff resources has an impact on oversight activity. As noted, the impact is probably less dramatic than a first glance at Figure 1 would lead one to think. However, even if one believes merely that some new staff people will haphazardly find their way into oversight, then further increases in staff will help maintain or even increase oversight activity. Staff earmarked for oversight duty are even more likely to have this effect, though one would realistically expect much slippage between the duties they are supposed to perform and their actual assignments.

The second factor, oversight units, potentially is important not because it is likely to increase oversight activity greatly, but because of its potential as a backstop. The data indicate that oversight units, particularly oversight subcommittees without major legislative authority, do spend a much higher proportion of their time in oversight activities than nonoversight units. They were by no means the major factor responsible for the increases in oversight activity reported in the data, but the empanelling of more oversight subcommittees should establish a base for a higher minimum level of oversight in the Congress.

In closing, let me say a few words about some priorities for future research. First, research of the type reported here will benefit from a longer time frame, particularly in terms of establishing a norm for oversight in the pre-Nixon years, testing the import of split partisan control, and gaining a better understanding of the relationship between committee staff size and oversight behavior. Second, oversight sometimes occurs in hearings and meetings held primarily for some other purpose such as authorizing or appropriating money for ongoing programs. A more comprehensive study design would take this fact into account through such means as content analysis of hearing and meeting transcripts and interviews with participants. It also would consider oversight which occurred outside of the formal hearing or meeting framework. Third, much more work needs to be done on the quality issue. Case studies of various types of oversight efforts probably would be the best way to begin to understand better the conditions leading to more comprehensive and systematic oversight. Finally, not enough is known about the impact of oversight activity on the actions of administrators. Just what effects does oversight really have? An assumption was made at the beginning of the study that more oversight, even if it is not comprehensive or systematic, is better than less because of its likely impact on administrators' behavior. This assumption, while plausible, is so central to making decisions about reforms aimed at increasing the quantity of oversight that we should find out all we possibly can about its validity.

NOTES

1. I use the adverb usually because oversight can be performed in a terribly destructive manner if Congress does not exercise a minimum level of self-restraint. The prime example is the McCarthy "investigation" of government personnel practices in the 1950s.

2. There are certainly benefits to be gained from reviewing a program in a persistent yet unsystematic manner. However, the major payoff from either sporadic or regular unsystematic oversight probably comes from the anticipation by the administrators that the overseers just might uncover something embarrassing.

3. See, especially Scher (1963), Ogul (1976) and Bibby (1968, 1974).

4. The data are presented in Appendix G of the report, pp. 267-275. The percentage of all hearing and meeting days devoted to oversight, in what must be a typographical error, is erroneously presented as 1.1% (p. 268) rather than 11% in that report. (The raw numbers show 231 days devoted to oversight out of a total of 2,095 days.)

5. The hearings or meetings of formal Joint Committees and those held jointly by House and Senate Committees were also excluded from the analysis. Hearings or meetings of party committees (e.g., steering, policy, and personnel committees) were not included in the data set.

6. I have not yet had the time to analyze these data fully, but one would certainly want to look at such factors as increasing staff resources, larger numbers of liberal Democrats, and changing patterns in committee and subcommittee chairmanships for explanations of the pattern presented in the table.

7. Split partisan control might also be very important as a contextual factor influencing the relationship between other variables and oversight, but one would require data from a period in which the same party controlled the two institutions in order to establish this. Relevant data for the Eighty-Seventh to Ninetyth and the Ninety-Fifth Congresses are now being processed.

8. It is food for thought that on the plane of general activity, staff increases were quite pronounced in the Senate committees between 1973 and 1975, yet overall committee hearings and meetings days actually dropped.

9. Staff has been on the increase for quite some time, although not quite at the recent rate. A longer time frame for the analysis will provide some additional evidence from which to infer the ways in which these variables operate in the Congress.

10. The assumption here is that the larger the number of subcommittees, the more dispersed power is likely to be. This assumption is probably a reasonable one in most cases but there are some potential pitfalls. For example, in a committee with many subcommittees the chairman and a small clique might control the key subcommittees which have jurisdiction over the crucial programs within the committee's jurisdiction.

11. The oversight activity indicator was coded as oversight = 1, other = 0.

12. The percentages for the Ninety-Second and Ninety-Third Congresses were 35.5% and 29.0%, respectively.

13. The House Government Operations Committee, I should note as supplementary evidence, was below the average of oversight units in its oversight efforts, although not as low as in the Senate.

REFERENCES

BIBBY, J. F. (1974) "Oversight—Congress' neglected function: will Watergate make a difference?" Presented at the 1974 Meeting of the Western Political Science Association.

——— (1968) "Congress' neglected function," pp. 477-488 in M. Laird (ed.) Republican Papers. New York: Praeger.

HARRIS, J. (1964) Congressional Control of Administration. Washington, DC: Brookings Institution.

OGUL, M. (1976) Congress Oversees the Bureaucracy. Pittsburgh: Univ. of Pittsburgh Press.

ORNSTEIN, N. J. (1975) "Causes and consequences of congressional change: subcommittee reforms in the House of Representatives, 1970-73," in N. J. Ornstein (ed.) Congress in Change: Evolution and Reform. New York: Praeger.

SCHER, S. (1963) "Conditions for legislative control." J. of Politics (August): 526-661.

SCHICK, A. (1976) "Evaluating evaluation: a congressional perspective," pp. 341-354 in Legislative Oversight and Program Evaluation. Washington, DC: Government Printing Office.

SINGER, J. W. (1978) "Labor and Congress—new isn't necessarily better." National J. (March): 351-353.

U.S. Congress, Commission on the Operation of the Senate (1976) Interim Report of the Commission on the Operation of the Senate, Senate Document, Ninety-Fourth Congress, 2nd session.

U.S. Congress, House Select Committee on Committees (Bolling Committee), Committee Reform Amendments of 1974, Report to Accompany House Resolution 988, Ninety-Third Congress, 2nd session, House Report 93-916, Part II.

U.S. Congress, Senate Temporary Select Committee to Study the Senate Committee System (1976) The Senate Committee System, Committee Print, Ninety-Fourth Congress, 2nd session.

The Courts as Monitors
of the Bureaucracy

DONALD L. HOROWITZ
Smithsonian Institution

In the United States, bureaucrats have always had to answer to the courts. The scope of judicial review of administrative action, the classes of petitioners who could seek it, and the enthusiasm of judges for the task have all varied over time.

Much has depended, of course, on the interplay of statutory provisions and judicial sensibilities. Statutes requiring fairly narrow administrative determinations, based on a precise evidentiary record, do not lend themselves to searching judicial inquiries into every dark corner of an agency's business. Even so, a suspicion of unfairness or irregularity can trigger the curiosity of the courts to know more about how the administrator makes his decisions. Laws that in the most general terms charge administrators with responsibility for doing bold things, however, invite the courts to pass equally broad judgments on bureaucratic performance. A good many bureaucrats have discovered in litigation that a statutory provision that "the decision of the administrator shall be final" does not necessarily mean what it says.

More and more, of course, bureaucrats have been given responsibility for solving public problems by statutes that only in the vaguest terms provide legislative guidance about how this is to be done. There are many reasons for this phenomenon, ranging from strongly held differences of opinion about the appropriate solution to no opinion at all about the appropriate solution. Almost all of these reasons insure that someone will be unhappy about the course ultimately adopted by the administrator. And since the legislative standards are vague, typically because legislators are unsure of the solution, their uncertainty frequently leads them to conclude that nothing will be lost if the courts are given equally broad authority to review how the adminis-trators perform. And so, for this and other reasons I shall touch on, we are now in a phase of active judicial oversight of bureaucratic per-formance—active in the dual sense that a judicial second look is frequently available to interested or even not-so-interested parties and that the review often ranges widely over the decisions made by bureaucrats.

Some courts have even begun to articulate a doctrine of general judicial "supervision" of administrative agencies or "partnership" with them. Such metaphors, however much they reflect current de-velopments in judicial review, also conceal some major differences between administrative processes and the judicial process. Bureaucrats and judges may be partners, but they tend to have different specialties. The prospects for judicial amelioration of bureaucratic maladies will be shaped by the way the judicial process works and the tasks it is structured to perform.

Of all the policy processes, the judicial process is the one that is formally most programmed for "rational" decision-making. Judicial decisions must rest on evidence. Judicial opinions state results in terms of reasons. Judges and juries are insulated from extraneous influences. They are shielded from the clash of opposing interests and the process of "give-and-take" that are supposed to constitute integral parts of the other governmental processes. The courts take pride in their ability to work their way through the tangle of "special interests" and to handle issues "on their merits." In the judicial process, no particular virtue is seen in giving everyone something; of far greater importance is reaching the "right result." The assumption of the judicial process is that where reason resides, the public interest will emerge.

There is a long tradition in the United States of appealing to the courts when efforts in other forums fail. Among other things, the fact that courts operate on avowedly different assumptions from other branches of government makes them attractive as alternative forums in which the play of interests can proceed. The predicate of such appeals is that institutions that are composed differently and proceed on different principles may well reach different results.

Yet the ability of the courts to proceed on different principles rests ultimately on the different burdens they have shouldered. Reason can reign when courts decide cases in which the number of unknowns is limited, in which doctrinal signposts exist, in which the relevant facts, though disputed, can be ascertained with a fair degree of reliability for purposes of the litigation, and in which the consequences of a decision one way or the other are limited in scope and generally foreseeable.

Courts still decide many cases of this kind, but their calendars increasingly include suits raising issues that tax their ability to ascertain the relevant facts, gauge the consequences of a decision one way or another, and reason to a conclusion. Most of these cases are challenges to governmental action, action usually taken by an administrative body. Many of them, involving matters such as the registration of pesticides, the regulation of effluent flows, and the approval of drugs and dyes, require complex assessments of risk and choice among alternatives. Some involve experimental social programs, while others deal with investment decisions having potential social costs, such as highway and power plant construction. Wholly new bodies of legal doctrine, such as the law of welfare rights and environmental protection, have grown up. The scope of judicial scrutiny has also enlarged, as the deference that judges formerly paid to administrative decisions has tended to wear thin. Courts today play a more prominent and less interstitial role in defining and protecting the public interest, often against agencies accused of neglecting it.

This chapter will trace some of the roots of the expanding judicial role in articulating the public interest, evaluate the prospects for resolving such issues through judicial review, and assess some of the consequences of judicial involvement in administrative decisions.[1]

THE ADMINISTRATIVE STATE AND
THE JUDICIAL THREAT

When the Administrative Procedure Act was passed in 1946, liberal proponents of the administrative state, eager to protect the New Deal agencies from the predatory attacks of a conservative judiciary and legal profession, were outraged. Among other things, they saw the Act's judicial review provisions as granting a license to the courts to thwart the creative work of the administrative process. Three decades later, the same battle is being fought, but the sides have changed. By and large, the business interests that wanted to use the courts in their crusade against regulation never got to do so. Instead, the liberal reformers now attack the federal agencies their predecessors proudly created. They invoke the aid of the courts against the same interests that earlier fought for access to the courts—and under the same statutory provisions. The courts, far from undoing the work of the federal agencies, have in general required them to do more and better. No one seems to play his or her appointed part.

How have we arrived at this paradoxical turn of events?

The reformers' fears were not wholly ill founded, but in the short run they proved quite mistaken. The Administrative Procedure Act (APA) was framed against the background of a long campaign to gut the New Deal agencies. With the American Bar Association in the vanguard, critics charged that the agencies were doing judicial work but without the independence of judges, that they often espoused the cause of one of the parties before them or were captives of their staffs. It was argued that agency procedures were haphazard, irregular, and unfair. The ABA in general favored the transfer of much of the work of the agencies to the courts, viewed as more committed to traditional principles of justice.

The Administrative Procedure Act did not do this. Instead, it spelled out basic procedural rules for the agencies to follow. The Act made many administrative determinations subject to judicial review, but often within a very narrow compass. This was far short of the hopes of those who saw creeping despotism lurking behind the "fourth branch" of government.

Nevertheless, the result was to regularize and in many ways to formalize administrative procedure. Beyond that, the Act allowed judges to sit in judgment on the way in which administrators had conducted themselves. These provisions alone were sufficient to offend those who had fought long and hard for the problem-solving utility of the administrative mechanism. These people wanted "results" rather than rules, and managerial technique rather than what they saw as legal obscurantism. What they most objected to was the sacrifice of flexibility—that most vaunted virtue of the administrative process—on the altar of an abstraction, due process of law. Judges, whose administrative expertise could hardly be acknowledged and whose sympathies were questionable at best, would now have the power to issue orders undoing the work of specialists. Worse still, implementation of administrative decisions might be delayed while the pleasure of the judge was awaited; "vested interests" might use and profit from the lapse of time. This was the ultimate conspiracy of the lawyers against the public interest (for exactly this view, see Blachley and Oatman, 1946: 213-227; see also Waldo, 1948: ch. 5).

Despite these forebodings, for the first fifteen or twenty years of its operation the APA kept the courts out of the work of the federal agencies and departments far more than it let them in. Particularly was this so on the broad policy questions where arguments for administrative expertise and flexibility were most strongly invoked. Resort to the courts was possible in the vast majority of cases only where a showing of procedural irregularity was made. Rarely was it possible to challenge administrative action in court on substantive grounds— that is, by showing that though the agency had followed the proper procedure, it had nonetheless reached an inappropriate resolution of the problem before it.

The drafters of the APA were only a decade removed from the excesses of the Surpreme Court in the 1930s. They were well aware of the Court's flights of fancy into "substantive due process," of the constitutional crises wrought by judicial immoderation, and the "Court-packing plan" it produced. Out of such concerns came the blanket exception to judicial review for matters "committed to agency discretion." The courts were not to second-guess wholly discretionary judgments. Nor were they to overturn agency action if the agency had followed the appropriate procedure, unless the action was "arbitrary, capricious, an abuse of discretion, or otherwise not in accordance with law" or "unsupported by substantial evidence."[2] The intention was to make the procedures of the agencies predictable, to confine them to decisions that had some demonstrated basis in fact, and to prevent them from acting in disregard of statutory law or fundamental constitutional principles. Courts were not to have a central role in formulating public policy, and for quite some time they did not seek such a role.

These conditions no longer obtain. Over the last decade or more, courts have become a more prominent part of the process of administrative decision-making. They have moved beyond protection of the rights of parties aggrieved by administrative action to participation in problem-solving and protection of more general public interests against agencies accused of indifference to the public interest. Judicial review has passed from matters of procedure to matters of both procedure and substance. Judicial scrutiny of records of administrative decision-making has become far more searching than it once was, and judges have often not liked what they have found. Courts have not merely sat in judgment on administrative action but on inaction as well; they have required agencies to do things the agencies themselves had declined to do.[3]

The signs of this more active role were everywhere—in legal doctrine, in frequency of litigation, in the sweep of decisions, and in judicial pronouncements on and off the bench.

The obstacles to carrying policy problems to the courts have been falling away over the years. The doctrines that barred litigants or certain classes of litigants at the threshold—requirements of standing, jurisdiction, and the like—are now much diluted, and the defenses available to government agencies once suit was begun have also been chipped away.

At the same time, the frequency of litigation challenging governmental action, especially in the federal courts, increased considerably between the early 1960s and the early 1970s, although perfectly accurate figures are difficult to come by.[4] The scope of the challenges raised in such cases seems to have broadened considerably. One indirect measure of this is the steady increase in the percentage of cases brought by nonprofit organizations suing to challenge governmental action. These organizations are more likely than the individual plaintiffs they have proportionately supplanted to challenge not some narrow determination, of interest to only one party, but the policy as a whole and the assumptions on which it is based.[5]

Finally, the scope of the exception to judicial review for matters "committed to agency discretion" has been steadily narrowed. Now even agency determinations of "feasibility" and "prudence"—the kinds of words opponents of judicialization might have made into slogans in 1946—are not immune from judicial scrutiny.[6] Far from eschewing discretionary judgments, some meliorist judges today see themselves as warriors in "the fight to limit discretion" on the part of administrative agencies.[7]

THE BACKWASH OF THE APA

In the long run, then, the anguished prophesies of the reformers have been fulfilled and overfulfilled. Courts have insisted that agencies abide by stringent procedural requirements, and in the main these requirements and the judicial role in enforcing them have been accepted without much question. By what the courts have done goes much beyond administrative procedure. Increasingly, the courts insist on having the last word on the merits of many issues of public importance. It is not anything so modest as the judicialization of the administrative process that is the issue: It is the role of the courts in sharing what was formerly taken to be the agencies' exclusive job.

Needless to say, courts have assumed such functions haltingly, unevenly, incompletely—but far beyond what opponents of the APA imagined they might do. Yet in certain ways, these developments were an outgrowth of that Act. As the APA and the courts whittled away many of the differences between agency proceedings and court proceedings, so too did they obliterate much of the distinctiveness of the administrative process. In some respects, agencies have simply become second-class courts. The new title, "administrative law judge," in lieu of "hearing examiner," is more than just an attempt to share in the prestige of the courts: It also marks the extent to which the trial-type hearing has become a norm of administrative practice. Judicial review of substantive issues is therefore the aftershock of the judicialization of agency proceedings. Why accept the counterfeit administrative version of a just decision when one can have the real currency, robes and all? The more similar the administrative and judicial processes become, the more the same functions will be performed interchangeably.

Furthermore, the APA and similar laws may have demanded of judges exceptional ability to compartmentalize their work. Once a judge has jurisdiction to review for procedural irregularities, how can he be expected uniformly to acquiesce in an "erroneous" decision, even if it is arrived at through impeccable procedure? Jurisdiction to review the one invites review of the other, and it is unrealistic to think that judges will always adhere to a restrictive "arbitrary and capricious" or "abuse-of-discretion" standard once the subject matter is opened up to them at all.

Broader currents have also shaped the judicial inclination to scrutinize agency action closely. The APA became law at a time of national quiescence, and it is not surprising that it should have been interpreted as it was during such a period. Equally, the courts were affected by the restlessness that affected other institutions in the 1960s, and their eagerness to probe grew apace. The bases of administrative legitimacy came under attack. Claims that once rang true began to ring hollow. "Expertise" can connote narrow-mindedness, and "flexibility" may mask political compromise. The courts have not been especially tolerant of either. Generalists themselves, judges are often disdainful of specialization. They tend to be rationalists, searchers after "solutions," suspicious of the political process and "special interests" as impediments to rationality. As they sensed the growth of clientelism in the federal agencies, departmental self-aggrandizement and bureaucratic rivalries, official sloth, inertia, and rigidity, the courts became less and less hospitable to administrative claims to immunity from judicial oversight and more and more disposed to weigh costs and benefits for themselves. What they saw made them, in a word, skeptical.

Those who now invoke the courts against the agencies tend to exalt these qualities of the judicial process: the generalist character of the judges and the distance from the political contest they seem to possess. Now it is the judges, rather than the managers, who are regarded as the expediters dissolving the sediment that has accumulated in the administrative machine. But do they have the equipment to do this job? In the race to the courthouse, this question has rarely been posed and even more rarely addressed.

HAZARDS OF JUDICIAL GUARDIANSHIP

Judges may be performing new roles in administrative-agency litigation, but they continue to act very much within the framework of an old process, a process that evolved, not to devise new programs or to oversee administration, but to decide controversies. The constraints of that process operate to limit the range of what can reasonably be expected from courts. The principal limitations derive from the way in which cases get to courts, the way in which issues are framed and reasons adduced, and the provisions for effectuating court decisions.

Courts are public decision makers, yet they are wholly dependent on private initiative to invoke their powers: They do not self-start. Parties affected by administrative action choose to seek or not to seek judicial redress on the basis of considerations that may bear no relation to the public importance of the issues at stake, to the recurring character of the adminstrative action in question, or to the competence of courts to judge the action or to change it. This basic feature of judicial review has a number of important consequences.

First of all, the fact that judges do not choose their own agenda makes it difficult for them to concentrate in a sustained way on any policy area. Judicial action tends to be spotty and uneven; some agencies may be subject to frequent correction in the courts, others to virtually none at all. The decisions that emerge are ad hoc; they are rarely informed by a comprehensive view of the agency's work, and they cannot aspire to anything approaching the status of a coherent policy. One of the catchwords of the administrative state—and now perhaps one of its biggest disappointments—was "planning." Few agencies do the kind of program planning that was once expected of them. But if this is a deficiency of the administrative process in need of rectification, the courts, whose own process is fundamentally passive and piecemeal, are not the place to seek it.

The fact that courts do not deal with anything resembling a random sample of the work of administrative agencies affects their perspective in another way. They are put in the position of having to prescribe on the basis of very special, indeed often highly atypical, cases— cases that come to decision one at a time. Small wonder that their outlook on the administrative process has tended to become skeptical: They base their inferences on a skewed sample. Courts see the tips of icebergs and the bottoms of barrels. If their perspective is detached, it is not necessarily well informed.

As courts decide only special cases, so do they decide them in a special way. The framing of issues is geared to the litigant and his complaint. The mission of the courts is to set wrongs right. This means that the facts of the single case are highlighted, the facts of all cases slighted. The judicial process has a bias toward the particular and against the recurrent. Judicial standards of relevance are strict. In consequence, everything that can be labeled context or background is relegated to a distant second place in litigation. Elaborate provision is made for proving and weighing the events that give rise to the litigation. Virtually no provision is made for proving anything more general about administrative behavior. Courts are, for example, often ignorant of the scope and nuances of the programs they find themselves judging, and nothing in the rituals of litigation alerts them to this omission. On the contrary, everything pushes them toward a narrow focus on the case before them. It is this feature of adjudication that so often gives outsiders the impression that courts are fascinated by questions that are at best tangential to policy.

The sources of judicial reasoning do of course reside in general principles. But those principles are to be found in yet more particular cases—often cases far afield from the administrative action being challenged. The principles tend to cut across the functional divisions along with agencies are organized and policies are formulated. For purposes of decision, reality is organized in terms of categories that seem to make no sense except in court. Thus, perhaps the only thing that social security recipients, produce handlers, and environmentalists have in common is that all must be accorded hearings by the administrators whose actions affect their interests—though the "actions," the "effects," and the "interests" may be completely different in kind. No doubt the propensity of courts to seek their analogies in far-flung places contributes to the development of an integrated jurisprudence, and there is much to be said for it in these terms. But this propensity again detracts from judicial attention to the program being reviewed. It also diminishes the value of the judicial decision as guidance to the administrator as he manages his program.

Judicial decisions thus embrace a limited species of reasoning. Equally important, they are *all reasoning*. The judicial process is tied to reason as the mode of decision and can scarcely be described apart from its resort to reason. Yet there are some questions that lend themselves to other modes of decision—particularly to negotiation and compromise. Sometimes that is the only way to satisfy conflicting interests and keep them from turning against the political system. Sometimes reason provides no clues to an appropriate answer. There may be a shortage of knowledge sufficient to provide answers or a shortage of resources to find the answers at the time they are needed, at a cost that makes sense. The administrative process has at least its fair share of such problems. Courts are not the place to look for their solution.

Perhaps the ultimate hazard of relying on courts to guard the public interest is that their decisions stand a good chance of being ineffective or effective in ways not intended. Some administrators have been known to act on the view that courts decide only individual cases. A succession of cases repudiating the lawfulness of agency policy brings a series of concessions to individual litigants but no change in policy.[8] Those with the resources, initiative, and foresight to bring suit may force a "policy change" applicable only to their cases.

Even more generous views of the authority of courts to lay down policy can raise problems of uniformity. Decisions of the federal courts, short of the Supreme Court, are binding only in the circuit or district in which the court sits. Although this principle is a useful safeguard against settling difficult policy questions prematurely, it also permits recalcitrant bureaucrats to wait until at least several courts have spoken before bringing general policies into line with court decisions. Typically, this time is measured in years, and there are some agencies that do not feel obliged to alter their course until the Supreme Court itself has spoken. Given the multitude of issues competing for Supreme Court consideration, this may be never. The fact that courts decide one case at a time and the fact that agencies show varying degrees of responsiveness to judicial decision make it hard for courts to force policy change all by themselves.

There is, however, a problem of impact beyond this. It lies in the propensity of all policies to have unanticipated consequences. In this respect, policies enunciated by courts are no different from the policies that emanate from other decision makers. But the courts are unusually short of machinery to detect and correct unintended consequences after they have occurred. They have no monitoring mechanisms, no inspectors, no grapevines (compare Kaufman, 1973). Quite the opposite: Judicial properties foster isolation of the decision maker from the environment in which his decisions must operate. Unless a litigant provides the courts with feedback about the consequences of their decisions, there is every likelihood that they will pass unnoticed—and unaltered. Here again, private initiative seems inadequate to protect public interests.

CONCLUSION

Different institutions tend to perform well at different kinds of tasks. Each has its own characteristic modes of operating, and these leave an indelible stamp on the matters they touch. In the case of the courts, I have argued, their procedures remain attuned to the disposition of individual controversies. This means that they function on a basis that is too intermittent, too spotty, too partial, too ill informed for them to have a major constructive impact on administrative performance. They can stop action in progress, they can slow it down, and they can make it public (their exposing function has been too little noted). Perhaps most importantly, they can bring moral judgment to bear, for moral evaluation is a traditional judicial strength. But courts cannot build alternate structures, for the customary modes of judicial reasoning are not adequate for this. When it comes to framing and modifying programs, administrators are far better situated to see things whole, to obtain, process, and interpret complex or special-ized data, to secure expert advice, to sense the need to change course, and to monitor performance after decision. Courts can limit the discretion of others, but they find it harder to exercise their own discretion where that involves choosing among multiple, competing alternatives.

Although the tendency to resort to the courts for the vindication of broad public interests continues unabated, the impact of judicial intervention on administrative behavior remains uncertain. There has surely been no rush in the federal agencies to embrace judicially enunciated standards of performance beyond what is minimally required by individual decrees. Even then, many government lawyers and program managers have been inclined to read judicial opinions as narrowly as the words would warrant, secure in the knowledge that many things escape the attention of the courts, that judicial correction comes not every budget session, but only every so often, and frequently in a different court and usually in a fresh factual setting.

But it is wrong to reckon the benefits and costs only by the effects of judicial action inside the departments and agencies. The growing judicial role has implications for the courts, too. They have so far been remarkably slow to enhance their ability to meet the new burdens they face. It is, as I have suggested, the fact that they continue to face new challenges with the old machinery very much intact that limits their ability to handle complex data, to monitor the consequences of their decrees, or to do the other things that might make them more effective partners in the process of defining the public interests.

Yet even in this failing, there is something to be celebrated. The outstanding characteristic of the judicial process remains the way in which it generalizes from the particular instance. So committed are the courts to the individual case that all their machinery is tuned to resolving it. From the standpoint of policy-making, this is a weakness. Retooling the judicial process means essentially giving it the capacity to function more systematically in terms of general categories, to draw probabilistic inferences, to forecast effects. Should retooling proceed beyond marginal improvements, it seems highly likely that it will occur at the expense of the commendable attention currently given to the individual case and that courts, in trying to improve other institutions, will become much more like them. The distinctiveness of the judicial process—which makes it unfit for much of the important work of government—lies in its willingness to expend social resources on individual complaints one at a time. That distinctiveness is worth preserving.

NOTES

1. In the second half of this chapter, I have drawn on my book (Horowitz, 1977).

2. Administrative Procedure Act, § 10, 5 U.S.C. § 701. I have omitted references to some refinements contained in section 10.

3. See Lau v. Nichols (1974); Adams v. Richardson (1973). Increasingly, too, the courts have required the agencies to provide for the fair representation of all interests affected by their decisions. See Stewart (1975: 1669-1813).

4. In the decade between 1961 and 1971, cases filed in federal district court against the United States, its agencies, and officials doubled—from 6000 to 12,000 per annum. Earlier decennial increases were far more modest. See *Annual Report of the Director of the Administrative Office of United States Courts*, 1941: 95-96; 1951: 130-131; 1961: 238; 1971: 262. The number of reported district court cases challenging agency action (excluding certain categories of heavily routine cases) more than quadrupled from the early 1960s to the early 1970s. But these are reported opinions only, and do not necessarily reflect total rates of case filing or disposition.

5. In the sample of reported cases described in note 4, individual plaintiffs declined from 72% of all cases in the early 1950s to 63% in the early 1960s and 49% in the early 1970s. Nonprofit organizations were plaintiffs in only 1% to 2% of the reported challenges to agency action in the early 1950s, but 23% by the early 1970s.

6. See Citizens to Preserve Overton Park v. Volpe (1971).

7. See Environmental Defense Fund v. Ruckelshaus (1971); see Wright (1972: 575-597).

8. This was the case with federal agencies that continued to withhold classes of documents the courts had ruled citizens were entitled to obtain under the Freedom of Information Act. For other examples, see my book (Horowitz, 1977a: especially ch. 5).

CASES

ADAMS v. RICHARDSON (1973) 480 F. 2d 1159.
CITIZENS TO PRESERVE OVERTON PARK v. VOLPE (1971) 401 U.S. 402.
ENVIRONMENTAL DEFENSE FUND v. RUCKELSHAUS (1971) 439 F. 2d 584, 597-598.
LAU v. NICHOLS (1974) 414 U.S. 563.

REFERENCES

Annual Report of the Director of the Administrative Office of United States Courts (1941, 1951, 1961, 1971) Washington, DC: Author.

BLACHLEY, F. F. and M. E. OATMAN (1946) "Sabotage of the administrative process." Public Administration Rev. 6 (Summer): 213-227.

HOROWITZ, D. L. (1977) The Courts and Social Policy. Washington, DC: Brookings Institution.

——— (1977a) The Jurocracy: Government Lawyers, Agency Programs, and Judicial Decisions. Lexington, MA: Lexington Books.

KAUFMAN, H. (1973) Administrative Feedback: Monitoring Subordinates' Behavior. Washington, DC: Brookings Institution.

STEWART, R. B. (1975) "The reformation of American administrative law." Harvard Law Rev. 88 (June): 1669-1813.

WALDO, D. (1948) The Administrative State. New York: Ronald Press.

WRIGHT, J. S. (1972) "Beyond discretionary justice." Yale Law J. 81 (January): 575-597.

Bureaucratic Autonomy
and the Public Interest

FRANCIS E. ROURKE
Johns Hopkins University

Throughout much of its early history, the effort to reform public administration in the United States was rooted in the belief that the public interest was best served by giving administrative agencies a great deal of independence within the political system. In the late nineteenth and early twentieth centuries, this was the animating force behind administration reform. It brought such innovations in American political institutions as a merit system designed to make competence rather than political allegiance the criterion for selecting public employees, and a decentralized administrative structure in which key functions of state and local government, including education, planning, and economic regulation were carried on by independent agencies isolated from the political sector.

In recent years, however, there has been a dramatic shift in the reform perspective. The reformers of the 1960s and the 1970s seem bent not on extending, but on curtailing the independence of bureaucratic organizations. They argue that bureaucracies represent formidable concentrations of power in contemporary society, and that executive agencies should be brought back within the political system and made more accountable. If traditional efforts at reform could be described as an attempt to depoliticize the administrative process in the United States, the reform movement in our day seems rather aimed at repoliticizing administration—at least in the sense of restoring public control over previously independent agencies.

This fear that bureaucracy has won too independent a position for itself in the political system is at the heart of a number of current reform measures. These include the move to strengthen citizen participation in bureaucracy, a move that continues at the federal level in spite of disappointing experiences with the poverty program, as well as the efforts currently being made to strengthen the oversight mechanisms through which legislative bodies monitor executive activities. Where reformers once worried about administration being too weak to resist outside control, they now fear that it may be too strong to allow it.

But it is possible to foresee that just as traditional reformers went too far in insulating administrative agencies from political control, current attempts at reform may well push too strongly in the opposite direction. There is a case to be made for the autonomy or semi-autonomy that administrative agencies were sometimes granted in the past—in terms of both the professional efficiency of the organizations involved or of their responsiveness to the publics they serve. This case should not be overlooked in the current passion to restore political control over areas of bureaucracy that presently seem to exercise independent authority.

FORMS OF BUREAUCRATIC INDEPENDENCE

There are two kinds of administrative agencies in modern American politics that have raised the problem of insufficient control over bureaucracy in a particularly acute form. First, there is a set of what might be called constituency agencies that are closely tied to some dominant group or cluster of groups outside of government. In the operation of constituency agencies public power is seemingly exercised not in behalf of the community at-large but for the benefit of special interests that seek favorable treatment from government officials. It is conventional to regard these constituency agencies as having been "captured" by the groups they serve—thus becoming governmental outposts of powerful or even predatory private interests.

A second set of agencies that generate serious difficulties of political control are organizations that have succeeded in establishing a position of autonomous self-determination within the executive branch. They are controlled neither by the public nor by any network of outside constituencies. They are dominated instead by the career officials who steer the agency and set its course. Power in the case of these self-directing bureaucracies is centered in the agency itself, rather than, as is the case with constituency agencies, in outside groups.

CONSTITUENCY AGENCIES

Public organizations in this category perform an agency role in its literal sense. They act as "agents" for others, although of course the employees of the organization may also use the power that flows from their base of outside support to enhance their own bureaucratic prerogatives and privileges. But what is usually clear in any case is that the agency is the "agent" and the constituency is the "principal."

Constituency agencies are commonly encountered in areas of policy where agencies control access to benefits and resources that are highly important to external groups that themselves have a great deal of leverage within the political system. Many of these constituency agencies are in effect clientele organizations—administrative institutions created to serve the needs of particular population groups—labor, agriculture, or veterans, for example. In the case of these agencies, domination by an outside constituency has been virtually mandated and certainly legitimized by the statutes under which they operate. The raison d'etre of a clientele agency is its ability to be of service to an outside constituency.

Public works agencies like the Corps of Engineers and the Bureau of Reclamation can also be included in the constituency category. These agencies make decisions on the building of dams and other public facilities that may impact heavily on the political prospects of office-holders or the economic well-being of local communities. These external beneficiaries of a public works agency's decisions often play a major role in the determination of its policies.

A common criticism of constituency agencies is that their effort to serve the needs of specialized segments of the population inevitably leads them to neglect the welfare of the public at large. The groups with which constituency agencies interact are often viewed by contemporary reformers as being exploitative in character as far as the general public is concerned; e.g., the oil industry, the airlines, and the pharmaceutical houses.

But it is important to remember that specialization in the groups being served is as much a characteristic of bureaucracy as is specialization in the skills bureaucrats bring to their role in government agencies. Specialization on the part of its employees has long been regarded as the distinctive attribute of bureaucracy. The division of labor within government agencies that both reflects and promotes this specialization has been looked upon as the key to the superior efficiency that Max Weber and others attributed to bureaucracy as an institutional form for the delivery of services in modern society. In the same way constituency agencies can be said to represent a specialization of concern that heightens the sensitivity of bureaucracy to the needs of particular population groups and thus improves its effectiveness.

Something else that needs to be taken into account in evaluating the role that constituency agencies play in the administrative process is the fact that the domination or capture to which these agencies are commonly subject can be imposed on them by groups with purposes that reformers themselves would tend to regard as benign. Handicapped persons, for example, represent one such constituency, disadvantaged groups another. Civil rights agencies are frequently dominated in their decision-making by the equal opportunity lobby. Ecology interests often hold conservation and environmental protection agencies under close control. In short, what would generally be conceived of as predatory interests are not always the groups that benefit when constituency agencies are held in something resembling protective custody by outside forces.

At their best constituency agencies can also be said to perform a representative function. In the past the concept of representation has usually been applied to bureaucracy to refer to the degree to which the demographic character of an agency's personnel corresponds with that of the population at-large, or, in the case of some agencies like the Bureau of Indian Affairs, with that of the group it serves (see Krislov, 1974, for the most recent full-scale treatment of the subject). The closer the resemblance, the more representative an agency is said to be. But regardless of the demographic character of its personnel, an agency can also be said to be representative if it accurately reflects the views of a particular population group in the deliberations of the executive branch, and this is what consituency agencies commonly claim to do.

SELF-DIRECTING AGENCIES

A second set of agencies whose independence reformers now seek to reduce are what have been referred to earlier as self-directing organizations. The policies of these agencies are usually determined by the career professionals who dominate their staff. Such agencies are not altogether immune from outside penetration; administrative organizations in the United States seldom are. But they are more strongly resistant to it than other bureuacracies. The forms of control to which they are primarily subject are internal rather than external—a system of self-control—such as can be enforced by a formal or informal code of professional ethics, for example.

The staff of these agencies usually possess some form of expertise that the community defers to. Whereas constituency bureaucracies are usually dominated by the outside groups with which they are linked, self-directing agencies normally deal with deferential publics. When capture occurs, it is the agency that captures the public rather than the reverse. The outside groups with which these agencies interact have very often been created by its activities. Without its presence, these organizations would not exist. The business firms that supply weaponry to the military are a case in point.

At the national level in the United States, one of the best illustrations of this kind of organization are the agencies dealing with national security affairs—the CIA, the FBI, and the like. A similar group of agencies at the state and local level are the law enforcement organizations—police departments and states' attorneys offices—that are established to preserve domestic security. A common characteristic of all agencies dealing with security matters, whether international or domestic, is that they operate with a good deal of secrecy. This secrecy contributes in an important way to their ability to set their own course. Decisions and activities that are concealed from the public can hardly be subject to its control.

Agencies which have a major scientific or technical component to their work also have a broad capacity for self-determination at all levels of government. The professional employees of these agencies are usually masters of some arcane discipline that the outside laity cannot altogether fathom. Such organizations trade on a certain air of magic or mystery that is associated with what they do. They do not need to resort to secrecy to preserve their independence. The public tends to accept the fact that much of what the agency does is beyond its comprehension. Illustrations of scientific agencies whose esoteric knowledge provides a basis for this kind of autonomy include NASA, NSF, and NIH. At the state level the independence that public universities have long enjoyed in the states' administrative structure is a product in no small measure of deference on the part of the public and the legislature to the wide range of professional skills that the faculties in institutions of higher learning are believed to command.

In the cases just described, the independence that administrative agencies enjoy ordinarily has a de facto quality. Nominally at least, the agencies concerned are under the same kind of political supervision as all other administrative units in the executive branch. But they have succeeded in winning by political strategy or strength an independence they cannot claim under law.

There is one group of agencies, however, that have been granted a position of actual legal independence, as administrative bodies. These are the independent regulatory commissions which monitor a varied set of social and economic activities at both the state and national level of government. The complexity and need for expertise in the policy areas under supervision as well as the desirability of continuity in administration were among the factors that led legislatures to hit upon independent commissions as the proper vehicle for the achievement of a primary objective of economic regulation—the pursuit and protection of the public interest.

A persistent and perplexing problem with these agencies is that they have so often seemed prepared to exchange their status as autonomous bodies for that of constituency agencies—serving the narrow needs of the industries they regulate rather than those of the broad public they were established to protect. The administrative metamorphosis to which these agencies are subject has often been criticized by reformers. While it is understandable if not defensible that agencies established to serve the needs of specialized groups should come under their control, it seems grossly inappropriate when an agency established to serve the public interest is captured by a specialized clientele.[1]

The transformation that occurs here can sometimes be traced to an ambiguity in the statute under which a regulatory agency operates, or to an unexpected turn in the historical development of the industry under its supervision. The Civil Aeronautics Board was established both to promote and regulate the infant airline industry under its jurisdiction, an ambiguous mandate that more or less invited the regulatory agency's capture even as it seemed to exclude it. The Interstate Commerce Commission was created to regulate the railroads at a time when the industry was strong, but soon found itself obliged to promote the industry's welfare, as the railroads began to face increasing challenge from other forms of transportation (see, in this connection, Huntington, 1952).

Eisenstadt (1959: 302-320) has described the process by which an administrative agency shifts from the pursuit of its own goals to those of the groups it serves as "debureaucratization." This he describes as a "subversion of the goals and activities of the bureaucracy in the interests of different groups with which it is in close interaction" (clients, patrons, interested parties)[Eisenstadt, 1959: 312]. No better term has yet been devised to describe the process by which many regulatory agencies in the United States have been transformed from agencies serving broad public purposes into organizations protecting specialized private interests.

THE CHANGING POLITICAL ENVIRONMENT

The portents are favorable today for a substantial expansion in public control over bureaucratic organizations that had once seemd immune to it, whether because of their close ties with powerful constituencies, or their success in winning a position as self-directing bureaucracies. Just recently we have seen two agencies—the FBI and the CIA—subject to challenge in the legislature, the media, and even the courts in ways that would have been unthinkable a decade or so ago.

One major development accounting for this change is the growing capacity evident in modern society for the political mobilization of citizens affected by the exercise of administrative power. Citizen action today means citizen organization, and the past two decades have seen the birth of a large number of new citizen organizations. Most of these organizations aim to speak for interests not previously represented or grossly underrepresented in political decision-making. A variety of new environmental groups has sprung up, older people are now represented by their own lobbying organizations, and women's organizations have acquired a new power and effectiveness. The list of new citizen organizations and of old organizations that have been in some sense "reborn" is a long one. A recent study of public interest groups shows that 63% of these organizations have been established since 1960 (see Berry, 1977: 34).[2]

This multiplication of new citizen organizations has a direct and significant impact on both constituency agencies and what have been called here self-directing organizations. Constituency agencies now find themselves subject to pressure by a much wider circle of groups and interests in framing their policies. It is no longer as easy as it once was for an administrative agency to link itself with a single, monochromatic constituency. The Corps of Engineers, for example, now confronts not only the Rivers and Harbors Congress, representing its traditional pork-barrel constituency, but also a wide range of new groups, concerned about the negative impact of some of the agency's water projects on the environment.

Self-directing agencies have also come under greater public control as a result of this new citizen capacity for political mobilization. Agencies like the CIA that were once allowed and expected to go their own way in austere isolation now find themselves subject to a kind of surveillance by outside groups that is entirely new for them. A major factor contributing to this change is the fact that the administrative process has become more highly visible in all sectors than it once was, and this increased visibility is incompatible with administrative autonomy. The assumption of a much more vigorous investigative role by the media is partly responsible for this new visibility. Partly responsible also are the freedom of information and disclosure laws that have been enacted at all levels of government—largely as a result of pressure exerted by the public interest lobby. Exposure legislation of this sort alerts more people to the fact that decisions affecting their interests are being made within bureaucracy and stimulates them to do something about it.

A second development that is helping to bring bureaucratic organizations under greater outside control is the weakening public faith in professional expertise. Such expertise has traditionally been one of the prime characteristics of bureaucracy, and it has led other institutions within government—the legislature and the courts, for example—to defer to its judgment on policy issues. The power of expertise and the power of bureaucracy are very much linked together in modern society, and whatever diminishes one tends to diminish the other.

This declining public faith in expertise can be traced to many factors. Among the most important of these are the negative impact a great many scientific advances in such fields as chemistry have had on the environment, the failure of military professionals to deliver the results expected in Vietnam, and the inability of economists to come up with solutions for the simultaneous onslaught of inflation and unemployment. Add to this the continuing decay of cities in spite of the best efforts of planners and the difficulties social workers have faced in trying to devise remedies for the phenomenon of the "permanently poor." These last decades have not been kind to experts and have done much to undermine the authority of expertise. People are now prepared to challenge—through, for example, malpractice suits—the competence of professionals to whom they would once have automatically deferred.

Both of these developments—the enhanced capacity for mobilization on the part of citizen groups and the declining faith in expertise—have helped set the stage for a variety of new efforts that have been made in recent years to exert better public control over bureaucracy. These efforts include experiments with citizen participation in bureaucratic decision-making, an increased focus of attention by public interest groups on bureaucratic rather than legislative behavior, government financing of consumer advocacy before regulatory commissions like the FTC, the passage of sunset laws, and the establishment of zero-based budgeting systems. All these developments testify to a growing awareness of bureaucratic power and an increasing public desire to do more to control its exercise.

If this objective were attained, it would do much to close the gap between bureaucracy and democracy that so long has haunted the liberal imagination. At the same time it is important to remember that a great deal of what contemporary reformers are trying to do is to undo the work of earlier reformers. In their day the merit system and the independent boards and commissions that once dominated the administrative structure were regarded as very great advances in the science and art of administration. The Achilles heel of reform in administration as in other areas has been the unanticipated consequence. If they are to avoid disappointment, contemporary reformers need to be more wary of surprises than their predecessors in earlier periods proved to be.

One pitfall seems worthy of particular note. Reformers need to remember that the independence that many administrative agencies have traditionally enjoyed is not necessarily without social utility. As the argument here has tried to show, constituency agencies that have been established to serve minority interests provide social benefits not only in helping these groups cope with their special problems, but also in preventing these problems from "spilling over" and having injurious consequences for the rest of society. The majorities to which advocates of improved political control seek to make bureaucracy more responsive may thus have a stake in the effective performance by constituency agencies of their specialized role of serving the needs of particular groups. Bureaucracy may thus pursue the public interest when it is responsive to minorities as well as majorities.

As far as self-directing agencies are concerned, it can be argued that the autonomy they enjoy is often indispensable for the effective performance of a public function. Agencies like the Bureau of Labor Statistics that are required to gather statistical or other kinds of information need to have a certain immunity from outside control if their reports are to be free of suspicion of a political slant that would render them useless to society. This is true of all agencies that perform primarily a research function, as well as organizations that carry on tasks that are essentially judicial in character and that need to be protected from political influence.

Thus, the search for better controls over a bureaucracy that seems to dominate contemporary politics should not obscure the fact that there are many functions of administrative agencies that can be best performed in the public interest if these agencies are allowed a certain degree of organizational independence. Coming to terms with this paradox is a major imperative as modern society seeks to maintain an effective administrative system that is not a law unto itself.

NOTES

1. For an interesting historical account of the way in which agencies designed to serve the public interest first emerged in the United States see Wilson (1975).

2. For a superb analysis of the role of public interest groups in American politics see Berry (1977: 34).

REFERENCES

BERRY, J. M. (1977) Lobbying for the People. Princeton: Princeton Univ. Press.

EISENSTADT, S. N. (1959) "Bureaucracy, bureaucratization and debureaucratization." Admin. Sci. Q. 4 (December): 302-320.

HUNTINGTON, S. P. (1952) "The marasmus of the I.C.C.: the commission, the railroads, and the public interest." Yale Law J. 61 (April): 467-509.

KRISLOV, S. (1974) Representative Bureaucracy. Englewood Cliffs, NJ: Prentice-Hall.

WILSON, J. Q. (1975) "The rise of the bureaucratic state." Public Interest 41 (Fall): 77-103.

Decentralization of Government Agencies

What Does It Accomplish?

ROBERT K. YIN
Massachusetts Institute of Technology

Several years ago, Douglas Yates and I completed a study of municipal decentralization (Yin and Yates, 1975). Such decentralization was in vogue then, as many mayors and city governments tried to broaden (some would say "dilute") the effects of the antipoverty programs by encouraging widescale citizen participation in government. Our study, which is summarized briefly below, reviewed the reports of 215 case studies of urban decentralization, with most of the efforts having occurred during the 1960s.

In contrast to these earlier activities in municipal decentralization, one of the hallmarks of the 1970s will probably be the continued attempts at federal decentralization. Thus, many of the initiatives taken by President Nixon as part of the New Federalism included attempts to decentralize—either by giving state and local units more discretion with federal resources (as in the general revenue-sharing program), or by giving federal regional and field offices greater administrative roles vis-à-vis their headquarters counterparts (e.g., see Haider, 1974: 257-282; Nathan, 1975). It had not occurred to me until recently that some of the lessons Yates and I had learned with municipal decentralization might be applicable to federal decentralization, in spite of the vast differences in programs and politics. Yet, it may certainly be claimed that decentralization of government, whether

Author's Note: *Presented at the 144th annual meeting of the American Association for the Advancement of Science, Washington, D.C., February, 1978.*

municipal or federal, usually begins with similar motives—i.e., to provide greater control and a sense of participation to those served by government (Richardson, 1976: 211-231). And, it may also be claimed that, for both municipal and federal governments, decentralization represents one of the few common options for trying to alter governmental behavior.[1]

The present chapter therefore focuses on the decentralization of governmental agencies and what it accomplishes from the perspective of both municipal and federal experiences. The chapter first discusses the main lessons from municipal decentralization, then outlines the characteristics of recent federal initiatives, and finally concludes with comments on the likely effects of decentralization.

MUNICIPAL DECENTRALIZATION

Our study of municipal decentralization (Yin and Yates, 1975) covered a wide variety of policy initiatives. Decentralization could occur through:

- the formation of little city halls;
- the creation of a community relations office;
- the establishment of a grievance or complaint procedure;
- the development of citizen advisory or governing boards;
- as well as many other bureaucratic mechanisms.

Whatever the mechanism, however, two dimensions always remained important: decentralization could mean an increase in actual power by the clients of a service (*client involvement*) or decentralization could mean greater territorial division in the administration of a service (*territorial dispersion*). An important realization was that the term "decentralization" often confused these two dimensions, but they were really independent—that is, attempts to give clients greater power were not necessarily synonymous with territorial dispersion, and vice versa (see Table 1).[2]

For instance, an effective grievance mechanism will allow feedback from clients to change services. Such a mechanism may be best organized, however, on a territorially centralized basis, with complaints coming from the entire city into a central office. The tabulation of

TABLE 1
Urban Decentralization Strategies Placed Along
Client-Oriented and Territorial Dimensions

Territorial Focus	Client Role in Administration of Service		
	Negligible	Informed	Dominant
City-wide	Community Relations	Grievance Mechanisms	— — —
Neighborhood	Physical Redeployment	Employment	Political Decentralization
	Administrative Decentralization	New Neighborhood Institutions	

SOURCE: Yin and Yates, 1975.

grievances and feedback to service practitioners might have greater impact because general patterns of service problems may be easier to discern. Conversely, a little city halls program (physical redevelopment strategy) involves much territorial dispersion. Storefronts or trailers are staffed by municipal representatives in numerous local districts. Such territorial dispersion, however, does not mean that any real power has been transferred to clients. The clients may receive better information about services, and they may be able to transact their services on a local basis (as in paying water bills at the little city hall rather than going "downtown"), but the territorial dispersion in itself is no guarantee that clients will have more power over the services that are delivered.

A second major finding in our study was that different services within the same municipal government responded differently to decentralization initiatives. Yates and I called this the "service hypothesis," noting that the relationship between residents and various street-level officials—i.e., teachers, police officers, fire officers, and so on— had different traditions and resulted in different bureaucratic rules. To take a simplistic example, the tradition of holding "open school night," when parents are welcome to speak to teachers and to browse through an entire school facility without regard to any particular complaint they might have, has no counterpart in the police service (or in the public health service, for that matter). We regarded some of these differences as being so strong that this lay behind our thinking in naming our work "Street-Level Governments," because we felt it useful to think in terms of each service agency constituting a system of governance of its own.

The service hypothesis can explain many of the outcomes of municipal decentralization. To begin with, some services such as law enforcement or public health are in a much more centralized state of organization, and only weak forms of decentralization can be attempted. In addition, such service differences make any attempt at district-wide coordination more difficult if not impossible. If one service cannot really decentralize authority to its district offices, for instance, then a district "cabinet" composed of the district officers of a variety of services will not be able to operate on an equal footing. In all, we regarded the service hypothesis as being so important that it led to the major lesson from our study: the possibilities for decentralization cannot be considered in the abstract, but have to be proposed in conjunction with a specific service.

A third lesson from our study of municipal decentralization covered the overall pattern of outcomes. Every case study was examined for any evidence of five types of outcomes: increases in the flow of information, changes in service officials' attitudes, changes in clients' attitudes, improved services, or increased client control. The type of evidence on these outcomes was spotty; however, the outcomes were generally positive (see Figure 1). About two-thirds of the case studies, for instance, indicated some improvement in services as a result of decentralization. Nevertheless, few included any dramatic changes in the quality of urban life that people had come to expect from serious decentralization efforts.

Thus, as I have previously written elsewhere (Yin, 1977a), the main outcome from decentralization must be considered an organizational or administrative one. Typically, decentralization produces changes in political or bureaucratic procedure, but the link to substantive effects in the urban quality of life is indirect at best. Such substantive effects are, in contrast, more readily produced by other types of governmental action than decentralization—e.g., highway programs, school desegregation laws, or even military engagements such as the Vietnam war.

These, then, were the three main lessons drawn from our work on municipal decentralization. The first was that decentralization could mean a client-oriented or territorial initiative; the second was that the specific service being decentralized was the most important factor in determining the outcomes of any decentralization initiative; and the third was that decentralization outcomes were generally of an administrative rather than service nature.

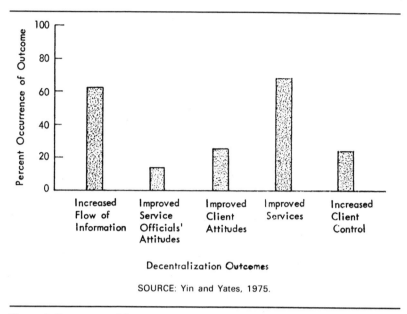

Decentralization Outcomes

SOURCE: Yin and Yates, 1975.

Figure 1: Frequency of Outcomes Identified by Case Studies of Urban Decentralization (n = 215)

FEDERAL DECENTRALIZATION

Before discussing some of the objectives and problems of the New Federalism, it is important to distinguish among various kinds of federal programs. When dealing with domestic federal programs, the balance is different from municipal programs (see Figure 2). On the one hand, the federal government may directly operate a service. Examples of these are the postal service, the Indian reservations and other special territories, and the unemployment service. By and large, these services do not dominate the domestic federal budget and therefore are not usually the main focus of organizational reform. On the other hand, the federal government may support aid or assistance programs, in which monetary payments, grants, or loans are made to recipients who may be individuals, units of state or local government, or other nonprofit organizations. Here, federal support of any specific service is indirect, but problems can arise in the way that federal agencies are organized to distribute funds or make awards. Such aid or assistance programs constitute a large proportion of the domestic federal budget and therefore reflect the types of programs most people associate with the federal government.[3]

Among the aid and assistance programs, the major shift that occurred during the Nixon administration was an attempt to give increased control over federal resources to state and local units of government. Thus, in an August 1969 television address the President gave his ideological justification—i.e., to make governmental decision-making more democratic by giving less discretion to federal bureaucrats or poverty-area citizens and by giving more discretion to those officials "elected to serve all the people" (Nathan, 1975: 85). Decentralization was then tied to another administrative goal—the decategorization of grant programs (Mirengoff and Rindler, 1976). The two initiatives together served as a potent force, threatening congressional prerogatives as well as the power bases of special target populations such as the poor.[4]

The early and political results of this shift in priorities are probably well-known (see Sneed and Waldhorn, 1975). Numerous general and special revenue-sharing bills were introduced, and several bills eventually became law, taking the form, for instance, of the revenue-sharing program administered by the Treasury Department, the comprehensive employment program of the Department of Labor, and the community development block grants of the Department of Housing and Urban Development. By the end of the Ford Administration, six years after the submission of the first special revenue-sharing bills, the shift in federal priorities was still being implemented, with Ford's fiscal 1978 budget, for example, containing renewed proposals for decentralizing programs in education and health (see Office of Management and Budget, 1977).

Other decentralization initiatives occurred with less public debate and were less well-known (Advisory Commission on Intergovernmental Relations, 1977c). These included the establishment of common boundaries for ten regions in the country (mandated by Executive Circular A-105 in 1969), the creation of ten federal regional councils (mandated by Executive Order 11647 in 1972), and a whole host of OMB circulars on grants administration that followed the Intergovernmental Cooperation Act of 1968.[5]

It is difficult at this time to assess the actual outcomes from the decentralization initatives taken under the guise of the New Federalism. Preliminary studies have generally focused on redistributive effects— which appear to have occurred—but there is no evidence that services have been altered dramatically from those produced under centralized programs.[6] Certain comments can nevertheless be made about the

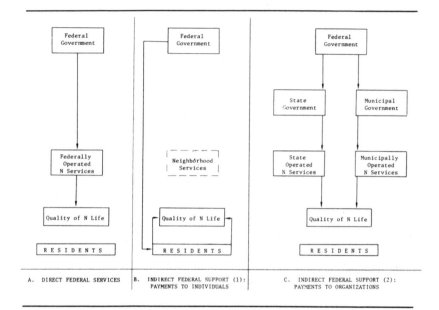

Figure 2: Classical Systems for Implementing Federal-Neighborhood Policies

decentralization process, and here the experiences appear to parallel those with municipal decentralization. First, although it is true that the federal initiatives were marked by political conflicts among client groups—low-income groups versus the officials of the general purpose governments—conflicts also resulted from client versus territorial concerns. For instance, national lobby groups, representing local jurisdictions and other special target populations, tended to support the continued centralization of federal programs on a territorial basis. Conversely, territorial dispersion did not necessarily mean greater control by clients. Thus, although the Department of Housing and Urban Devolopment, the Economic Development Administration, and the Small Business Administration developed area or district offices at the local level—which have considerable discretion in allocating federal resources—little control has been passed on to state or local governments. Most local governments, in fact, still only control a minority proportion of the federal funds expended in their jurisdictions. In short, the first observation might be that client and territorial differences are just as dramatic with federal as with municipal programs, and that few initiatives accomplish both types of decentralization simultaneously.

Second, vast differences among the various services exist, providing a federal counterpart to our "service hypothesis." Figure 3 shows an illustrative prototype of the various headquarters and field units that can be involved in a federal aid program. For different federal programs, power and authority tend to rest at different levels. At the most decentralized extreme of territorial dispersion, the 100-odd district offices of the Small Business Administration perform the major function of reviewing and approving loans to local businesses; similarly, for the most extreme form of client-oriented decentralization, the Treasury Department has only a staff of about 150 persons that allocates the $6.8 billion general revenue-sharing program, in which the clients—e.g., state and local units of government—play the dominant role in deciding how federal funds should be used. At the most centralized extreme, mass transit project applications have traditionally been reviewed by the headquarters staff in Washington, D.C.. Similarly, in the newly mandated Urban Development Action Grant (UDAG) program, projects will be reviewed and approved by headquarters staff in the Department of Housing and Urban Development.

These service differences have made any attempt at horizontal coordination extremely difficult. This is true whether such coordination is attempted at headquarters, regional, or state or local levels. With each service having a different degree of decentralization, there is no single level at which officials of different agencies have comparable responsibilities. In this sense, it is very difficult to speak of the overall decentralization of federal aid programs. As Pressman (1975) has so imaginatively put it, the intergovernmental system really consists of a pattern where "fragmentation meets fragmentation." These implementation patterns have been further examined in a study of the organization of federal economic development programs (Yin et al., 1978; Yin, forthcoming). As but one example, a pilot study in Milwaukee has shown that there can even be mixed organizational patterns for different programs even though they are part of the same federal agency.

Although the outcomes from federal decentralization are difficult to assess, decentralization initiatives may nevertheless produce two administrative shifts that are worth noting. And these may, in the long run, serve as the main effects that any federal decentralization will have.

The first administrative shift occurs within single agencies that are the target of decentralization. For instance, in creating the Com-

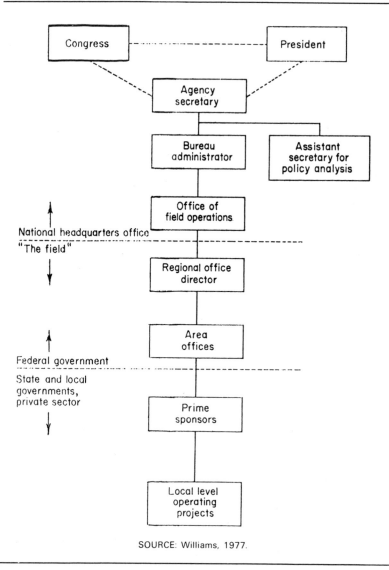

SOURCE: Williams, 1977.

Figure 3: Illustrative Policy and Operations Structure for Federal Aid Programs

munity Development (CDBG) and Comprehensive Employment (CETA) block grant programs, shifts in authority and responsibility did occur in the Department of Housing and Urban Development and in the Department of Labor (Williams, 1977). Prior to the block grant program, the headquarters offices of the Department of Labor had direct responsibility for over 10,000 project awards annually. This responsibility has been passed on to the DOL regional offices as well as to local "prime sponsors" who are the main recipients of the block grants. Similarly, HUD area offices now have major responsibilities with regard to CDBG projects. Decentralization, in short, served in each case as an impetus for reorganizing a federal agency and thereby for changing bureaucratic rules and behaviors that may have become overly rigid and unresponsive. Such an effect may be far different from the substantive outcomes (e.g., more neighborhood revitalization or decreased unemployment) that policy makers and the public may seek, but *decentralization may nevertheless serve as one important way of shuffling bureaucratic organizations and thereby keeping them responsive to their overhead agencies.*

The second shift has been in the new opportunities for control and power in the intergovernmental system. Various decentralization initiatives, even if made in isolation from each other, will produce new political alliances and balances of power. Although it is difficult to say which groups have benefited most—i.e., whether mayors or county executives are now more powerful than in the past vis-a-vis either federal or resident organizations—*decentralization initiatives can provide new opportunities for elected officials to assert themselves in a manner different from their predecessors.* This means that newly elected officials, for instance, can at least stylistically create a unique trademark and can appear to be trying new and different approaches to serve their constituents. This is as true at the federal level, where the Nixon Administration will historically be remembered in part for its New Federalism, as well as at state and local levels.

In summary, both federal and municipal decentralizations appear primarily to produce administrative achievements. These include reorganizing specific agency bureaucracies as well as opportunities for new relationships among different levels of governments. Both of these effects are eminently justifiable according to any theory of bureaucratic organization or political science (e.g., see Downs, 1967). However, the larger question still remains. Are services better or are citizens' lives improved in any substantial manner? The answer is probably not. The intergovernmental system has become so complex, and the role of government in individual lives is now so pervasive, that initiatives such as decentralization (or centralization) will only be unevenly implemented at best and hence have marginal effects on service delivery or the equitable distribution of services.

NOTES

1. Some of the other options are covered by the other chapters in the book. However, not all are equally relevant to municipal and federal bureaucracies.

2. The distinction appears more critical in understanding decentralization than the standard one between "administrative" and "political" decentralization (see Kaufman, 1969).

3. The twofold distinction between direct service provision and aid programs is intended for discussion purposes only and does not attempt to describe the whole range of federal policy instruments; e.g., fiscal policy, tax policy, regulatory initiatives, and others.

4. For a description of the continuing conflicts at the neighborhood level, see Yin, 1977b.

5. The OMB Circular A-95, establishing a project notification and review system at the local level, is but one of several examples of these circulars (see Comptroller General of the U.S., 1975).

6. Examples of some early assessments include: Comptroller General of the U.S. (1974) on the federal regional councils; Nathan and Adams (1977) on the revenue-sharing program; Nathan et al. (1977) on HUD's block grant program, and Mirengoff and Rindler (1976) on the CETA program. In addition, the Advisory Commission on Intergovernmental Relations has issued two reports on these programs (1977a, 1977b).

REFERENCES

Advisory Commission on Intergovernmental Relations (1977a) Community Development: The Workings of a Federal-Local Block Grant, A-57. Washington, D.C. (March).
—— (1977b) The Comprehensive Employment and Training Act, A-58. Washington, D.C. (June).
—— (1977c) Improving Federal Grants Management, A-53. Washington, D.C. (February).
Comptroller General of the United States (1975) Improved Cooperation and Coordination Needed Among All Levels of Government—OMB Circular A-95. Washington, D.C. (February).
—— (1974) Assessment of Federal Regional Councils. Washington, D.C. (January).
DOWNS, A. (1967) Inside Bureaucracy. Boston, MA: Little, Brown.
HAIDER, D. H. (1974) When Governments Come to Washington. New York: Free Press.

KAUFMAN, H. (1969) "Administrative decentralization and political power." Public Admin. Rev. 29 (January/February): 3-15.

MIRENGOFF, W. and L. RINDLER (1976) The Comprehensive Employment and Training Act. Washington, DC: National Academy of Sciences.

NATHAN, R. P. (1975) The Plot that Failed. New York: John Wiley.

——— and C. F. ADAMS, Jr. (1977) Revenue Sharing: The Second Round. Washington DC: Brookings Institution.

NATHAN, R. P. et al. (1977) Block Grants for Community Development. Washington, DC: Brookings Institution.

Office of Management and Budget (1977) Issues '78. Washington, DC (January).

PRESSMAN, J. L. (1975) Federal Programs and City Politics. Berkeley: Univ. of California Press.

RICHARDSON, E. (1976) The Creative Balance. New York: Holt, Rinehart & Winston.

SNEED, J. D., and S. A. WALDHORN [eds.] (1975) Restructuring the Federal System: Approaches to Accountability in Postcategorical Programs. New York: Crane, Russak.

WILLIAMS, A. (1977) Draft manuscript on CDBG and CETA programs.

YIN, R. K. (forthcoming) "Creeping Federalism: the federal impact on the structure and function of local governments," in N. J. Glickman (ed.) The Urban Impacts of Federal Policies. Baltimore: Johns Hopkins Univ. Press.

——— (1977a) "Goals for citizen involvement," pp. 50-52 in P. Marshall (ed.) Citizen Participation Certification for Community Development. Washington DC: National Association of Housing and Redevelopment Officials. [Also presented at the 141st Annual Meeting of the AAAS, New York City (January 1975)].

——— (1977b) "What a national commission on neighborhoods could do." J. of the Amer. Real Estate and Urban Economics Association 5 (Fall): 255-278.

——— and D. YATES (1975) Street-Level Governments: Assessing Decentralization and Urban Services. Lexington, MA: Lexington Books.

YIN, R. K. et al. (1978) "Federal aid and urban economics development: a local perspective." Rand Corporation. (unpublished)

Solving Problems of Bureaucracy

Limits on Social Science

DAVID K. COHEN
Harvard University

CHARLES E. LINDBLOM
Yale University

Remedies for the problems of bureaucracy take many forms, ranging from simply pruning existing organizations to creating new organizations or procedures. One remedy, increasingly popular in recent decades, is better information and analysis for decision-making. Bureaucracies work badly, it is often argued, because inadequate information and analysis are brought to bear on decisions. Typically the inadequacies are said to arise from the experience of workers within bureaucracies: their information and analysis are said to be anecdotal, fragmentary, and powerfully shaped by the perspective of their particular agency or bureau. Better information and analysis would be more impartial, more independent of particular perspectives, and it would be generalizable rather than fragmented and anecdotal.

Authors' Note: *This chapter is a revised version of Chapter Four from USABLE KNOWLEDGE: Social Science and Social Problem Solving, by Charles E. Lindblom and David K. Cohen, published by Yale University Press.*

In a word, it would be the product of disinterested social science research[1] rather than the product of the experience of practitioners in bureaucracies. Importing or imposing PSI knowledge and analysis—in the form of planning, evaluation, policy analysis, and systems analysis—is thus a common and increasingly popular remedy for the problems of bureaucracy. Improve the information and analysis on which decisions are based, the argument goes, and you will improve decisions.

Several assumptions underlie these prescriptions. One of them is that PSI is more authoritative than other inputs to decision-making. PSI is thought to be better than the ordinary knowledge of bureaucrats because it is more sure, or conclusive. Decisions based on scientific knowledge, it is thought, will thus provide a better basis for action than decisions based on ordinary knowledge. Another assumption is that scientific knowledge is more impartial. It is thus thought to t. less limited, and hence more closely approximate to a "public interest." Decisions based on PSI would thus be a better basis for action than decisions arising from the interplay of partisan interests and the information connected to them.

Is PSI as authoritative as scientific reformers of bureaucracy—and other advocates of an expanded role of PSI—argue?

We think not. The character of PSI is such that it is not, and in all likelihood cannot be, more authoritative than other inputs to decision-making. In this chapter we explore the limits on PSI's authoritativeness. These arise first in a very simple way: PSI is costly, so much so that it cannot be practiced for most social problems nor pushed to conclusive answers on those issues on which it is practiced. Second, even if it were a free good and thus available without constraint of manpower, materials, or money, it cannot achieve scientifically definitive or conclusive answers on certain kinds of questions. At core both of these explanations trace to the complexity of the social world and, in the face of that complexity, man's limited cognitive capacity. To stretch that capacity is enormously costly; and even if stretched as far as imaginable, it cannot handle certain kinds of questions.

At least some of the implications of the costliness of PSI for good practice are obvious. Since PSI cannot cover the whole terrain of problems to be solved, good practice requires discrimination in what is attempted. The difficulty of finding funds to support their research requires pPSI to give at least some attention to cost. Even the most apparent implications of cost for good practice are, however, often missed, as when, for example, it is recommended that "the level of spending on basic research should be such as to allow funding of all meritorious research proposals," a prescription that recommends the impossible (National Academy of Sciences, 1965: 276).

Implications of costs for the conclusiveness with which PSI can establish propositions on those questions it attacks pose more difficult and interesting issues. They intertwine, however, with other issues that also concern the conclusiveness of PSI propositions—specifically, those arising out of PSI incapacities other than its costliness.

CONCLUSIVENESS AND AUTHORITATIVENESS

For our purpose—which is that of developing issues bearing on the usefulness of PSI in social problem-solving—the conclusiveness issue needs to be somewhat amended. PSI knowledge might be scientifically conclusive—or reasonably so—yet for some other reason be rejected for social problem-solving. Let us therefore distinguish between the question of whether a proposition is reasonably verified scientifically and the question of whether anyone will act on the belief or assumption that it is true. PSI might establish as scientifically highly verified the proposition that children learn as well in large classes as in small; yet no school superintendent might be willing to act on such a conclusive finding—even though he knows of it—in agitating for new policies, in establishing class sizes in his schools, or in advising parents on the educational needs of their children. He may be skeptical or hostile to it for many reasons. If he is not willing, we will say that, however conclusive the knowledge is by scientific standards, it is not *authoritative* for him, it does not in his eyes warrant his acting on it.

Conclusiveness is necessary but not sufficient for authoritativeness.[2] Moreover, since scientific conclusiveness is a matter of degree, so also is authoritativeness. And authoritativeness of knowledge, we suggest, varies from person to person even more so than judgments of conclusiveness.

We also need to distinguish between two kinds of authoritativeness, or two ways in which it can at least hypothetically be achieved. In the first case, a proposition is authoritative because its degree of scientific conclusiveness is high (and there are no positive obstructions on other grounds to its authoritativeness). In the second case, it is authoritative because, although its conclusiveness leaves a great deal to be desired, the scientific or professional tests confirm or are confirmed by ordinary knowledge (fallible as both may be). In the second case, PSI achieves a sufficient degree of conclusiveness to make the knowledge authoritative, but only because PSI adds to the weight of ordinary knowledge. In the first case, we shall say that PSI is independently authoritative; in the second case, dependently authoritative.

Some practitioners at PSI (pPSI) may be disturbed at the thought that ordinary knowledge can confirm PSI knowledge or that it is appropriate to think of so powerful an instrument as PSI being cast in the role of confirming ordinary knowledge. Yet in fact PSI knowledge is often less conclusive than ordinary knowledge. That increased market demand usually means higher prices, that war will occur again somewhere in the world, that decades from now some people will still live in poverty, that newly invented technologies will on some counts greatly raise our standard of living in the future, that political democracy will arise in some nations and vanish from others within the next generation—all are more conclusive propositions for social problem-solving than most formally tested propositions of PSI. Indeed most ostensibly scientific PSI propositions, such as those statistically tested at great expense in the controversies over the educational consequences of school desegregation, are extremely shaky and widely challenged as soon as first asserted.

MISPERCEPTIONS

With these distinctions, we now suggest that its practitioners frequently misperceive PSI. They mistakenly believe that: pPSI should strive for independent authoritativeness; pPSI should above all strive for the scientific conclusiveness that is necessary to authoritativeness, with little attention to the other requirements for authoritativeness; and there is no other significant role for PSI than the attainment of authoritativeness.

The contrary views we suggest are that: PSI can ordinarily not be independently authoritative; pPSI will be more effective if they were to strive only for dependent authoritativeness; for independent authoritativeness, even where it is possible, is not enough (since in addition PSI has to be confirmed by ordinary knowledge); consequently, pPSI must always attend in addition to the relation between their knowledge and the ordinary knowledge that confirms it; and, finally, there are in any case alternative roles for PSI that do not require authoritativeness, either independent or dependent.

In this article we go no further than to indicate why PSI cannot usually be independently authoritative—and why it should then discriminatingly pursue no more than dependent authority.

The misperceptions, we suggest, arise from a traditional deeply rooted belief that scientific inquiry is the pursuit of verified propositions. Science is, in such a view, the pursuit of truth, a method of eliminating false opinion, a way to perceive reality correctly. Even if they allow for persistent error and longstanding differences in findings, most scientists and pPSI find it difficult to conceive of science and professional investigation as other than a process that ultimately moves toward convergence on propositions, toward an increasingly correct representation of reality (see, for example, Mulkay, 1975; White and Rein, 1977). All these notions seem to imply that pPSI should pursue confirmed knowledge or scientific conclusiveness. And from the aspiration to achieve scientific conclusiveness, it is assumed that one can take a quick short jump to authoritativeness.

FAILURES OF AUTHORITATIVENESS

That these are indeed fundamental misconceptions will become clearer if we look at various aspects of failures of authoritativeness, beginning with some that can be passed over quickly because of their familiarity.

NONRATIONAL RESPONSES TO PSI

Perhaps the most familiar failures to achieve authoritativeness of either kind (and for that reason the least interesting for present purposes) stem from many irrational and nonrational human resistances to believing what pPSI, or scientists generally, say. The skepticism or hostility of the government official toward the professional researcher, for example, is much commented on. So also is his reluctance, for many irrational and nonrational reasons, to take the trouble to digest PSI knowledge even when it is made easily available to him. All these familiar considerations bearing on authoritativeness we pass over, not because they lack importance but because they are already widely identified and their implications for the practice of PSI much discussed. Their general tenor is to lay blame on users of PSI and to suggest how the practice of PSI, especially the presentation of its results to potential users, has to be adapted to the shortcomings of the users.

PSI INCOMPETENCE ON NORMATIVE ISSUES

We are more interested in pointing up failures of authoritativeness that arise out of problem complexity and PSI inconclusiveness in the face of complexity. Of these, one is, again, sufficiently familiar to warrant only the briefest attention. That is the alleged incompetence of scientific inquiry to settle the value or normative questions that always arise in social problem-solving. According to this allegation, PSI cannot even go so far as to achieve scientific conclusiveness or any approximation to it on normative questions, and instead remains silent on those issues. That being so, it can hardly be authoritative on them.

The allegation, if true, throws light immediately on one of the many reasons why inescapably people turn to ordinary knowledge and why, alternatively, many normative issues are thrown into an arena for an interactive rather than analytic settlement.

The allegation is not entirely true. Ostensibly normative analysis, we suggest, is overwhelmingly empirical in form. That is, social scientists, philosophers, and other people typically argue about values and norms by making statements most of which are in principle factual (for example, see Wellington and Winter, 1971).[3] An objection, for example, to higher taxes is that they will impede business incentives, which is a statement factual in form. Evaluative discourse thus appears to be open to the contribution of PSI; and pPSI are misdirected when, as is often the case, they permit a misconception on the point to direct them away from normative issues.

But the allegation is not entirely false either. We do not challenge the widespread opinion among pPSI that not all normative propositions can be translated into empirical ones, that one is eventually driven back to end-of-the-line propositions that have to be treated as axioms, or as articles of faith, or as expressions of preference or emotion. Clearly, then, as is well recognized, even if PSI is scientifically conclusive on its empirical propositions, it cannot achieve authoritativeness for action without normative propositions that lie beyond its competence to establish.[4]

DIVERGENCE

Much less familiar an obstacle to authoritativeness—specifically to independent authoritativeness—is one that goes to the very foundations of social science and PSI. Standing in sharp contrast to the customary belief in the tendency of scientific investigation to converge on increasingly correct representations of reality is the phenomenon of divergence that marks much of social science and PSI. Examples abound. Commenting on fifteen years of PSI analysis of productivity, profits, and living costs designed, at least in part, to illuminate policy on wage inflation and unemployment, John Dunlop, economist and former U.S. Secretary of Labor, notes: "Some analysts have concluded the relation among these variables to be strong, others that it has been quite weak; some hold that wage responses to increasing employment are moderate while others hold that wage responses are becoming more inflationary" (Dunlop, 1977: 30).

Our ignorance grows, as Popper has observed, with our knowledge. Or, in the words of another, "the outcome of any serious research can only be to make two questions grow where one question grew before" (Veblen, 1961: 33). We suggest that the usual effect of PSI is to raise new issues, stimulate new debate, and multiply the complexities of the social problem at hand.

Divergence can of course be passed off as transitory, in which case it does not challenge the widespread faith in the power of PSI finally to reach agreed propositions. Yet it appears that in many fields the increase in conflict over issues is not transitory but remains or even grows as PSI continues to uncover even more complex aspects of reality (see Cohen and Weiss, 1977). Research on social stratification and school busing illustrate the indefinite proliferation of diverse issues, findings, and hypotheses, instead of convergence.

Although the question of divergence can be posed with brevity, its significance for social science and PSI is enormous. The frequency of divergence rather than convergence will open up in some minds the possibility that, whenever it is divergent, hence not conclusive and hence not authoritative, PSI in fact has no important contribution to make to social problem-solving. Elsewhere we have examined a more reasonable inference to be explored: that PSI makes its contribution, despite its muddying of waters, in ways other than those leading to independent authoritativeness via convergence of opinion. In any case, questions have to be asked: Under what circumstances does PSI move toward divergence? In what specific ways might PSI be valuable despite divergence? What kinds of PSI best take advantage of those ways?

In the face of divergence of scientific findings, although independent PSI authoritativeness becomes impossible, it seems clear that dependent authoritativeness remains possible. One of the divergent views (which like its rivals enjoys some degree of scientific confirmation) confirms or is confirmed by some people's ordinary knowledge. They then take that view as authoritative, thus act on it. It appears that a great deal of PSI offered to problem solvers is of just this kind.

DEFINING, BOUNDING, OR CONSTRUCTING PROBLEMS

A common failure to achieve an authoritative solution to a problem arises because critics or skeptics of the solution easily can—and do— allege that the problem has been incorrectly defined.

Suppose we begin, as an exercise in defining a problem, with the familiar "Why Johnny can't read." To specify the problem more precisely, someone will suggest that the problem is one of reading difficulties among certain urban ethnic groups. But then it will be said that the problem is one of inadequate family incomes for these groups. And to that it will be responded that income itself is not the problem; the problem is basically a deficiency in the family's ability to implant an incentive to learn to read in children. Hence the problem becomes that of the inadequacy of the urban ethnic family as a social institution—an institution that is failing to perform its required functions. That may provoke the suggestion that the problem is that of defective socioeconomic organization; socioeconomic institutions do not integrate these families into normal social functioning. But perhaps then the problem is one of faulty political organization in the society at large, since presumably the right kind of political decisions could remedy the faults of the economy, the structure of urban society, and the place of the family in it. At this point someone is also certain to suggest the politics is not an independent influence on economy and society, being itself dependent upon them. It might then be suggested that the problem is one big interlocked problem of social organization—to which formulation one may or may not add some additional problem specification, such as that the phenomena of social class are the "real" problem. But problem definition at this level can perhaps be counted on to produce another abstract formulation. Any big interlocked problem of social organization, it will be suggested, can only be understood as a product of history and culture. The problem, then, is a fundamental one of an historically produced culture that is inadequate. From which it seems only a small step to the conclusion: the world is not what it might be. That is the problem.

Of all these attempts to define *the* or *a* problem, none is correct (or incorrect). The notion of an authoritative PSI is therefore strained. We do not discover a problem "out there"; we make a choice about how we want to formulate a problem. And, of course, opinions will also differ as to whether a *phenomenon* is or is not a *problem*. War is often taken to be a problem, but nations use war as a solution to problems. And is decline of parental authority a problem, or an indication of a desirable social trend?

FACT AND PROOF VERSUS EVIDENCE AND ARGUMENT

Another way to look at some of the failures of authoritativeness, we suggest, is to observe that, despite the convention that pPSI are engaged in the pursuit of conclusive fact and proof, they are instead engaged in producing inconclusive evidence and argument. Problem complexity denies the possibility of proof and reduces the pursuit of fact to the pursuit of those selective facts which, if appropriately developed, constitute evidence in support of relevant argument. We do not here mean that evidence is manufactured without respect to data, or that contrary evidence is suppressed, or that argument is indifferent to such facts as can be established. We mean only to call attention to the inevitably incomplete character of attempts at proof, the consequent reduction of such attempts to informed argument, and the highly selective search for just those facts that bear on argument as evidence for or against the argued position. There is, consequently, a need for new rules of verification or proof suitable to what PSI can actually accomplish.

Majone (1977: 202 and throughout) had made these points with reference to policy analysis. We suggest that his insight can be generalized to almost all forms of PSI, including much of its social scientific component as well.

POSTDECISION PSI

Judges write their opinions after they make their judicial decisions. The opinion serves to commend the decision to others. Writing it may also clarify the judge's mind on the relation of the decision to other decisions he has made, thus organizing his mind in ways helpful to his coping with future decisions. The relation of issues in the judicial opinion to those issues that actually brought him to his decision may be either close or distant.

Majone (1977) goes on to suggest that by a very rough parallel, a good deal of PSI is contracted for or otherwise produced in order to display the rationality of decisions reached through ordinary knowledge. PSI is not simply a rationalization of decisions already reached—in the pejorative sense of the term "rationalization." It may test the decision, that is, ask whether grounds can be found through PSI for setting aside a decision reached by ordinary knowledge and analysis. It also may commend the decision to others without whose consent it cannot be made effective. It also satisfies strong desires of decision makers to see their decisions in a perspective of rational thought, and that is in many cases a useful form of self-testing (Majone, 1977).

In all these postdecision uses of PSI, it is not authoritative for action, coming as it does after the act. Some pPSI will allege that these are misuses of PSI. Clearly, however, much of PSI is of this character; and it is important to clarify, by further research, the possibility that much or most of PSI is destined, in ways that cannot be escaped, for unauthoritative uses of these kinds. The closer PSI moves to direct engagement in social problem-solving—as, for example, when the pPSI takes a policy-making organization as client—the more difficult it is to find examples of PSI that are in their impact unquestionably pre- rather than post-decision, hence authoritative for the decision.

It is just possible, at an extreme, that PSI infrequently achieves a greater degree of authoritativeness for action than, through putting previous decisions in intellectual order by postdecision defense of them, indirectly altering the perspective through which subsequent decisions are made. Think of the *Wealth of Nations* in this light.

OBSOLESCENCE OF PSI KNOWLEDGE

Finally, PSI fails on authoritativeness because, as is familiar, it tries to describe or predict the ever-changing behavior of learning human beings, and it even provides them with learning. From all their experiences and sources of information, human beings learn to behave differently with each passing month or year; and they constantly render PSI generalizations about their behavior obsolete.

Contrary to the general assumption that valid scientific knowledge cumulates, much of the midtwentieth century investment of American political science in survey research on voting, a body of generalization to which the profession pointed with pride when claiming a new scientific status, is already obsolete. There are even signs that some of the general propositions of macrotheory in economics, once among the most secure holdings of social science, have become obsolete in a changing society that now displays inflation and depression simultaneously. (Of course, much of the statistical reporting done by social scientists, social research institutions, and government agencies rapidly becomes obsolete, sometimes even before it can be published, although it remains part of the historical record.)

In some periods of rapid change, it is a possibility—although we do not know how one could firmly establish such a fact—that PSI falls behind; specifically, pPSI lose more knowledge than they gain. And if the common presumption is that PSI produces a cumulation of knowledge, the cumulation may be at best extremely slow.

Commenting on the obsolescence of voting studies, the authors of a recent study write:

> the description of the electoral process of the late fifties no longer holds, and that change in the electoral process came in response to political events. Does this mean that all political processes are contingent on the events of the day and that generalization is impossible about political matters? The electrolysis instruments continue to produce hydrogen and oxygen decade after decade. The survey instruments produce different results now than they did a while back. Nevertheless, we remain convinced that generalization is possible, even about matters as volatile as politics. But the generalizations will have to take time into account. [Nie et al., 1976: 9]

In principle, authoritativeness is still possible if only PSI is thus focused on the unchanging aspects of human behavior. But it is the changing aspects that are often pertinent to social problems and their solutions. Businessmen's behavior, not in its unchanging aspects but in its specific 1970s pattern, may be the crucial element in economic policy. Hence, we suggest, useful PSI is destined for steady obsolescence and on that specific ground—in addition to all the others—cannot, as a consequence, attain authoritativeness.

PSI knowledge, we have argued, is almost never conclusive, hence for that and other reasons almost never independently authoritative. If the common pPSI aspiration is that PSI become a source of independent authoritative knowledge, the actual fact is, we suggest, that PSI acquires no more than dependent authoritativeness together with other inputs into problem-solving. A PSI finding, never itself independently authoritative, will often become authoritative if it confirms ordinary knowledge, and often not if it contradicts. And, as is familiar, it will become authoritative in some users' minds if it squares with their ideology, but not otherwise. Or if it conforms to their general world view or epistemological position.

Hence PSI knowledge is, again, best seen as an increment to other knowledge. Now and then it adds sufficient weight to carry a proposition across the line of disbelief. In presumably rare circumstances, it achieves an outright challenge to a substantial body of established belief. In these circumstances, however, it probably achieves its impact on that body because it is an increment to another body of established belief that has been in conflict with the first. In any of these cases, we may be tempted to speak of it as authoritative (hence also conclusive); but, strictly speaking, it is not. It is only when PSI and other knowledge are joined in mutual support that knowledge about the social world is authoritative.

The reform of decision-making in bureaucracies or other settings therefore will not occur simply as a result of increasing PSI. Because PSI is typically no more authoritative than either ordinary knowledge or other inputs to decisions, when offered as an input competing with these other inputs PSI competes only weakly. As many studies of policy analysis, evaluation, and other PSI inputs show, PSI can make no compelling independent claim to the assent of decision makers.

There probably are ways, however, in which PSI might increase its usability. All of these would involve renouncing a claim to independent authoritativeness through scientific conclusiveness. They also would entail different roles for PSI. It seems likely, for example, that PSI is better suited to rationalizing decisions after the fact than it is to weighing alternatives in advance. Such retrospective rationality may well be of use to many problem solvers in their persistent efforts to understand existing policies or programs. Another possibility is that while PSI is rarely able to offer conclusive proof on the effects of decisions under consideration, it might nonetheless be useful in structuring evidence and argument about decisions or their effects. Many of the rules governing PSI seem to be oriented to producing true propositions about the social world, but it might be more appropriate to devise or borrow other rules —such as those found in law, or earlier in rhetoric—which aim as much at good argument and proper uses of evidence as they do at truth. This might be particularly helpful in bureaucracies, for PSI is increasingly the vehicle for debate about policy.[5] Reforming the rules of discourse to better conform to the character of PSI might improve policy argument.

There are other important roles for PSI which also are nonauthoritative—such as providing "enlightenment," or constructive conceptual tools for setting social problems, and others. But a full discussion of them is impossible here.[6] Indeed, more exploration and experimentation with such alternatives would be in order before a satisfactory discussion would be possible. We are not sure about the chances of acceptance of new roles for PSI—indeed, we acknowledge that they may be small. One reason is that all such changes would require that practitioners of PSI and workers in bureaucracies alike would have to accept much more modest claims for the authoritativeness of PSI knowledge. This might be easier to accept in principle than in practice.

NOTES

1. Henceforth we will use the term Professional Social Inquiry (PSI) to cover both social science narrowly conceived and those many other forms of professional knowledge allied to social science but not properly or entirely scientific (such as opinion polls, policy analysis, census work, and so on). We shall use pPSI to denote a practitioner at PSI.

2. Some knowledge (including misinformation) is for some people under some circumstances decisive even though it is without a shred of scientific confirmation. That is to say, it is in their eyes a sufficient basis for their action; it warrants their acting on it. You make your plans for the day on the supposition that it is Tuesday, a belief you hardly need subject to scientific testing. But pPSI are not greatly concerned with decisiveness, as just defined. They wish to develop knowledge that warrants action because of its scientific conclusiveness, because of the professional care that has gone into producing it. It is this quality that we wish to capture in the idea of authoritative knowledge: knowledge that serves as a basis for commitment or action because it has met to significant degree professional standards for verification.

3. Almost any book or article on a policy issue seems to serve as evidence of the truth of the hypothesis. But for one example, see the empirical character of various arguments over public policy toward labor unions in municipal public employment in Wellington and Winter (1971).

4. Practitioners of PSI sometimes suggest that, if their clients will provide them with the required normative propositions—that is, their values—then PSI can proceed to authoritative conclusions. In that simple faith are several issues that need unravelling. The client is often, of course, multiple, and the multiplicity of them is in disagreement on values. The client also often explicitly or implicitly asks the pPSI for advice on values and cannot tell the pPSI what values to take as given. Even if the client is single and is willing to declare his own values, subsequent policy recommendations made by the pPSI will not be authoritative for any persons whose values are different.

And, finally—and perhaps most important in signalling issues that call for intense further study—it appears to be impossible to articulate values with any precision prior to empirical analysis of issues to which the values are relevant. To say, for example, to practioners of PSI that they should take full employment as an important value in their analysis, say, of problems of fiscal policy does not tell them how important, or whether more important than many other values that will appear as relevant only as the empirical analysis proceeds, or—in short—what the schedule of trade-offs should be between full employment and ever-emerging other values at issue. These are, however, all familiar reasons for rejecting the naive view that PSI can achieve authoritativeness if only clients will provide the required normative elements in analysis.

5. Giandomenico Majone (1979) has suggested this in conversation.

6. A more adequate discussion is found in Chapter 5 of *Usable Knowledge*.

REFERENCES

COHEN, D. and J. WEISS (1977) "Social science and social policy: schools and race." Educational Forum (May): 393-413.

DUNLOP, J. T. (1977) "Policy decisions and research in economic and industrial relations." Industrial and Labor Relations Rev. 30 (April).

MAJONE, G. (1979) "Process and outcome in regulatory decision-making." Amer. Behavioral Scientist (May/June).

——— (1977) "The uses of policy analysis," in Annual Report. New York: Russell Sage.

MULKAY, M. J. (1975) "Three models of scientific development." Soc. Rev. 23 (August).

National Academy of Sciences (1965) Basic Research and National Goals. U.S. House of Representatives Committee Print, Committee on Science and Astronautics (March).

NIE, N., S. VERBA, and J. PETROCIK (1976) The Changing American Voter. Cambridge: Harvard Univ. Press.

VEBLEN, T. (1961) The Place of Science in Modern Civilization. New York: Russell & Russell.

WELLINGTON, H. H. and R. K. WINTER, Jr. (1971) The Unions and the Cities. Washington, DC: Brookings Institution.

WHITE, S. and M. REIN (1977) "Can research help policy?" Public Interest 44 (Fall).

Think Tanks

A New Invention in Government

YEHEZKEL DROR

NEED FOR INVENTIONS IN GOVERNMENT

Study of ancient statecraft is a frustrating experience: Despite delusions to the contrary, modern governments are not fundamentally different from classical Chinese machinery-of-state in their dependence on a few rulers and their advisers interacting with quasi-professional bureaucracies.[1] The primary novel feature of modern governments, namely representative mass democracy combined with a distinct career-group of mediocre politicians, makes the tasks of government much more demanding. However useful institutionalization of turnover of rulers and their control by legislatures and "the public" may be for some aspects of the quality of government and however desirable democracy is in terms of values, they complicate the tasks of governing.[2] Advances in technology, especially in communications and information processing, provide some limited help. But no breakthroughs have occurred in the capacities of governments, which continue to be constrained by inherent limits of rulers, politicians, organizations, and mass behavior.[3]

Comparison of slight improvements in the capacity to govern on one side, with radical changes in intensity of expectations and demands, in complexity of issues, and in consequences of mistakes on the other side, reveals a negative balance of growing relative incapacity to govern.[4] To overcome this increasing inadequacy and obsolescence of contemporary governmental systems—new inventions in government are urgently needed. This chapter is devoted to exploratory examination of one of the more interesting U.S. inventions in government, namely policy research organizations, better known as *think tanks.*

To put the matter in correct perspective, some other relatively recent inventions in government in various countries should be mentioned. These include, for instance, in no particular order: conscious use of redundancy as a design strategy for important organizational components; methods for relating budgeting to operations within a longer-term perspective; analytical approaches to decision-making, such as "policy analysis"; a range of regionalization, devolution, and decentralization designs; specialized concern with the future and its consideration in policy formation by specific units; procedures to reconsider periodically inherited structures and assumptions; opening up of government through "freedom of information" rules; modern forms of control organizations, designed to make bureaucracy work through structured competition and conflict between organizations; independent evaluation arrangements focusing on outputs and effectiveness; a variety of ombudsman units to handle citizen complaints; national suggestion box experiments, soliciting proposals from the public on national problems; a range of debureaucratization schemes, such as negative income tax or vouchers, to substitute macropolicy instruments or quasi-market mechanisms respectively for bureaucratic management; public financing of party leadership training and party research to improve the quality of politics; advisory services to legislatures; improvements in crisis management systems to handle emergencies; public policy schools to train professional policy advisers; a variety of advisory staff supports for rulers going beyond traditional court advisers; interactive computers as aids in decision-making; and new ideas on the recruitment, training, and career patterns of top level officials.

This looks like an impressive list, but, as yet, most of these innovations are in their initial phases, far from providing the necessary breakthroughs in the capacity to govern. Some of them may in fact decrease capacities to govern. In any case, they constitute interesting starting points for urgently needed comparative study[5] and systematic evaluation.

Think tanks are an especially interesting and important innovation in government, ripe for evaluative study. Foreseen by Francis Bacon in *New Atlantis,* think tanks were first institutionalized in the United States more than thirty years ago, with the establishment of the Rand Corporation and the Brookings Institution. Since then, a variety of think tanks have been established, some working mainly for various government agencies and others for the public at large.[6] Partly overlapping with a whole range of advisory organizations, such as policy analysis units, brains trusts, and more traditional consultant firms, think tanks are nevertheless characterized by a set of features which take quite a unique form distinguishing them as a new invention in government.[7]

Thirty years is quite a short time for maturation of a new governmental institution. This is reflected by the scarcity of good literature on the subject and its neglect in many political science texts.[8] Nevertheless, enough experience has accumulated to permit some evaluation of the functions of think tanks, their potentials and their limitations. This is an urgent task, both because of the importance of think tanks and the potential utility of further expanding their roles in governments,[9] and because of the lessons that can be drawn from their experiences as ex post facto experiments on governmental innovations in general. This chapter is a kind of prolegomenon to such an endeavor, presenting some initial findings and preliminary hypotheses.

PURE-TYPE THINK TANK FEATURES

Rand Corporation, Brookings Institution, Heritage Foundation, Institute for Defense Analysis, Hudson Institute, Urban Institute, American Enterprise Institute—these are only a few out of the large number of think tanks in the United States, each one of which is characterized by features of its own. Nevertheless, a unique cluster of characteristics which are specific to think tanks can be identified. These can best be brought out and discussed through construction of a "pure-type" model of "think tanks," with inbuilt variability.[10]

In essence, a think tank can be described as an island of excellence applying full-time interdisciplinary scientific thinking to the in-depth improvement of policy-making, or as a bridge between power and knowledge.

A pure-type model of think tanks is composed of six main interdependent features, with some variance:

(1) Mission. Interdisciplinary science-based contributions to policy-making—this is the central mission of think tanks. This mission distinguishes think tanks from other research organizations, aiming at the advancement of pure knowledge or at product-oriented R&D

(though it is possible to regard think tanks as a kind of Research and Development laboratory on complex policy issues). This mission also distinguishes think tanks from other policy-oriented structures, such as parties, interest groups, and advocacy units, as well as from regular public administration agencies, which are based on pragmatism and professionalism but not science. The range of policy-making they aim at as well as the scope of their scientific base vary among different think tanks. But the mission to make interdisciplinary science-based contributions to policy-making constitutes one of their most important characteristics.

(2) Critical Mass. Think tanks are distinguished by a minimum critical mass of five types of interrelated resources devoted to their mission: number of full-time professional staff; quality of staff; scientific diversity and disciplinary range of staff; time; and information. In these respects, there are quite a number of differences between smaller and larger think tanks; but I believe that a certain critical minimum mass differentiates think tanks from other forms of policy-oriented work. (These are not necessarily less useful—a single person on his own can invent brilliant policy ideas.)

About fifteen to twenty professionals from at least five to six disciplines, including a few outstanding scientific thinkers, working in open-ended teams on at least three to four policy issues, each one of which receives a number of man-years, with full access to nearly all existing information on those issues—something like this constitutes the minimum critical mass for constituting a think tank.

(3) Methods. There is quite a difference between Rand Corporation-type think tanks and Brookings Institution-type think tanks in basic work methods: Rand-type think tanks develop a range of interdisciplinary languages, approaches, and methods for analyzing problems. However tacit and open-ended they may be, these techniques constitute an accumulating "policy analysis" frame that inform but do not dominate the work.[11] Brookings-type think tanks are based more on the work of individual scholars working on their own, in interaction with their peers and within a creative and supportive environment. Both of these approaches[12] (as well as mixed approaches) produce their own contributions to policy-making,[13] the Rand approach probably being stronger in careful analysis of detailed policy alternatives and the Brookings

approach probably encouraging policy inventions and contemplation of fuzzy "grand policy" issues. In principle, more fusion of these two approaches seems desirable. This may be difficult, however, both because of "research climate" contradictions and because of underdevelopment of heuristic policy analysis methods fitting needs of "grand policy" consideration and innovative sociopolitical architecture.[14]

One important feature of all think tanks is that they are "thinking" outfits, not engaging directly in laboratory work and field work. Brains, papers, and computers—these are the equipment of think tanks.

(4) Research freedom. We reach now one of the basic needs of think tanks, which is also one of its main constraints: research freedom. To make a significant contribution to policy-making, as well as to avoid corruption of the scientific base of their work, think tanks must be free not only in arriving at their findings, but in formulating and reformulating the questions on which they are working. Certainly, think tanks operate within acknowledged assumptions and within the constraints of basic sociopolitical paradigms. (There is variety in this respect between independent extra-establishment and even slightly anti-establishment think tanks such as the Center for the Study of Democratic Institutions at some phases of its operations and intraestablishment think tanks such as the Rand Corporation.) But if constraints and paradigms become narrow, go beyond general social values, and inhibit questioning of concrete policies and their assumptions—then think tanks cannot make positive contributions to policy-making. Reconsideration of basic policies rather than more efficient implementation of doubtful present policies—this is a main function of think tanks. Permissible limitations on their activities are strictly limited. The trouble is that this requisite contradicts fundamental political and bureaucratic dynamics, resulting in a barrier to the utilization of think tanks for making governments work.

(5) Clientele-dependency. The inherent limitation on think tanks caused by the need for research freedom is accentuated by their dependence on clients—for financing, information, access, and feedback. There are differences in this respect too between think tanks working for the public at large and enjoying independent financing, and think tanks working for a defined clientele of public agencies and dependent on them for financing.[15] The problem is not only one of money and information, but the more subtle one of being able to

interact with policy-makers and receiving some response from them—
without which continuous policy-oriented work becomes futile. This
creates a degree of clientele-dependency which contradicts research
freedom and inhibits the establishment and proper utilization of think
tanks.

(6) Outputs and impacts. The main nominal outputs of think tanks
are written documents and oral briefings that present ideas, analysis,
and positions on various aspects of policy issues, including also the
policy-making process, adding rather than detracting from its complexity. This is not necessarily a bad thing, as there is no hope of
handling complex problems with simple processes. But the complexities
of the policy-making process create a gap between the inputs of think
tanks and the outputs of policy-making, which is justified in principle
because think tank outputs are only one of the legitimate and necessary
inputs into policy-making. Nevertheless, this gap may reduce the
impact of think tanks to zero (and even make it negative, by provoking
counterreaction), posing the problem of adjusting policy-making as a
whole to the proper use of the inputs of think tanks (as well as of other
thinking and analysis inputs). Methodologically, this hiatus also
prevents measurement of think tank contributions to policy results
except by case studies, which necessarily are selective.

Additional important products of think tanks are professionals
experienced in policy thinking and policy analysis as well as explicated
methodologies.[16] On another level, think tanks may influence policy-
making culture and policy debates as a whole. More diffuse but not less
important is the impact of think tanks on the bureaucracies with which
they interact in a complex love-hate help-compete relationship: To
protect themselves, the bureaucracies must, as a defensive reaction,
establish an in-house countercapacity which upgrades their policy-
considering qualities.[17]

This concise pure-type model of think tanks needs further elaboration. In particular, additional features of think tanks must be considered, such as the specific organizational culture of think tanks and
inbuilt tensions and role conflicts, such as those between commitment to
clients and identification with them on the one hand and individual
values and scientific norms on the other.[18] Also needed is at least some
guesstimate of their net contributions to policy-making in the United
States, perhaps through a series of case studies and systematic

evaluations by main clients as well as by think tank staffs themselves. These tasks go beyond the scope of this chapter, indicating urgently needed research on this invention in government. Here, in order to reach at least some tentative conclusions on the potential contributions of think tanks to making governments and bureaucracies work, some of the interfaces between think tanks and the policy-making system must still be explored.

THINK TANKS AND THE POLICY-MAKING SYSTEM

On a first look, think tanks appear to be a very attractive idea for improving the capacities of governments: Concentrated work by highly qualified persons on main policy issues—what could be better than that to help overloaded governments and bureaucracies augment their in-house capacities? Nevertheless, despite some progress, the contributions of think tanks to government are limited. In particular, attempts to broaden the scope of work of think tanks by moving from the defense domain to domestic issues have been hard going, and the results are by no means clear.

These difficulties have systemic reasons, an understanding of which is essential for evaluating the implications and potentials of think tanks as a new invention in government.

Relatively easy to consider are facts like scarcity of qualified professionals and underdevelopment of adequate methodologies for handling the fuzzy complexities of domestic issues, as well as "grand strategic" defense issues. Given time and effort, these problems can and will be overcome. Somewhat more difficult are inbuilt biases of rationalistic approaches and especially of economic thinking, which at present serve as a main basis for policy analysis methods: For instance, these hinder cognition of "crazy" behavior[19] and limit adequate consideration of political and psychological variables. This too is a temporary weakness of contemporary methods, not difficult to over-come once diagnosed. Similarly, emotionalism and intolerance of clinically detached concern with national problems is less a problem in the United States than in many other countries, though this may change.

I think the fundamental systemic difficulties of think tanks and their roles in government stem from more deeply rooted contradictions between essential think tank features and basic political-bureaucratic dynamics. These include the following:

(a) Clarifying options, explicating decision criteria, increasing the number of realistic alternatives, foreseeing problems—these are among the most important contributions of think tanks to policy-making. All these are quite dysfunctional for politics and bureaucracies: They overload collective decision processes, undermine consensus and coalition maintenance, and disrupt incremental decision-making patterns.

(b) Exposing fallacies in accepted assumptions and identifying innovative and clearly superior policy designs—these are additional important contributions of think tanks to policy-making. These are quite unpleasant and often counterproductive to politicians and bureaucracies alike: They hurt esteem, provide weapons to oppositions, hit sunk investments, and discredit the relevant agencies. If think tanks do not come up with innovative ideas, they are a waste of money and effort; if they come up with new ideas contradicting established policies, it is much worse, because it endangers and attacks what the organizations have done and stand for. Only if think tanks come up with new ideas after politicians and bureaucracies are in a state of despair—or concerning issues about which the politicians and bureaucrats are indifferent—is this accepted as a pure blessing.

(c) Think tanks base their work on scientific knowledge and professional analysis. If successful, this undercuts the experience-based legitimation of most bureaucracies, hurting both their self-image and their external image.

(d) In the final analysis, influence on important policy decisions is a scarce good subjected to intense competition, which has the characteristics of a zero-sum (or fixed-sum) game. Therefore, if think tanks gain influence, this constitutes a real change in the power map, with some other units and groups losing influence. This puts think tanks squarely into bureaucratic politics. The more they disclaim this notion and present themselves as neutral communicators of "objective scientific findings," the more dangerous and strange they are for politicians and bureaucracies.

(e) The skills of think tanks emphasize some very important considerations and variables, but neglect others. In particular, despite growing interest in "implementation," political and organizational considerations tend to be ignored in much think tank work. This reduces the objective utility of their results; more importantly, it makes their findings often either naive or dangerous and sometimes both from the perspective of politicians and bureaucracies. That is not an accident, but an inherent feature theoretically justified by the hypothetical division of labor between think tank analysis and other, more political and organizational inputs in policy-making. If public policy think tanks did go deeply into political analysis, including, for instance, electoral results of various policies, their basic functions would be corrupted and their legitimation would be annihilated. But this necessary limitation on their perspective seriously reduces their utility to top decision-makers and diminishes their strength in policy formation.

Additional functional tensions, conflicts, and contradictions between think tanks on the one hand and governmental, political, and bureaucratic needs and dynamics on the other can be identified. But the five points presented above suffice for a major conclusion which serves to explain the actual difficulties in utilizing think tanks for making governments and bureaucracies work: However promising when looked at as pure models by themselves, think tanks are not easy to integrate into policy-making systems, and they involve real costs from the perspectives of political and bureaucratic institutions.

TENTATIVE CONCLUSIONS

My overall conclusion is that think tanks are a very interesting and very useful invention in government which can make significant contributions to the improvement of policy-making. But they also involve substantive political and organizational costs. This is a major part of the explanation for the greater contributions up until now of think tanks in the defense domain, where the costs are easier to absorb and contain, than in the domestic domain.[20]

Therefore, expansion of the use of think tanks is not a natural and easy process for governments and bureaucracies. Only if driven by the shock of serious failures and/or by enlightened reformers and innovators on the inside and from the outside do think tanks fulfill significant roles in government.

To move from behavioral findings to prescriptive recommendations, it seems that think tanks are a very promising institution which, if suitably encouraged and developed, can serve one of the most urgent needs of modern democratic governments—improvement of fundamental policies. This requires upgrading of the capacity of think tanks themselves and adjustment of some features of the policy-making system to their utilization. What is needed is a network of diverse think tanks interlocked at various locations into main policy-making processes. This is not easy to achieve, but it is probably less difficult than changing the basic features of governmental organizations so as to permit them to fulfill think tank functions as part of their normal in-house operations.

The United States is at present the most advanced country in that direction. Therefore, its experience is of broad comparative interest. At the same time, the United States still has a long way to go before think tanks realize their full potential as an aid to governing. Much work remains before they can effectively serve as an innovative bridge between power and knowledge in an age of harsh turbulence.

NOTES

1. On ancient Chinese statecraft, see especially Creel (1970, 1974). Similarly illuminating is the noninnovative history of advisers to rulers—a very important and quite neglected role in governments. See Goldhamer (1978).

2. I am speaking here about the basic features of the machinery-of-government, not political culture and its socioeconomic infrastructure. The latter have undergone radical transformations, much more so than the Central Core of the machinery-of-government—causing the gap and obsolescence mentioned in the text. Historic-comparative study of the machineries-of-government is a neglected subject in modern political science and governmental studies. This is a serious omission because in-depth understanding of the fundamental problems of government—such as "how to make bureaucracies work"—requires a long-range perspective and comprehensive case studies on the successes and failures of different types of government and their main components.

3. Especially disturbing is the frustration of hopes that mass education would produce enlightened democratic citizens, as expressed for instance by Karl Mannheim. Unless overcome by radical changes in education which are still unclear, the combination of the educated nonenlightened mass citizenry and the growing challenges faced by governments may well tax to the utmost the potentials of democracy and perhaps, under some conditions, overburden them. Looked at from this perspective (detailed elaboration of which is beyond the scope of this chapter), the search for radical improvements of governmental capacities through innovations may well become critical for the survival of democracies in harsher internal and external environments. Thought-provoking in this context, even though dealing with specific circumstances not shared by most Western democratic countries, is *The Breakdown of Democratic Regimes* by Linz and Stephen (1978).

4. I prefer the terms "capacity/incapacity to govern" over "governability." The latter is a misconception implying that it is up to populations to be "governable," while neglecting the more significant side of the equation ideologically as well as operationally, namely, the capacities/incapacities of governments. It is a pity that the Trilateral Commission committed such a mistake (Crozier et al., 1975).

5. In addition to more fundamental historic-comparative study mentioned in note 3 above, at the very least, intense comparative study on the experience of modern Western democratic governments is essential as a basis for mutual learning, despite obvious and tacit differences in political institutions and political culture. As a matter of fact, there are many efforts under way in a number of countries to improve governmental capacities, probably as a result of growing feelings of inadequacy by politicians as well as senior civil servants. To pick just an example accessible to the reader limited to the English language: on the United Kingdom, see the broad surveys in Stacey (1975) and Thornhill (1975), as contrasted with the insightful but conservative perspective of Heclo and Wildavsky (1974).

6. A good survey is provided in Dickson (1971). Still the best in-depth study of a think tank, though quite outdated, is Smith (1966). The ease of misunderstanding the nature of think tanks is illustrated by Slee Smith (1971). One of the best essays on the subject is still Levien (1969). This author serves now as Director of the International Institute for Applied Systems Analysis, mentioned in note 9 below.

7. Reality moves on a multidimensional continuum between different types of units, with one merging into another. Nevertheless, I think quite clearly a distinction can be made between "policy analysis units," "brain trusts," and "think tanks." Adopting a pure-type methodology, I propose the following characterizations for policy analysis units and brain trusts, as distinct from the features of think tanks presented in the text.

Policy analysis units are small organizations working mainly on important current decision-issues, for and in close contact with top decision makers; their main mission is to improve decisions through providing a more comprehensive, systematic, and longer-range perspective. Some parts of the presidential advisory structure in the White House staff, including some phases of National Security Council staff work, illustrate this function in the United States. The Central Policy Review Staff in the Cabinet Office and the Policy Advisors of the Prime Minister illustrate different functions of such policy analysis units in the United Kingdom.

Brain trusts are small groups of "wise persons," advising top decision makers on an ad hoc and temporary basis.

The history of presidential advisory structures and habits in the United States illustrates various versions of such "advice to rulers" systems. For examples, see Tugwell, (1968); Cronin and Greenberg (1969); Hess (1976); and, more prescriptively, George (1979). It will be interesting to see whether any of the ongoing studies of the presidency (e.g., by the National Academy of Public Administration) will come up with innovative proposals on advisory supports to the President, which are both a sensitive and quite critical component of any government.

8. It is bad enough that many standard texts in American government still neglect and frequently completely ignore think tanks and their roles in U.S. policy-making; it is even worse that a report of the Commission on the Year 2000 on the future of U.S. government fails to discuss think tanks as well as other important innovations. See Perloff (1971).

9. It is interesting to note that quite a number of governments are considering the establishment of think tanks in their countries, and some have already been set up, such as the Institute for Research on Public Policy in Canada, the Netherlands Scientific Council for Government Policy, and—on an international level—the so-called "East-West Think Tank," the International Institute for Applied Systems Analysis. These three think tanks were all established in 1972! The establishment of a European think tank, an idea strongly supported by the Ford Foundation, is presently being discussed.

10. Compare Dror (1971: 90 ff.).

11. The evolution of Rand-type policy analysis methods can be followed by examining some main Rand books in order of publication. Especially relevant are: Hitch and McKean (1960); Quade (1964, 1975); Novick (1975); Quade and Boucher (1968); and Fisher (1971).

These books do not reflect and present all the craft and skills of policy analysis at its best, not to speak about the involved wisdom and clinical qualifications. Parts of these are on the level of tacit or subjective knowledge (as discussed by Polanyi and Popper) and therefore are inherently difficult to explicate. This is a serious problem for the further development of think tanks and their credibility, as well as for the transferability of such skills and their application to broader policy domains. The danger that explicit microanalysis tools may displace as yet implicit macroanalysis approaches and thus limit the contributions of Rand-type think tanks to narrow issues continues to be a real one, especially as it is reinforced by the preference of most clients for marginal improvements which do not endanger their basic assumptions and policies. This matter is discussed later on in the text.

12. Again, I am following a "pure-type" simplification procedure. Both Rand and Brookings are complex and multidimensional organizations, with much contemplative policy thinking going on at Rand and many highly structured methods (e.g., macro-economic models) being utilized at Brookings.

13. I leave aside the fascinating sociology of organizations and bureaucratic-politics question of what functional needs and historic accidents predispose a think tank to move toward either one of these main approaches. Let me just observe that the International Institute of Applied Systems Analysis devoted much work to methodologies, as illustrated by their books published in an "International Series on Applied Systems Analysis." My hypothesis is that the difficult internal and external political environments of a think tank shared by Western democratic countries and Communist countries encourages utilization of "value free" strict methodologies.

14. This is a main missing link in supplying scientific aids to the capacity to govern. Some of the related problems are interestingly considered in Lindblom and Cohen (1979).

15. Optimally a mixture of clientele-financing and independent financing is desirable: Total dependence on clients inhibits in-depth and innovative research, even with the most enlightened of clients. Thus, some path-breaking work at the Rand Corporation was financed by Ford and other independent foundations. But total financial independence may encourage too Olympian an attitude, overdetached from reality and overisolated from implementation and impact considerations.

16. Both the Brookings Institution and the Rand Corporation ventured into advanced teaching. The Brookings Institution did so for a number of years and then stopped its teaching activities (though it still is accredited as a degree-giving institution). The Rand Corporation eight years ago set up the Rand Graduate Institute, which runs a doctorate program in policy analysis and which is one of the more advanced of the novel public policy schools. I tend to view the more innovative public policy and policy analysis graduate teaching programs as a spin-off of the think tanks—which have produced the knowledge, the teachers, and the teaching material essential for the university programs. It will be interesting to observe whether the same will happen with policy analysis as happened after World War II with operational research in England: After being moved to universities, the subject became dominated by strict methodologies which meet the traditional criteria of science, losing its utility as a broad problem-solving approach. Recent books written as texts for policy analysis teaching demonstrate this danger, with rare exceptions. For example, compare MacRae and Wilde (1979) and Stokey and Zeckhauser (1978) on the one hand with Wildavsky (1979) on the other. This danger is related to the already mentioned absence of a "grand policy analysis" methodology and approach, which could serve as a specific and adequate core for advanced university teaching.

17. The history of systems analysis in the Department of Defence illustrates all the phases of such a process, from the development of relevant methods and personnel at the Rand Corporation, to their transplantation under McNamara into the Pentagon, up to their partial absorption by the traditional defense agencies. E.g., compare Enthoven and Smith (1971) with Sanders (1973).

18. An extreme expression of these tensions is the publication of the top-secret Vietnam papers by a senior Rand analyst. Without presuming to judge this instance, it is clear that repetition of such cases would completely ruin think tanks as a bridge between semi-independent scientific thinking and governmental in-house policy-making processes.

19. See Dror (1980), especially Chapter 1.

20. Other reasons for the greater success of think tanks in defense issues include the relative lower complexity of many defense problems, the pressure of real costs of failures, the shocks of rapid changes in defense issues and technology and the inability of regular organizations to cope with them, and an attitude of respect toward R&D and technological innovation. Also very important is the ability to absorb unpleasant conclusions through classification and thus to avoid or at least delay high external costs. Accident and personalities also played a role in the establishment of the prototype of all defense think tanks, the Rand Corporation.

Having worked a number of years ago on a comparative evaluation of think tank operations for the military and for the City of New York, the relative open-mindedness of military clientele compared with the restrictive approach of urban bureaucrats (with a few distinguished exceptions) was really striking.

REFERENCES

CREEL, H. G. (1974) Shen Pu-Hai: A Chinese Political Philosopher of the Fourth Century B.C. Chicago: Univ. of Chicago Press.

——— (1970) The Western Chou Empire. Volume 1, The Origins of Statecraft in China. Chicago: Univ. of Chicago Press.

CRONIN, T. E. and S. D. GREENBERG (1969) The Presidential Advisory System. New York: Harper & Row.

CROZIER, M. J. et al. (1975) The Crisis of Democracy: Report on the Governability of Democracies to the Trilateral Commission. New York: New York Univ. Press.

DICKSON, P. (1971) Think Tanks. New York: Atheneum.

DROR, Y. (1980) Crazy States: A Counterconventional Strategic Problem. Millwood, NY: Krause.

——— (1971) Design for Policy Sciences. New York: Elsevier North-Holland.

ENTHOVEN, A. C. and K. W. SMITH (1971) How Much Is Enough? New York: Harper & Row.

FISHER, G. H. (1971) Cost Considerations in Systems Analysis. New York: Elsevier North-Holland.

GEORGE, A. (1979) Presidential Decisionmaking in Foreign Affairs. Boulder, CO: Westview.

GOLDHAMER, H. (1978) The Adviser. New York: Elsevier North-Holland.

HECLO, H. and A. WILDAVSKY (1974) The Private Government of Public Money. Berkeley: Univ. of California Press.

HESS, S. (1976) Organizing the Presidency. Washington, DC: Brookings Institution.

HITCH, C. J. and R. McKEAN (1960) The Economics of Defense in the Nuclear Age. Cambridge, MA: Harvard Univ. Press.

LEVIEN, R. E. (1969) Independent Policy Analysis Organizations—A Major Social Invention. P-4231. Santa Monica, CA: Rand Corporation.

LINDBLOM, C. E. and D. K. COHEN (1979) Usable Knowledge: Social Science and Social Problem Solving. New Haven, CT: Yale Univ. Press.

LINZ, J. J. and A. STEPHAN [eds.] (1978) The Breakdown of Democratic Regimes. Baltimore, MD: Johns Hopkins Univ. Press.

MacRAE, D., Jr. and J. A. WILDE (1979) Policy Analysis for Public Decisions. Belmont, CA: Duxbury.

NOVICK, D. [ed.] (1975) Program Budgeting: Program Analysis and the Federal Budget. Cambridge, MA: Harvard Univ. Press.

QUADE, E. (1975) Analysis for Public Decisions. New York: Elsevier North-Holland.

——— [ed.] (1964) Analysis for Military Decisions. Chicago: Rand McNally.

——— and W. BOUCHER [eds.] (1968) Systems Analysis and Policy Planning: Applications in Defense. New York: Elsevier North-Holland.

PERLOFF, H. S. [ed.] (1971) The Future of the U.S. Government: Toward the Year 2000. Englewood Cliffs, NJ: Prentice Hall.

SANDERS, R. (1973) The Politics of Defense Analysis. New York: Dunellen.

SLEE SMITH, P. I. (1971) Think Tanks and Problem Solving. London: Business Books.

SMITH, B.L.R. (1966) The RAND Corporation: Case Study of a Nonprofit Advisory Corporation. Cambridge, MA: Harvard Univ. Press.

STACEY, F. (1975) British Government 1966-1975: Years of Reform. Oxford: Oxford Univ. Press.

STOKEY, E. and R. ZECKHAUSER (1978) A Primer for Policy Analysis. New York: Norton.

THORNHILL, W. [ed.] (1975) The Modernization of British Government. London: Pitman.

TUGWELL, R. G. (1968) The Brains Trust. New York: Viking.

WILDAVSKY, A. (1979) Speaking Truth to Power: The Art and Craft of Policy Analysis. Boston: Little, Brown.

Civil Service Reform
as a Remedy for Bureaucratic Ills

ALAN K. CAMPBELL
U.S. Office of Personnel Management

With its passage in October 1978, the Civil Service Reform Act provided the legal basis for the first comprehensive overhaul of the federal bureaucracy in nearly a century.

The Act embodies provisions which it is believed will increase government efficiency, an emphasis quite different from that which had dominated public activity during the previous two decades. During that time, America was in a period of substantial economic growth and challenged by compelling social problems. There was little inflation, unemployment was low, and productivity was high and increasing. The time was ripe for government to divide up the growth increment of the nation's economic pie for the benefit of those in need.

Government responded with the "New Frontier" of President Kennedy and the "Great Society" of President Johnson, which pioneered new social programs built on the foundations of Roosevelt's "New Deal." Medicare funded health care for the aged, and the Head Start Program provided preschool training for the disadvantaged. There were child nutrition programs and, for the first time, substantial federal financial support for education. The new and increased programs sought to house the poor, to rebuilt the downtown areas of central cities, to rehabilitate the disabled, and to train the unemployed. These times also produced the Civil Rights Act and the Voting Rights Act, which opened the system to equal job and educational opportunities, still an unfinished task, but one which is well started.

These programs were products of an expanding economy and of a political climate which demanded them. They grew out of racial awakening, youth revolt, and a new, politically sophisticated women's

153

movement. The need for the programs was magnified by a redistribution of population from farm to city and from city to suburb, which left cities with disproportionate numbers of the black and the poor and made new political demands on the central government. Talk of government efficiency was muted, because many perceived it to be a subtle, conservative attack on the new social programs.

To say that the situation today is different would be an understatement. Candidates of every political persuasion run for public office under the banner of "greater efficiency" or, as it is more directly and frequently put: "Cut Taxes." The electorate, disappointed that the problems were not being solved or were not being solved quickly enough, became increasingly disillusioned with government. Despite lowering the voting age and opening the processes of government to more people, the disillusionment caused a decline in voter interest and participation and a rise in the power and influence of single-issue interest groups. These changes, combined with the adoption of many state primaries for the selection of presidential nominees, have produced a decline in the influence of political parties; this in turn has resulted in both a lack of leadership on the legislative side and the declining influence of the chief executive.

Vietnam, the energy crisis, an economic downturn, Watergate, and a political process that does not seem to work well, have shaken the country's self-confidence. The enthusiasm and idealism that characterized the programs of the 1960s has been replaced by a mood of caution, wariness, and skepticism. Across the country, that mood is expressed by what journalists and scholars have called a "taxpayer's revolt."

The "taxpayer's revolt" is a reaction to what many believe to be an inefficient bureaucracy. This revolt has been examined carefully by public opinion experts. These experts have found that it is not programs to which people object; rather, they believe that the programs are not well run, that they are inefficient, and that the funds do not go to the people who need them most. In one poll, 71% of those questioned indicated they would vote against tax cuts which meant major reductions in aid to the elderly or the poor and the disabled. Nearly two-thirds of those responding said they would vote against tax cuts which reduced the amount spent for public education. But when asked if they were getting full value for their tax dollar, the overwhelming majority at local, state, and federal levels said no.

Throughout the 1976 election, President Carter demonstrated that he perceived and understood this national mood, yet he also maintained his steadfast belief in the value and necessity of the previously adopted social programs. To reconcile these perspectives, he made increased government efficiency through reorganization and improved management a central theme of his campaign, and it has formed a major part of his program since assuming office.

ELEMENTS OF THE REFORM TRADITION

Historically, government reorganization has been motivated not only by a desire to increase efficiency, but also by a desire to reduce the influence of "politics" on government, to make government more responsive, and to place decision-making closer to the people. It is not a new idea. Reorganization has played a significant role, if not a dramatic one, in the history of American government at all levels. From the Taft Commission on Government Efficiency early in this century to the passage of the Budget and Accounting Act and the maturing of the City Manager Movement in the 1920s, from the Brownlow Recommendations of the 1930s to the two Hoover commissions of the late 1940s and early 1950s, we have experimented with reforming or reorganizing our governmental institutions for at least three-quarters of a century, with particular emphasis on the executive branch.

Although each of these efforts at change was influenced by particular problems of the time, there are common themes. Certainly, all responded to the gradual growth of the governmental role in society. This growth led to a continual increase in the proportion of the country's economy used and influenced by the government, and to a proliferation of government agencies as the purposes of government expanded.

The role of politics in the government decision-making process also influenced many reorganization efforts. Some reorganizations attempted to reduce the political role by introducing more professionalism and expertise into government. Others worked to expand the electorate and provide opportunities for greater citizen participation in public decision-making. As government expanded, there was a tendency to fragment the executive branch. In carrying out new programs, executives at all levels of government, but particularly at the national and urban levels, found their spheres of responsibility becoming greater and greater, with literally hundreds of units reporting to them. In some instances, as new programs were undertaken, the agency administering them was headed by an independent or semi-independent board or commission responsible to the executive in indirect and noncontrolling ways.

This situation led to demands for consolidation of like activities within larger departments and agencies, with direct line of responsibility to the chief executive. Such consolidation had considerable success, even though there remain too many units for effective control at all government levels in the United States. The demand for consolidation through restructuring remains a common theme in both the literature about governmental organization and political debates about governmental effectiveness.

Related to the reasons for the movement toward consolidation has been the belief that responsibility should be more clearly established. Of course, this demand cannot be accomplished in its entirety, since the very nature of government institutions, with their divisions of power, cannot and should not be modeled on strictly hierarchical systems.

The executive branch of every democratic government feels multiple pressures from responsibilities to its chief executive, to legislative bodies, to the courts, and to special interest groups. Despite this characteristic of government, there have been moves to increase the strength of the line of responsibility running from the executive departments to chief executives. At the state and local levels, this has led to a gradual decline in independent commissions and boards and to a reduction in the number of elected executive department officials. At the federal level, this has been accomplished by increasing the influence of the executive office of the President through the gradual growth in dominance within the office of the President's chief budgetary agency, the Office of Management and Budget.

This move toward centralization and consolidation was altered somewhat in the 1960s, not through conscious reorganization programs, but rather as an adjunct to the growth of social programs. Based on the proposition that many of the problems relating to racism, sexism, and poverty were caused by the lack of political power in the hands of affected groups, new social legislation often called for considerable decentralization of the administration of new programs. The phrase was "maximum feasible participation." It was to be accomplished by opening up governmental decision-making processes through a variety of legally required hearings, establishment of new kinds of governmental institutions at the neighborhood level, and through other decentralizing techniques.

During the last decade, the concept of decentralization reached its most extreme manifestation in "revenue sharing" legislation which provided federal grants to state and local governments with practically no strings attached. The common description of how this system works is that the federal bureaucrats leave the money on a stump in the middle of the night for it to be picked up the following morning by state and local officials to spend as they see fit.

Those who championed government restructuring believed it improved public management. Increased efficiency was to be an indirect result of the restructuring, rather than a specific purpose for doing so. The civil service reforms now being implemented emphasize improved management as their primary goal.

The reorganization and management improvement initiatives of the Carter Administration are a continuation of the historical trends just described. They also constitute new directions. Associated with the past is the emphasis on consolidation and the placing of related activities in the same departments and agencies. The movement of all equal employment opportunity programs, formerly scattered through half a dozen departments and agencies, to the Equal Employment Opportunity Commission is one example. Another is the placement of all programs concerned with natural resources in the same department. Bringing economic initiatives together, particularly on a regional basis, is also being discussed as a possible restructuring effort.

THE NEW DEMAND FOR EFFICIENCY

Many of the Carter Administration's efforts to improve administrative efficiency depart from the organizational trends of the past. Perhaps because of this new aspect, they are somewhat difficult to categorize. The changes are a product of the problems with which American society and government are now struggling. These problems give a greater significance to the effectiveness of the machinery-of-government issue than has ever before been the case in the United States.

The most important current influence is the slowdown in our rate of economic growth. Many explanations are being given for this. We do not know whether the slowdown relates to the increasing costs of environmental regulations, to the decline in capital investments, or to the reduction in expenditures for research and development. We do know that the rate of economic growth has declined by almost 80% in the last ten years. As a result, there is no new growth increment to redistribute to accomplish social purposes. And it is much easier politically to redistribute a growth increment than to redistribute resources which people have already become accustomed to using.

This new economic reality affects government policy in regard to the private sector and encourages within government an emphasis on improving management of the resources it has. The federal government is working toward policies to reduce the impact of its regulation on private sector productivity—an effort which has been substantially successful in the area of air transportation, and which new legislation will attempt to expand to other transportation modes.

There also are efforts to place increased emphasis on public sector productivity itself. In November 1978, President Carter established a National Productivity Council, reporting directly to him, to improve productivity in both the public and private sectors. One of its principal assignments is improvement of productivity in the federal sector. The issue of public sector productivity is a relatively new one; it has emerged in the United States as an important issue only in the last decade. In part, this emergence is a result of the increased proportion of the total economy consumed by government activities. Perhaps, more significantly, it is a result of political leaders recognizing public resistance to increasing taxes in order to maintain service levels.

The attention to public sector productivity immediately raises the problem that it is difficult to measure with the same systems used to measure private sector productivity. There is the additional problem that governmental systems contain more disincentives than incentives to increasing productivity. The rewards granted to those responsible for running the public sector tend to be unrelated to improving efficiency in governmental operations. There are practically no disincentives for performing a task with more people and more resources than are necessary. If one operates with a lower budget or reduces the number of people supervised, one may even risk a decrease in civil service rank.

The history of the evolution of the federal civil service has been primarily one of increasing the protections of the career members. Civil service legislation originally adopted in the last century had its origin in an effort to curb the spoils system. That original emphasis has dominated subsequent legislation, rules, and regulations. The new emphasis is to modify these protections sufficiently to encourage initiative, flexibility, and productivity. The civil service reforms which President Carter recommended to Congress in 1978, and which are now law, attempt to move the system in these directions.

THE CARTER ADMINISTRATION'S
CIVIL SERVICE REFORMS

On January 19, 1978, in his "State of the Union Address," President Carter said he considered reform of the civil service "to be absolutely vital." This marked the first time an American president included civil service reform among his major legislative priorities (Carter, 1978).

President Carter then sent the Congress two major initiatives aimed at better execution of the laws governing federal personnel management and better management of the people who operate within those laws. The first initiative was a reorganization plan which reassigned the functions performed by the U.S. Civil Service Commission to two separate agencies—the Merit Systems Protection Board and the Office of Personnel Management. This reorganization plan provided the framework necessary to carry out the second initiative, the Civil Service Reform Act. This legislation was the product of the most comprehensive review of the civil service system since its inception nearly a century ago. It aims, as the President pointed out, to "restore the merit principle to a system which has grown into a bureaucratic maze. It will provide greater management flexibility and better rewards for better performance without compromising job security" (Carter, 1978).

Despite the fact that the views of federal managers and staffers, careerists and noncareerists, union members and nonunion members frequently are at odds, all agreed that the personnel system within which they operated needed change. All of these groups complained of serious problems in the system, yet to balance their competing interests in reform proposals was very difficult. For example:

- How could widespread manipulations of the merit system be prevented without imposing constraints which would stymie the system?
- How could an appeals system be designed to guarantee the procedural rights of employees without making managers reluctant to initiate legitimate adverse actions?
- How could managers be given the authority with which to manage and employees be given protection from abuses of that authority?
- How could efforts to bring about a federal work force representative of the American population be accelerated without comprising merit principles?

It could be argued that these complex problems suggested almost contradictory reforms.

The Civil Service Reform Act responds to the challenges posed by these questions and attempts to reconcile their potential conflicts. It was constructed on the historical lessons and experiences of the federal service.

BETTER APPEALS
AND INVESTIGATORY STRUCTURES

In the past, the entangling web of safeguards created to protect the federal personnel system from political assaults and cronyism may have, in reality, spurred such abuses. It was not uncommon for managers to feel they had to shortcut procedures to accomplish even legitimate objectives. Heavy pressure to subvert merit principles from the White House, members of Congress, agency heads, and special interest groups conceivably could have resulted in the promotion of partisan political interests. The watchdog of the merit system, the Civil Service Commission, could not always adequately prevent these abuses.

Legitimate concerns were raised by employees and managers over the often incompatible roles of the Civil Service Commission—as the author and overseer of personnel regulations and policies; as the advocate for, and adviser on, sound personnel management; as the adjudicator of appeals and protector of employee rights; and as the investigator of alleged merit system abuses. The reorganization plan separated these competing roles by creating the Merit Systems Protection Board for appellate and investigatory functions and the Office of Personnel Management for personnel policy-making. Within the MSPB, in addition to the appeals function, there is an Office of Special Counsel with independent investigative jurisdiction over prohibited personnel practices, vested with the authority to initiate investigations to protect the public interest. This includes cases of alleged political interference with personnel decision-making or of reprisals against employees who legitimately disclose information related to violations of law. Charges resulting from these investigations are brought before the Merit Systems Protection Board of administrative law judges designated by the Board.

It is in the public interest for federal employees to bring instances of political abuse or of gross waste and inefficiency to public attention; yet, in the past, "blowing the whistle" was not easily done with impunity. There were too many cases where employees who legitimately complained about improper or illegal actions were subjected to harassment or other retaliatory actions. The Office of Special Counsel will eliminate these injustices.

The new Merit Systems Protection Board (MSPB), as a single independent agency, now performs the appellate and quasi-judicial functions formerly carried on by the three levels of appeal organizations which were under the jurisdiction of the Civil Service Commission. Formerly, employees who wished to appeal what they felt were arbitrary personnel actions faced a bewildering tangle of rules, procedures, and deadlines. The process could take three years or even more. The new Board provides timely review of most appeals and complaints. This aids managers, who in the past may have felt the appeals system was so complex that it was easier to retain or shift incompetent employees than to initiate disciplinary actions.

MEASURES TO PROVIDE FLEXIBILITY AND INCENTIVE

The federal personnel management functions of the old Civil Service Commission are lodged in the Office of Personnel Management, the President's principal agent for managing the federal work force. OPM develops personnel policies governing all aspects of civilian employment in executive branch agencies, as well as in certain agencies in the legislative and judicial branches. It is headed by a director, appointed by the President and confirmed by the Senate. OPM evaluates the effectiveness of personnel programs in federal agencies and conducts investigations to insure compliance with laws, rules, regulations, and policy directives. This agency also provides technical and professional assistance to the heads of executive agencies in improving the management and utilization of human resources. It performs for the President the same role relative to personnel management that the Office of Management and Budget does for financial management.

Among the specific problems which the new agency is addressing are the disincentives to management now created by personnel rules and regulations. Rules which originated as a defense against spoils and the ineffective government which widespread patronage provided have resulted in as much inefficiency as they were designed to prevent. The system is so encrusted that many managers feel it is almost impossible to manage effectively. One review of the staffing process revealed that between 17 and 610 calendar days could be required to hire a new employee (The President's Reorganization Project, 1977: 25).

Disciplinary actions could drag out even longer. A classic example often cited is an attempt by a supervisor to fire an employee whose repeated absences from her duty station placed undue pressures on her coworkers. The supervisor spent 21 months preparing documentation and conferring with personnel officers, and finally succeeded in building his case. However, at the end of that time, the supervisor received a poor performance rating from his superiors for the neglect of his other duties. Had the employee appealed, the case might yet be unresolved.

The traditional personnel system provided few incentives for managers to manage or for employees to perform. Unless unsatisfactory performance was documented and withstood challenges in the appeals system, pay increases were automatic for most employees. For example, in fiscal year 1977, while half a million federal employees received within-grade increases, only 700 were denied them. Though it should be a prime motivational tool, performance appraisal was not the basis for developing, rewarding, reassigning, demoting, promoting, retaining, or separating employees. Because of this, the image of the federal government as "the incompetent's best friend" (Reed, 1977) was given credence, even if it was not generally true.

Senior federal managers—those at grades 16 and above—were subject to even more cumbersome laws, regulations, and procedures which particularly impeded their ability to select, motivate, and manage their staffs. The rules did not prevent calculated attempts to politicize the career service, nor did they recognize legitimate needs for agency heads to fill critically important positions which personnel of their own choosing. In addition, career employees who accepted noncareer positions relinquished their career status. Positions were classified so that career employees could not easily be reassigned to make the best use of their talents.

The compensation system for senior federal employees provided even less incentive than for lower ranking employees. Ceilings on the pay of top executives caused their salaries to fall behind those of their counterparts in the private sector, despite increases in the cost of living. Among top executives, pay ceilings also prevented rewarding those whose performance was outstanding—many whose performance records were dramatically different received the same salary. As a result, the more capable executives were more inclined to seek other employment than were marginal managers. The government and the public have suffered as a result.

In response to these many shortcomings, the Civil Service Reform Act established processes to improve management, stimulate performance and efficiency, provide needed protections for employees, and help achieve the equal employment opportunity expectations to which the federal service is committed and the public is entitled.

To the extent that agencies have the capacity to assume them, the Office of Personnel Management has authority to delegate to individual agencies personnel management authorities which historically have been the province of the central personnel agency. These delegations move decision-making authority closer to the point of responsibility for results. A likely and beneficial spin-off of this could be the elevation of personnel management within the organizational hierarchies of federal departments and agencies. Joseph Califano, former Secretary of Health, Education, and Welfare, recognized the need for making personnel a more integral part of the total management process by establishing the position of Assistant Secretary for Personnel. As the first appointee to that position, a long-time career civil servant, Thomas McFee, said, "I am confident that my chances for success in turning goals into realities are far greater now that I sit as an equal with the other top management officials of HEW" (McFee, 1978).

The Civil Service Reform Act also provides a new merit pay plan for midlevel managers (GS 13-15). Pay increases for these employees will be based on the quality of their performance and contributions to their organizations, rather than on their length of service. Although within-grade pay increases will be eliminated for employees covered by the plan, larger and more timely cash awards will be provided to those whose performance warrants them. An incentive pay system is also provided for managerial employees in Grades 16-18 and at Executive Levels IV and V, grouped within a new Senior Executive Service.

THE SENIOR EXECUTIVE SERVICE

The key feature of the Senior Executive Service is that grade and rank for both career and noncareer executives is assigned to the individual rather than a position, much as in the military and foreign service systems. Noncareer positions in the SES will be limited by law to 10%. (Previously, there was no real limit on the number of noncareer positions.) For the sake of impartiality, a number of positions in the new service will be reserved for career executives. The remainder may be filled by either career or noncareer executives, as long as the number of noncareer executives does not exceed 10%. Managers, then, can place career executives into positions previously held by noncareer executives, or vice versa, depending upon organizational needs.

Admission to the Senior Executive Service is based on managerial qualifications, and retention and pay are based on performance. Compensation for executives is set within a limited range of salaries. There are no automatic pay increases, yet productive executives can receive substantial bonuses for outstanding performance.

Upon entering the service, career executives will serve a one-year probationary period during which they will be evaluated for performance. Those removed from the service for performance reasons during this period will be moved to suitable positions outside the service without salary loss.

THE CLIMATE FOR CHANGE

The problems we have faced in federal personnel policies and processes are not especially new. Nor, for that matter, are many of the solutions that have been advanced. For example, much of the conceptual base for a Senior Executive Service dates back to the second Hoover Commission. What is distinctive about the current reform effort is a disposition on the part of political decision makers to contemplate changes in the entire personnel management system. Though the 95-year history of the basic Civil Service Act was one of repeated reform efforts, the necessity of reform and the feasibility of reform have seldom been in concert.

The crucial impetus for the 1978 Act came from the White House. Every new administration feels the negative aspects of the bureaucracy's pressure for continuity. New policy makers arrive with mandates for change and find that though they can change structures and appearances, it is very difficult to make dramatic changes in direction. In signing the bill which granted him general reorganization authority, President Carter expressed his commitment to "move as quickly as possible to improve the efficiency and the effectiveness and the sensitivity of the Federal government bureaucracy in dealing with the needs of the American people." This, he stated, "was one of the campaign issues that induced the American people to give [him] their support "(Office of the White House Press Secretary, 1977).

The President sensed a broad public concern for improving the delivery of government service. Though a Louis Harris survey, issued in January 1978, showed significant increases in Americans' confidence in basic institutions, confidence in government at all levels remains quite low. In 1977, 23% of those surveyed said they had a "great deal of confidence" in the executive branch of government, compared with only 11% in 1976. However, ten years earlier, 41% had expressed such confidence.

Whether or not the public's views about government services and the productivity and reliability of career employees are accurate, the frequently negative perception has played a major role in transforming public management from an obscure topic for professional discussion to one of concern to all public officials. In the 1960s, for example, social pressures pushed the federal government to launch many new and exciting programs rapidly. Attention is now focused more closely on making these programs operate more efficiently and effectively.

It is no secret that federal personnel policy issues generate little sustained political attention. There are only a handful of Congressmen who come from districts where a substantial portion of their constituents are federal employees. Yet in every district and state of this country, there are numerous people who receive social security or veterans benefits, who fly in and out of airports, who travel on interstate highways, who use national parks, and who receive the many other vital services provided by federal government. The relationship between the public's stake in effective government and the need for improved public management is then a sufficient basis for presidential and congressional concern.

This concern seems all the more reasonable when one realizes that the public sector now consumes about one-third of the Gross National Product every year. Public sector performance, therefore, substantially affects the national economy. Quite rightly, the public expects it to be at least as productive and efficient as the private sector.

Standing alone, the changes embodied in the Civil Service Reform Act will not suddenly and dramatically improve the quality of performance of the federal work force. They will have to be combined with effective performance appraisal systems, with a productivity measurement system, and with other techniques which will help answer the question: "How well are we doing?"

Some may argue that this emphasis on government efficiency overlooks other important purposes of government. They would not necessarily be wrong in making that accusation. There are purposes served by government which reach beyond, and may even be inconsistent with, governmental efficiency. Participation in governmental decision-making, for example, is not provided in order to increase efficiency, but in order to achieve other very appropriate social goals. It is also fair to ask whether decentralizing within administrative structures themselves or decentralizing to subnational governments increases or decreases the efficiency of delivering government services.

Whatever the answers to these questions, the emphasis is heavily upon improving efficiency in the performance of governmental activities. It is important to understand that many who have been advocating the social programs of the past recognize the new call for efficiency as being necessary to the survival of those programs.

President Carter said it well, I believe, during the 1976 presidential campaign, when he pointed out, "there is no inherent conflict between careful planning, tight management, and constant reassessment, on the one hand, and compassionate concern for the plight of the deprived and the afflicted, on the other. Waste and inefficiency never fed a hungry child, provided a job for a willing worker, or educated a deserving student."

REFERENCES

CARTER, J. (1978) "State of the Union Address." January 19.

McFEE, T. S. (1978) "There's an ASPER in Your Future." Civil Service J. (April/June).

Office of the White House Press Secretary (1977) "Remarks of the President Upon Signing S. 626 Reorganization Bill." April 6.

The President's Reorganization Project (1977) Personnel Management Project. Volume 1, Final Staff Report (December).

REED, L. (1977) "Firing a federal employee: the impossible dream." Washington Monthly (July/August).

Competition Among Government Bureaus

WILLIAM A. NISKANEN
Ford Motor Company

Maybe I should first describe my own preferences: one of my favorite fantasies is a dream that Washington might once again be a quiet southern town with several major shrines and minor universities and where everyone, other than tourists, has the good sense to leave town in the summer. My favorite prescription to balance the budget is to turn off the air conditioning in Washington as a symbol of the government's commitment to conserve energy. My dream, alas, is not likely to be realized in the near future and, in the meantime, it would be useful to improve the responsiveness and efficiency of the organizations supplying the many services we seem to expect from government.

One of the many manifestations of academic parochialism is the difference in views concerning how economic activity in the private and government sectors should be organized. Most economic departments still teach that competition among profit-seeking firms supplying similar products is desirable to achieve responsiveness to consumer demands, efficient supply, and incentives to innovate. Some economists confuse competition with the number of firms in an industry and some antitrust laws confuse competition with the preservation of weak firms, but there is a broad consensus that competition is both a natural and desirable characteristic of private markets. And the empirical evidence provides overwhelming support for this consensus. At the same time, most public administration departments, based on a literature of German sociology and Wilson's Presbyterian maxims,

Author's Note: *The views expressed in this chapter are personal and do not necessarily represent the position of the Ford Motor Company.*

still teach that monopoly bureaus are desirable to achieve responsiveness to the political authorities, the coordination of similar government
services, the elimination of redundancy and overlap, and all those
presumably good things. Aside from the few public administration
scholars who have done any empirical research, there is a broad consensus that government services should be supplied by functionally
specialized monopoly bureaus. The periodic attempts to reorganize
government bureaus into functional monopolies, however, suggests
that monopoly is not the natural condition of a bureaucracy. And
there does not seem to be any empirical evidence to support the view
that monopoly is a desirable characteristic for the supply of government
services.

Most scholars seem not to have noticed this difference in views.
Some venturesome scholars have noticed the difference, but have
proceeded to do their own thing in deference to the sensitivity over "turf"
in the academic community. Could both groups be correct? Is it plausible that businessmen and bureaucrats are such different people that
profits are a necessary incentive in private firms but that the "public
good" is a sufficient incentive in government bureaus, that competition
is a necessary discipline in private firms but that monopoly is a desirable
characteristic of bureaus? Only a few scholars have even expressed any
curiosity about these issues.

A SIMPLE THEORY

Some years ago, I sketched out a theory of bureaucracy and representative government, based on the central, radical assumption that
bureaucrats and politicians are basically similar to the rest of us mortals
(maybe even more so) (Niskanen, 1971, 1975). In general, they are
assumed to value income, perquisites, power, prestige, the public
good, and an easy life in roughly the same proportions as other people.
The formal model of a bureau is based on an assumption that bureaucrats try to maximize the budget of their bureau, subject to the constraint that, on the average, they must supply the level and quality of
service expected by the politicians. The politicians, in turn, are assumed
to prefer reelection but to have no special concern about public issues
that do not bear on their reelection. A bureau makes the initial budget
proposal and is assumed to know the cost of supplying a service. Some

set of the politicians determine the level of the budget but are assumed to have no special information on the cost of the service.

This model generates the following general conclusions:

- for a given demand for a government service (as revealed by the politicians), the budget of a bureau is too large, i.e., larger than the budget that maximizes the net benefits of the service;
- the amount of the excess budget increases as a function of the cost to acquire the same service from another bureau or a private supplier;
- the excess budget is spent on some combination of inefficiency and oversupply, the specific combination depending on the personal motivations of the bureaucrat and the reward structure of the bureau.

In the limit, thus, the excess budget of a monopoly bureau is limited only by the total demand for the services and by its own costs. Any alternative source of supply, even if it is not used, reduces the excess budget of a bureau by permitting the political officials to reduce the budget of a specific bureau without reducing the level of the service.

Some personal reflections beyond my formal model also bear on the role of competition in a bureaucracy. Competition among bureaus supplying a similar service increases the amount of information available to the politicians and the public, because the competition for budgets is forced to the political arena. A monopoly bureau, in contrast, is more effective in suppressing information about costs, failures, and risks. Competition among bureaus increases the range of technologies used to produce a service, reducing the risk of failure of a given approach and accelerating the evolution to a new technology when demand, production, and cost conditions change. A monopoly bureau is more likely to rely on a smaller range of dominant technologies. The consolidation of similar services in a monopoly bureau, by facilitating "coordination," is likely to increase the range of outcomes, increasing the probability of doing everything right only at the cost of increasing the probability of doing everything wrong. And finally, competition among bureaus will appear messy, uncoordinated, and lacking direction. A monopoly bureau, in contrast, may seem as trim and majestic as the Titanic. Competition among bureaus is likely to be favored by those who understand evolutionary processes and tolerate complexity. Monopoly bureaus are favored by the medieval theologians among us who confuse coordination with direction, order with the organization chart. Competition among bureaus, in summary, reduces costs, increases the potential for political control, and increases insurance against major failure. A messy organization chart seems like a small price to pay for these effects.

SOME EVIDENCE

For those who care to look at the evidence, several types of empirical studies are now available that bear on the relation between bureaucratic structure and government spending. These studies suggest that the unit cost of government services increases with both the extent of monopoly and the absolute size of a bureau and that the consolidation of similar services in a monopoly bureau significantly increases total spending.

Some sense of the effects of competition on governmental efficiency can be derived from a recent study of output per man-year in the federal government (U.S. Congress, Joint Economic Committee, 1972). This study estimated the output and man-years for 114 elements of 17 agencies constituting 55% of the federal work force for five years from fiscal 1967 through 1971. The estimated annual percent changes in the output per man-year from this study are presented in Table 1. These estimates are almost perfectly correlated with the extent of existing competition among bureaus and with private firms. The federal government does not contract for any final services, and their output is difficult to compare across bureaus. The government contracts for some support services and for most industrial services. Among activities, the rate of increase of productivity is correlated with both the extent of contracting and the ease of comparing output across bureaus. The output measures are necessarily crude and the productivity estimates do not control for changes in other factors, but this pattern is too strong to dismiss. Bureaucrats, like other people, appear to shirk when they can get by with it and are efficient when they have to be. These estimates suggest the value of developing satisfactory output measures to permit contracting for final services and for noncomparable activities with either other bureaus or private firms.

Several studies of the economies of scale in the provision of local government services conclude that the unit cost of these services increases with the absolute size of the local government (Niskanen, 1971: 636). My own study of student performance in California public schools indicates that median scores on standard reading and mathe-

TABLE 1
Increase in Federal Output per Man-Year

Increase in Federal Output per Man-Year	
Service/Activity	Annual Percentage Increase
Final Services	1.25%
Operating	.84%
Processing	3.62
Support Services	3.24
Management	1.32
Procurement and Supply	1.11
Maintenance	6.32
Industrial Services	5.38
Overhead and Repair	5.05
Manufacturing	6.53

matics tests at both the sixth and twelfth grades are a significant negative function of school district size for districts larger than 2,000 students. Other studies of the school district size issue reach a similar
conclusion. These studies control for family and community characteristics and for school expenditures per student but not for other possible
outputs of the school system. Several similar studies of police performance conclude that police efficiency is a negative function of the
size of the police district. These studies are consistent with a conclusion
that the efficiency of bureaus is a negative function of the size of both
the government and the bureau. A larger government has more monopoly power, and the incentives of both voters and politicians to
monitor the bureau are smaller. The costs of monitoring the bureau
are larger, both to the politicians and the bureau chief, because the
"control loss" is a function of the number of managerial levels.

In summary, these studies suggest that inefficiency is not a necessary
characteristic of the supply of government services. For a given output,
these studies suggest that costs can be reduced by increasing the competition among bureaus, by contracting with private firms, and by
reducing the absolute size of bureaus.

The periodic reorganizations of the federal bureaucracy also provide an empirical base to test the effects of bureaucratic structure. These reorganizations, reflecting the conventional wisdom of public administration theory, have led to the consolidation of bureaus and agencies supplying similar services into larger departments. My theory suggests that the creation of these new departments would increase total spending for the consolidated functions. Several years ago, I tested for the effects on federal spending by function of the establishment of the departments of Defense, HEW, HUD, and Transportation, controlling for the other conditions that have affected the spending by function (Niskanen, 1971: 640-643). The pattern of these results is generally consistent with the hypothesis that the establishment of these four departments increased spending. The coefficients on the departmental effect are generally positive, highly significant for the two largest functions (defense and income maintenance), and nowhere both negative and significant. The magnitudes of the spending increases associated with the establishment of DOD and HEW are substantial— around 34% for defense, maybe as high as 25% for health, and around 25% for income maintenance! There is no evidence that this type of reorganization contributes to efficiency and economy. One wonders how soon Schlesinger's baby DOE will be overwhelmed by a herd of bucks.

The performance of these four departments, however, is even more disturbing than the increased spending. Since the establishment of the Department of Defense, the United States has fought one war to a draw against a second-rate military power, lost another war to a third-rate military power, and lost its strategic nuclear superiority over the Soviet Union. Since the establishment of HEW, health costs have skyrocketed, educational test scores have progressively declined, and there have been perennial demands for welfare reform. Following the establishment of HUD, our major cities have experienced riots, fiscal collapse, and continued decay. Following the establishment of the Department of Transportation, a large part of the railroad system has gone through bankruptcy to nationalization. Many other conditions, of course, have contributed to these problems, but there is no evidence that the establishment of these departments has reduced the developing problems in these areas. Somehow, I do not expect the Department of Energy to resolve the energy problem either.

What is the alternative? Can we afford an uncoordinated, redundant bureaucracy? My answer is there is an optimal positive amount of bureaucratic conflict and redundancy. It is a bit awkward to rationalize the combination of an antismoking campaign and tobacco subsidies, but these are trivial matters. The primary reason why some conflict and redundancy are important is that, in many areas, it is not clear what is the best thing to do. In many areas, competition among bureaus has been the primary reason why the government did something right, rather than everything wrong. Some of the more dramatic examples have involved the competition among the armed services in the development of weapons systems. In the hectic months following the launch of Sputnik in 1957, the Army and Navy launched the first U.S. satellites, the Army developed the first intermediate-range missile, and the Navy developed the fighter-bomber that has been the backbone of the tactical air forces since that time; in each case, the Air Force had the assigned responsibility for these tasks. The competition between the Polaris and Minuteman missile systems accelerated the deployment, improved the quality, and reduced the vulnerability of both systems. The continued competition between the Navy and Air Force to develop tactical aircraft and armaments has produced the best tactical aircraft systems in the world. The present competition between the Department of Labor, HEW, and HUD has made it possible to make an intelligent choice among a jobs strategy, an incomes strategy, and a cities strategy. Competition among bureaus may reduce the probability that the expected task is accomplished, but it increases the probability that the right task will be accomplished, often in unexpected ways.

POSTSCRIPT

Competition among bureaus is the *natural* condition of a bureaucracy. Cartels among bureaus, such as the Key West agreement among the armed services, tend to break down under the pressure of changing conditions and budget constraints, unless reenforced by the political authorities. Every new president, however, seems compelled to propose some consolidation of bureaus, and President Carter has made such reorganization a major issue. (One of the more ironic elements of the Carter plan is to create a government monopoly of the authority to prosecute private monopolies.) President Carter will learn that government reorganization is a tarbaby; it involves a huge amount of time, energy, and political capital to achieve, with little prospect of graceful withdrawal. More importantly, the consolidation of competing bureaus is the *wrong* type of reorganization, even if it were easy to achieve. The President would be better advised to exploit the natural competition among bureaus—to elicit information, to assure different approaches to important issues, and to permit the use of budgetary sanctions and rewards to specific bureaus without changing the total budget for a given function. My favorite fantasy may not be realized, big government may be around for some while, and there is no reason to tolerate a continued record of inefficiency and poor performance.

REFERENCES

NISKANEN, W. A. (1975) "Bureaucrats and politicians." J. of Law and Economics. 18 (December): 617-643.
——— (1971) Bureaucracy and Representative Government. Chicago: Aldine-Atherton.
U.S. Congress, Joint Economic Committee (1972) "Measuring and enhancing productivity in the federal sector," Joint Committee Print.

The Working Bureaucrat
and the Nonworking Bureaucracy

STEPHAN MICHELSON
Urban Institute

Government functionaries work hard and accomplish little. Many people would question the first part of that statement. But if it is true, then the malady of small accomplishment requires more explanation than the supposed inability of large government (or maybe just government) to induce work from its labor. I contend that it is largely true that government functionaries think that they work hard. That is, few are actively engaged in "ripping off" the system. Most, though ineffective, see themselves as conscientious. That is a start. The situation has two possible explanations: government employees have misconceptions about what "to work" means; or they really do work hard. By some objective measures I can imagine, but cannot imagine actually applying, I think most of these people put in a day's work. If I can't say it is a "good" day's work, the question is, why not?

Government functionaries, though they work hard and long, accomplish little because they have inherently unproductive jobs. The purposes which agencies, programs, offices are supposed to accomplish are poorly conceived, and then the tasks required to produce these unproductive outcomes are also poorly conceived. Sometimes the program is inherently contradictory or futile. I will give one example of such a program at the end of this chapter. Sometimes, with a reasonable programmatic concept, there is a mismatch between personnel

---

Author's Note: *Several people presently or formerly associated with programs whose management is challenged here have contributed to this chapter with helpful comments. They have also requested anonymity.*

and tasks. To those who have observed such problems I say "amen." But more common is a set of jobs the tasks of which are not understood, and even if well performed would not contribute to the aims of the program.

This isn't sabotage. It's just plain bad management. It's not bad management at the functional level, assigning and monitoring doable tasks, although that may occur. It's bad management at the conceptual level, devising relevant tasks. This distinction may help us understand how government employees can correctly feel that they "put out" each day while taxpayers can equally correctly feel that they have not been well served. I hope to demonstrate, using one program as an example, that good, hard-working folk can completely fail to run a program for lack of the theoretical concepts of what the program is and how it should work, which is to say, lack of management to devise those concepts and put them in place at the task level. This may not be the most glamorous theory of government malaise, but I think it is one of the most important.

COMMUNITY ECONOMIC DEVELOPMENT

Title VII of the Community Services Act is one of the more interesting, less-known parts of the "poverty" program. Except for ad hoc grants from Congress (as in the Alaska native land claim settlement), and occasional Economic Development Administration grants, it is the only overt wealth redistribution law I know of. It is true that mineral depletion, accelerated depreciation, investment tax credit, or subsidized loans all could be considered subsidies to wealth, not income. But only Title VII continually distributes general tax revenues in large lumps to nongovernmental bodies called "Community Development Corporations" (CDCs) for the purpose of putting community-owned capital in place in poor communities. The program started in 1966 as a Robert Kennedy and Jacob Javits add-on to the Economic Opportunity Act. In operation, it is a disaster. Most participants know it is a disaster, though because of the peculiar governmental concept of having agencies sponsor and supervise their own "evaluations," the program has been and will be called a success.[1] Furthermore, most people know *why* it is a disaster: the bureaucracy in Washington makes wrong decisions, right decisions too late and too unreliably, any decision when it should make none, and none when any decision would be preferred. The workers in the agency are by and large as sincere and as hard working as any equivalent bunch in industry. Individually, they are fine people; together, they are incompetent.

Starting in urban areas, inevitably (and quickly) the Community Development Program became both urban and rural since, whatever else it did, it gave away money. It gave the money to community corporations, some of which turned out to be just business development organizations, and were terminated. The CDC, said Washington, was supposed to be more. It was to reflect community values, to perform community services, to assess development needs, formulate an overall economic development plan, and direct the development of the community. To assist in that effort, the Office of Economic Development (OED), the arm of CSA which manages Title VII, also has supported groups such as a legal center in Berkeley, a business advisory firm in Belmont, Massachusetts, a research organization in Seattle, a training center in Palo Alto, the national organization of the CDCs in Washington, and CCED, a "research and advocacy" center in Cambridge. I joined CCED (the Center for Community Economic Development) in 1974, became Research Director in 1975, and left in 1978. My experiences there provide the base of my information.

THE CDC

In many ways a Community Development Corporation is a contradiction in terms. "Development" of most communities occurs by moving the former (poor) residents out, and moving new (rich) residents in (Cassidy, 1978). The hope for the original residents must lie in bringing into the community productive capital which employs the currently unemployed and upgrades the currently employed. Whatever else it does, one of its functions must be the placement of capital which employs the community. Seeing this far, OED designated two categories of grant funds to CDCs: CDC operating funds (flow) and venture capital funds (stock).

For the designation "CDC" to be meaningful, one would have to expect venture capital decisions made by a CDC to be different from those made by some other venture capitalist or land developer. A theory of what a CDC does would specify at least some way of observing the differentness of CDC decisions. Such a theory should guide the operation of a program so that the program's incentive system would nudge the CDC toward making those decisions that are consistent both with the CDC itself and with the program. The same theory, matched with evidence, would be used to convince Congress that *community*-based development is viable and important—if it is.

This is not the place to explore such a theory (see Michelson, 1978; Lilly and Miller, 1977).[2] Suffice it to say the program has none, and suffers because of it. Ideology is not theory; neither is lip service to the idea of "communityness." The insistence that CDCs have a certain form does not lead inexorably to knowing what they will do, or judging what they do as "development."

The CDCs are corporations; some are nonprofit, some are for profit. Every CDC has a president or executive director. All but one federally funded CDC has an elected board of directors. Most CDCs attempt to have some relationship with the community besides just being there and sponsoring business development. Some CDCs outside the Special Impact Program (see below) are very limited in purpose, such as housing rehabilitation, monitoring of public services or the like. Any community-based (open) organization which says it is interested in "development" is a CDC if it calls itself one. But the CDCs sponsored by Title VII are a special breed.

First, the average CDC receives about $1 million in total grant funds a year. For a nongovernmental but quasi-public body, placed in the middle of a poor area, this is power. There have been struggles for power within the CDC, struggles between the CDC and the local authorities, and (in contrast) recognition of the public authorities of the de facto political power of the CDC.[3] The deliberate bypassing of the local government was a daring move by the Congress—not repeated in subsequent development legislation—although there is little writing in the movement about this phenomenon. The Washington bureaucracy, in particular, has no theory about the meaning of this feature of the program, what it might say about policy of selection of CDCs, how it affects behavior of CDCs, how relations with government might be judged and how that judgment might be used.

Second, of course, is the price the CDC pays for the money: regulation. Only the Title VII funded CDC is an agent of a federal program. Other CDCs are agents of their boards. The board of a Title VII CDC has more money to play with and less ability to set its own rules. This is a source of continued tension which should be dealt with by finesse, not by fiat or finance.

MANAGING THE PROGRAM

I asked for three documents upon joining this program:

- the document which describes the program, which sets out its goal, its objectives (and how they relate to the goal), its strategies (and how they relate to the objective), and so on;
- the public document which sets out the basic accounting for all the funds (how much went to CDC staff, how much to equity capital, how much to service programs, and so on) and highlights the "accomplishments";
- the internal, honest document which assesses the performance of the program against its objectives, and assesses the overall plan and operation of the program.

It was truly naive of me, to be sure. There were no such documents. There still aren't. It's really quite simple to go from there to realizing that no one in the program has a rational basis for functioning. But it is of some interest to set that finding out in some detail. It is also important to emphasize here that I think the Act, Title VII of CSA, is a fine piece of legislation. It specifies legislative intent, but allows managerial discretion. It spells out purposes, goals, and tools, and lets the program administration refine the terms, set priorities, and choose from the legislature's menu. Its purpose, creating wealth in and under the control of poor communities, is admirable. If it was misconceived, as I think it was, still the legislature was open to being instructed by the program to rethink its concepts. It is true that Congress at times has threatened to end the program, and this has diverted program efforts from its program goal to saving its life. I don't want to slight the many and complex political realities which surround any program, and poverty programs most of all. The point here, though, is to analyze the day-to-day tasks of the workers in OED, to see how the self-image of the bureaucrat as hard working cannot be dismissed as folly, while it should not be confused with the objective reality of ineptness.

THE SETTING

The legislation says, in effect, here's some money to give to CDCs for the purpose of having an "appreciable impact" on poverty and community deterioration. Indeed, with CSA, this is called the "Special Impact Program" (SIP).[4]

The purpose of this part is to establish special programs of assistance to nonprofit private locally initiated community development corporations which (1) are directed to the solution of the critical problems existing in particular communities or neighborhoods (defined without regard to political or other subdivisions or boundaries) within those urban and rural areas having concentrations or substantial numbers of low-income persons; (2) are of sufficient size, scope, and duration to have an appreciable impact in such communities, neighborhoods, and rural areas in arresting tendencies toward dependency, chronic unemployment, and community deterioration; (3) hold forth the prospect of continuing to have such impact after the termination of financial assistance under this part, and (4) provide financial and other assistance to start, expand, or locate enterprises in or near the area to be served so as to provide employment and ownership opportunities for residents of such areas, including those who are disadvantaged in the labor market because of their limited speaking, reading, and writing abilities in the English language.

Over the years, language has been developed articulating such concepts as "appreciable impact," but there is no need to bore you with that here.[5] Let us take as given that the program managers have performed a basic task of putting down some language which officially interprets the legislation.

The key to any government program is who initiates and who determines the activities which are reported as "results." For any objective, the question is, who (or what) is directly responsible for achieving it. I call such key actors the "agents" of the program. The function of the rest of the program is to select and monitor the agents, establish incentives (rewards and punishments), judge the results, and fix-up by replacing the agents, changing the incentives, or revising the objectives.[6] With all the corporate structure behind and within a baseball team, eventually the pitchers pitch, the batters hit, and the fielders field. They are the agents. In the SBIC and MESBIC programs[7] the activity is the placing of financial capital, so the SBIS or MESBIC (not the entrepreneur) is the agent. In many EDA programs, the government employees (especially field representatives) are themselves the agents. They determine where grants and loans will go. The receivers of these funds do not care about the goal and objectives of the program; they care only about their own. The agent is essentially the last person or organization which incorporates by structure the program's purposes into its own.

The CDC is clearly the agent of the Special Impact Program. One CDC held out for some time before joining the program, just because it would have to incorporate the program's view of the world in its daily operation.[8] As the agent, it must direct its activities toward pleasing the Washington bureaucracy. Success is measured by the continued flow of funds. That is assured by having Washington think the agent is doing a good job. So we might like to know what a "good job" is and how doing it is demonstrated. That is, it should be the aim of the federal bureaucracy to establish an incentive system with rewards for good behavior and punishment or corrective action for bad. What constitutes good or bad behavior should be clearly spelled out, along with the consequences for deviation. The theory I am advocating provides a picture for the bureaucracy of what "good" agent behavior, or the results of such behavior, would be. Next there should be a line of communication established so that correct information flows to Washington, and correct feedback flows to the agent. Finally, there should be authority in Washington which leaves the agent alone when the objectives of the program are being realized, and takes action—consistent, helpful, but strong action—when necessary.

MAINTAINING FILES

OED is set up something like the State Department: there are "desk" people in Washington assigned to the CDCs. Each desk analyst monitors more than one CDC. Formal communication between CDC and Washington is through a quarterly report which is sent in multiple copies, to the desk analyst. However, actual communication is by telephone, visits of the CDC director to Washington, and the analyst to the CDC. The quarterly report is unlikely to contain anything the analyst doesn't know. By and large the quarterly reports are inaccurate and incomplete.[9] One can hardly expect the analyst to bother making corrections on his copy, which is stored in his files, though even if he does, a copy of the *incorrect* report goes to the microfiche room to create the only official repository of this information. At times OED has considered setting up a computer-oriented data system, but it would be worth nothing if it reflected the information flowing in.

Thus one aspect of the organization is that there is no one with an incentive to maintain correct records. The analyst is not held accountable, nor is the CDC. The analyst feels he "understands the situation" which is probably half correct. There is no program ability to know what has happened over time, unless an analyst has kept a separate (private) record, which would hold only for his CDCs for a limited period. There is no way at all to aggregate CDC activity into programmatic summaries.

Understanding the record-keeping system provides one level of explanation for why that second document, the one describing the program's operation over time and current status, does not exist. But if such a record were to exist, what would it contain?

We can look closer at the quarterly report to see what information OED officially asks for. The report is based on forms developed by Peat, Marwick and Mitchell, who did a reasonable job of setting out some ordinary accounting items one might like to know in any program: income statements and balance sheets of ventures, other program uses of funds, flow of funds for maintenance of the CDC, descriptions of activities in various stages, and minutes of board meetings. PMM, knowing this was just a stab at a moving object, strongly recommended that the forms be reviewed after a few years to see whether they satisfied the informational needs of the agency. Since the only information the agency uses is the informal information brought in by the desk analyst (and periodic "field reviewing"), no revision of the reporting mechanism has been undertaken, nor does anyone miss it. Apparently the quarterly report's function is the ability of the agency to say there is one.

The analyst, therefore, may be even more of a key figure than an organizational chart might imply. It bothers many people that these analysts are unskilled and untrained. It doesn't bother me, because no one has set out what skills they should have and what training it would take to achieve those skills. The fault cannot lie in selection or training of the analysts, if there is no model of what an analyst should be.[10]

THE ANALYST CLOSER UP

The analysts see the problem this way: to the CDC they represent the agency; to the agency they represent the CDC. They are paid by the agency but are emotionally involved with the CDC.[11] They are supposed to care for both the good of the agency and the good of the CDC, with no rule to determine when these values conflict, or to know what to do in such a circumstance. The analyst's position is inherently precarious. If he is not a vigorous advocate for the CDC within the agency, the CDC director will (correctly, from his point of view) take steps to go around the analyst. The director can establish his CDC's credibility in the "movement" through NCCED (the national organization to which most CDCs pay dues), because people confuse the director with his organization. He can develop other power bases: other CDC directors, legislators, and other staff at OED. He can cultivate personal friendships within the agency. If the analyst does become a strong advocate for the CDC, the agency soon grows immune. Though the analyst might like to think he is the "lifeline" to the CDC, and in some cases this is true, the shrewd CDC director does not let this occur.

The analyst, then, is in a double bind. In the first place, he doesn't know whom he represents or where his loyalties lie. In the second place, it often doesn't matter, since his authority can be circumvented.

AUTHORITY OF THE BUREAUCRACY

Let's think about authority. First, there is the authority of the agency. Legislative language is vague. Under Part A there is a stricture that the CDC—the receiver of funds—must have a governing body "not less than 50 percentum of the members of which are area residents." Other general requirements are left to the agency. The law then calls for appropriate coordination, adequate assistance, a need for the project, development of local skills and upward mobility for area residents, and community participation. As general as these conditions are, they are not even firm prerequisites to funding, since other parts of the Act contain even more broad language. One can say that Congress has provided enough language to point the administering agency in a clear direction. Ultimately, though, the agency maintains discretion and authority over its funds.

Second, then, is how that authority is located within the agency. Is power centralized or decentralized? If decentralized, is it by agent (all decisions concerning an agent located in one place, but different places for different agents) or by function (say, CDC staff, plans, venture approval, and the like)? Who has control of which money, and under what conceptions does that party operate? Can there be conflicting signals? The discussion here will not dwell on intraoffice politics, much of which revolves around obstructions created by the employees' union. Such impediments to management must be recognized, though I have nothing more to say about them.

In this program, as in most, there are only two fundamental aspects to the agency's authority: choice of agent and choice of activity. Both are regulated by the decision to put out money: who gets it and what is it spent for? If we locate authority within an agency, this is the authority we are looking for—the authority to select to whom money goes and the authority to approve the activities that party engages in.

CHOOSING THE AGENT

Since the program's agents are supposed to have "appreciable impact" on their areas, one might expect that the selection of agent would start there. There are two ways to have a large impact on an area: choose a small area or put a lot of resources into a larger area. The rural impact areas chosen are multicounty (ten in Kentucky, ten in Tennessee, for two examples). The urban areas are smaller than a city, but may contain several hundred thousand people. Whether this is big or small depends on the resources flowing to the CDC. I know of only one limited attempt to compare the CDC resources with a definition of the problem to ask if there was any possibility that the CDC could have appreciable impact (Michelson, 1976).[12] Somewhere one would like to see the scope of the problem laid out and an attempt made to structure the agency such that at least according to some theoretical calculations the program is a solution to the problems specified in the legislation. In this agency, and in others, the use of agency funds is such that there is not even in principle much chance to achieve the objectives of the legislation. One reason why the bureaucrats seem ineffective is that no matter how effective they might be, the program would be observed to fail.

Besides a measure of "impact," one should consider the capacity of the field agent, the CDC, to absorb the amount of capital which would be necessary to correct the poverty problem. In a theory which first estimated the problem, I would next estimate the rate at which one might expect the problem to be solved from federal funding. Then, since the CDC is not expected to end community poverty alone, I would estimate the kind of activities which would be so noticeable that other activities would come in on top of them—other federal grants, private funds, or community energy (self-help). This would give me a picture of what the agent of the program should look like: how big, what skills. Since there won't be such agents waiting for the program to fund them, it is especially necessary to have a picture of what the agent should look like, so proper assistance can be provided to those potential agents which are actually there.

Someone in the agency, in OED in this case, still has to have the authority to choose the field agent. Now we see that it must be a conditional selection: "You would be an adequate field agent for this program if you made changes X, Y and Z, of which we are willing to support X and Y." Language like this does in fact come from OED to CDCs. Grant applications are seldom approved in their orginal form. However, there is no way for a CDC to anticipate what changes will be called for.[13] To them (and to me) it seems like arbitrary bureaucratic actions. There is a "planning grantee" stage which sounds like a probationary period and does eliminate some clearly disfunctional CDCs. It does that which it takes no theory to do.

If the analyst had the authority to approve the CDC's application, it would be a sign of lack of communication to see changes being requested. The nature of the application would have been discussed before hand. The application itself would be only a formality. The analyst does not have this authority. He negotiates a proposal with his CDC, and then submits it to higher authority. At this point the analyst has "bought into" the proposal, and is the advocate for its adoption. The actual approval is a high-level affair, including the heads of branches which will have further dealings with the CDC and the Director of the program. Whether the bureaucratic model in which the agency's supervisor of the CDC, the analyst, periodically plays the role of advocate is a good model, I don't know. My concern in this article is the theory of the program which would provide the analyst the arguments for his advocacy. My concern in this section is where and on what basis authority lies for selecting and funding the CDC.

Since there is no theory of the problem, the resources required for its solution, the point at which "impact" toward the solution is achieved, and the nature and scope of the institution which could achieve that impact, there is no analytic determination of how many CDCs there should be, of what size, or shape. In the absence of such a determination, an experimental approach would be useful: fund several CDCs at different size levels, controlling for environment (size and demography of impact area, urban/rural and so on) as well as possible. After all, if you can't explain to the public in rational, consistent terms why X CDC was funded and Y was not, or why X got more dollars than Y, an agency could always explain that this variation was part of the "design."

Politics, for the limited purposes here, can be defined as the practice of dealing rationally with the arbitrary. Since the selection and funding decisions are not based on a theory and are not predetermined by an experimental design, they are perceived as "arbitrary" with respect to the goals of the program. That does not mean that the criteria are inconsistent, though they may be. "Arbitrary" means that there is no known or hypothesized relationship between the selection and funding criteria and agent performance. OED management has never attempted to determine which characteristics of agents lead to success partly because no one has thought to ask the question, and partly because they don't know what "success" is in the first place. But one should not slight the *effort* which goes into a funding decision. A team of analysts and other OED staff visit the site and review the grant application documents, often sending them back to the CDC for revision before approval. Although the agency has no uniform approach to grantee selection, each analyst has specific factors in mind, reflecting his individual views, of development and grantee success.

Since there is no adequate reporting and accounting system at OED, the review team knows only what it is told, plus what its members know from hanging around the CDC and the program. There are neither OED-developed indexes of CDC performance nor comparative measures (other CDCs, other development agents) available from the accounting system. Nor does such data exist at OED from which a system could be developed. This is only *apparently* due to the inadequacy of the reporting system described above. More important than the inability of the system to generate an accurate record is its inability to generate a relevant record. That is, having correct information is important only when that information is conceptually relevant. Since the quarterly report system is neither conceptually adequate nor accurate, it would be folly for the review team, even if they thought of it, to ask for the program to provide them with comparative data and standards for grantee review.

The result is that the review team and the analyst-advocate appear arbitrary and hence amenable to political pressure. Occasionally this pressure is of the overt, public conception of "political": one planning grantee was the outgrowth of the Democratic Party machine in an area whose representative to Congress was on the congressional oversight committee. One planning grantee was fully funded in a last-minute gesture to his ethnic peers by a departing program director. These are the stories which make the newspapers and hurt the program. They are not typical. By and large the reviews are carried out by sincere people who would like to help poor communities self-develop; and they put many hours into that effort. By and large their recommendations are followed by the high-level people who make the ultimate decisions.

What "political pressure" means, more commonly, is the ability of one community to find an argument which can sway members of the review team that this CDC is (a) in a really deserving community (poor),

(b) nonetheless has the requisite management skills, (c) has community support, (d) has new but practical ideas, and (e) would give the program a new image. This last item is not trivial. There having been no Chinese-American CDC in the program, such groups in several cities were encouraged to apply recently, as one of them was sure to be funded (and one of them was). After the Standing Rock Reservation was terminated, the program clearly wanted an Indian CDC. Dineh was funded on no basis I know of, and then a year later OED funded a CDC on the Northern Cheyenne Reservation in Montana, which quickly failed.[14] Roxbury and East Boston were funded together some years ago in a kind of black and white balancing act which had some political shrewdness to it, though no noticeable community development.

How the other pieces of information—deservedness, skill, support, and ideas—are determined, I do not know. Nor does it matter here, much though it matters to the program and to an individual CDC. The point is that a program with a clearly analytic end—having impact on problems of poverty through community-controlled small-area organizations—has an agent selection system which is based on the ability of the CDC to convince a review team or upper management of its worthiness, where neither the team nor the CDC has a conceptual or factual basis which relates "worthiness" to the program's goals.

It must be stressed here that there is no reason to believe the Special Impact Program is unique in these regards. The details provided for this program could as easily be provided for others. The necessity for the authority of any agency to be exercised in pursuit of that agency's goals, the idea that such authority is largely held to choosing and funding agents, and the conclusion that the exercise of that authority in practice is divorced from a cause-effect theory of program operation, is a fundamental bureaucratic malady.

APPROVING THE ACTIVITIES

Along with the grantee, a plan is approved. The contradiction between being a venture capitalist and having a development plan has struck others before me. Those CDCs that want to be venture capitalists submit a "search" system and criteria for venture selection as their plan. Others act more like development agencies, knowing what they want their area to look like and planning for that to occur.[15] In either case, although the plan has been accepted, specific venture funds still are subject to approval by OED before they are released. Therefore the agency retains this second authority, and we can try to find where it resides and how it is used.

In addition to the desk analysts, there are "business analysts" whose job it is to look over venture business plans and approve, disapprove, or recommend changes. Final approval authority rests with the program division branch chief or the program director, who receive recommendations from both the desk analyst and the business analyst. Although CDCs can either acquire or start up ventures, obviously the acquisition process is greatly hampered by the delay of OED reviews.[16] It sounds reasonable, though, to have Father Washington review business plans of child CDCs selected for their existence in places where business development is seldom attempted and usually fails. But is it?

Good business school graduates like to play with money. That's the fun of it. One might think, it would be more difficult to attract better people to a review-approval agency than to the field. If the reviewers are not better than the field developers, review makes no sense at all.[17] Management might want to devise ways to test whether and to what extent OED business review improves CDC venture performance, but OED hasn't done that. The more relevant issue here is the set of criteria which are to be applied in the review. Apparently the *business* review is separated so that strictly business criteria may be applied. Therefore the final decision is based on business and "other" considerations. That ought to mean first of all that there is a known set of "other" considerations which can override business concerns, and second of all, that a venture which is funded under these other considerations should not be held only to business performance standards.

I have never been able either to locate the criteria by which nonbusiness considerations would override business considerations, or to determine which ventures were approved on the basis of these other criteria.[18] Recall that the final decision is made at the branch chief or director level. This is the management level which, I am claiming, should be responsible for having a theory of development, and a theory of the program from which its organization and decision criteria should flow. However, such an explicit theory would take away from that same management the arbitrary authority that it now exercises, the ability to approve or not approve venture proposals on ad hoc grounds. The political process—the personal relationships with CDC directors, pressures from political powers, ethnicity, and so on—is one which many managers will prefer, since they are bound only by their "judgment" and ad hoc rationales for decisions.

Indeed, we should expect that it is what most program directors prefer. Note that management skill per se is purchasable by the director. I am not asking here for directors who are better managers, but for directors who bring more intellectuality, more program conceptualization to their position. They must combine that with a management capable of involving lower-level bureaucrats in the concepts of the program, and capable of understanding what a person can do in a day. But "better management" per se is not sufficient.

So stated, the possibility of achieving a "reform" of the kind I would like to see is obviously bleak. The rise to the top in Washington is itself such an overtly political process, a process of "playing ball" in the right way with the right people, that people with appropriate conceptual skills are seldom considered. A study of the Action program, which may be a counterexample, could usefully illuminate the ideas presented here. However, even if such a study found that that program was effectively managed in the way I am discussing, it would give little guidance. We cannot systematize drawing federal program managers from national protest movements.

THE ANALYST REVISITED

The analyst is the "bureaucrat" in the CDC's eyes. Although the analyst seems to act as the conduit of information, he both shouldn't (there should be a functional reporting system) and can't (if he doesn't report favorably, the CDC bypasses him; if he does, his credibility is lowered). The analyst is responsible for monitoring the CDC, and does have some authority. Major decisions are made with analyst participation, but most are not made by the analyst. He is not really the repository of authority, and the CDC knows that. On the other hand, in the vacuum created by unsure management, the analyst sometimes takes the authority he has not been given. And he could cause trouble—you don't want your advocate in grantee reviews not to like you. The CDC knows that, also.

Also, the analyst has no skills which the CDC values except political skills inside the agency. The analyst has an idea what kind of Overall Economic Development plan might be approved, but does not know what kind of plan is helpful.[19] The analyst receives quarterly reports which are in large part copies of previous reports with inadequate and inaccurate data. The CDC does not respect the analyst because he does not require real reporting; but if he did, then he would appear as a nit-picking bureaucrat who "can't see the broad picture." Though the analyst may on his own know more about a particular CDC than could be contained in a report, he has no standards against which to compare his knowledge. This is the meaning of my statement above that the analyst is "half" correct. He can make no sense of his knowledge without a conceptual basis for asking questions, and a comparative basis for answering them. He has neither.

EVALUATION

The rules of the Special Impact Program game were not formally specified until November 1975, when CSA Instruction 6158-1 was issued. These rules are now contained in the regulations. They empha-size that Title VII should be seen as a demonstration program, not an operational program. This would argue for deliberate variation and evaluation—not in terms of development of communities, but in terms of determining the best ways for the federal government to support community-based development, as well as a measure of how good this "best" is. One of the ways in which CDCs might vary is their emphasis on the profitability of their ventures. An alternative to directly produc-ing profits, as a model of development, might be to find areas of non-profit, but catalytic activity.

However, the regulations specifically call for an emphasis on profit.[20] One can ask no more of an evaluation than to take the program at its word, and evaluate its achievements against its objectives. The only large-scale evaluation of the program completed so far, except for the one after its first year of operation, considered the program success-ful on the basis of *projected* profits of ventures (Abt Associates, 1973). In most cases these projections were hopelessly optimistic. The evalua-tors would have been closer to the truth had they predicted that all ventures would fail (Center for Community Economic Development, 1977).[21] By its own major criterion, venture profits, the Special Impact Program continues to fail.

More importantly, the question of what "communityness" a success-ful business venture should have has never been answered. It might be argued that any CDC venture is "community" based, since it is approved by the community-representing board. That would imply that at most only business decisions should be made in Washington. Whether Washington's review helps business decisions is unknown, since program evaluations never investigate the operation of the OED staff. Since venture approval decisions are arbitrary, they could always be called "business" judgments no matter who makes them.

Reports to Congress have carefully avoided generalizations about ventures, which in any case cannot be made given the disarray of the data. Since there are CDCs which have equity positions in profitable businesses, "success" stories can always be brought out to please the crowds. At oversight hearing time, analysts are put to work finding these stories, and they do. Despite the inadequacy of program performance (both from its own criteria, as above, and by others) and the inadequacy of the bureaucracy's performance, the individual bureaucrats can work hard and produce what is requested of them.

THE COMMUNITY

Since the outlook for management reform on its own initiative is bleak and the need is clear, is there hope that some outside force could exert pressure? Specifically, would more community involvement either cut through the bureaucratic inefficiencies, or make the bureaucracy "shape up?" The issues this question raises are too complex for a direct answer. Here are a few pessimistic considerations.

First, in any ongoing program, there will have been a selection of agents through arbitrary (political) criteria, as described above. If one asked now for increased "involvement" in fundamental decision-making by the CDCs, he would be asking for a very peculiar version of "community participation." Why should *these* CDCs suddenly be the ones to call for or articulate rationality in CDC selection? Surely these CDCs would rationalize selection criteria which would choose themselves, and venture-approval criteria which would approve their activities.

It is difficult to make a person or organization accountable to anyone other than the provider of funds. That is what places the SIP-CDC, which is supposed to be accountable to its community, in such a difficult situation in the first place. The bureaucrat, also, will respond to the holder of the purse, which is program management. If the first problem is that giving power to current agents would freeze the arbitrary criteria by which they are selected, the second problem is to conceive of how effectively to give them this authority in the first place. The experience of the Parental Advisory Councils in Title I of the Elementary and Secondary Education Act indicates that community oversight can be effective in review and exposure, and in the growth of the people who serve on them. But in that program federal funds came by formula, and did not go to the parents. One cannot expect a board of CDC representatives to act on the one hand as discretionary program grantees and on the other as program monitors.

It might be hoped that an association of agents could act to protect the individual agent interest, without either exposing an individual agent to retribution or preventing an individual agent from receiving proper sanctions. NCCED was formed partly for that purpose. However, such an association makes the weak CDCs stronger (by their numbers and by their association with stronger CDCs) and the strong CDCs, who can operate better alone, weaker. Therefore, the association management must act to protect the weak (the management's constituents) while the strong CDCs make their private deals and use the association's numbers as a political power base. It is difficult to see how any such agent organization, based on one agent one vote, can apply pressure on bureaucrats to run a more effective program. Recent scandals with associations of Community Action Agencies, in requiring CSA to monitor *them* more closely (not the other way around), seem to bear this out.

Third, one could grant complete autonomy to all CDCs, overtly endorsing the *process* of community development and making no judgments about outcomes. This would grant to a CDC a limited term tap on the U.S. Treasury, subject only to legal (theft, fraud, and so on) restrictions. It would make the CDC program equivalent to revenue-sharing, being a direct slap in the face of locally elected authority. It cannot happen.

Fourth, one can hope to put some market forces on individual analysts. Give them pots of money and goals. Giving the bureaucrat more power is exactly the opposite of giving the community more power, unless the goals are structured so that the bureaucrat enlists the aid of the community toward achieving his ends. This solution does speak to the source of accountability: the analyst would be accountable to higher level management for production of certain outcomes; but *what* outcomes? Would managers who cannot devise a nonarbitrary reward system for agent performance be able to devise one for analysts?

Fifth, one could think of establishing several Special Impact Programs, with completely separate bureaucracies. They would compete for communities, which would give the CDC some bargaining power it now does not have, facing a monopoly agency. However, at some point these competing agencies must be judged. How would we know which was the best? The problems are similar to judging competing analysts. Which program is the most effective in generating community-based economic development? Answering that question requires some of the same theoretical conceptions and data which the current program management does not have. Granted, it requires conceptualization only of outcomes. But it assumes that *someone* can direct an organization toward those outcomes. Why not hire such a person as deputy director in the first place? I don't see how competing bureaucracies would accomplish much beyond multiplying costs, although some deserving groups which have not played the political game sufficiently well might get some funding that way.

If we can agree that there are societal goals which are to be produced by federal programs, then specifying the program outcomes, specifying a relationship between program processes and outcomes, and specifying a management structure to effectuate the processes, is unavoidable. Suggestions about community input, which I support whenever they are relevant, simply don't speak to the particular management problem which I have been describing.

GENERALIZABILITY

To what extent is the argument that what bureaucrats need is better management, and that what "better management" requires is better theory a valid generalization? I think it can be demonstrated time and again that ineffective appointments at key management levels have created the situation that the public views as ineffective bureaucratic functioning. As a counter example, consider the processing of complaints by the Equal Employment Opportunities Commission. In my view, Eleanor Holmes Norton brought a new conception of complaint processing to the Commission when she assumed the Chair. It was that complaints are often emotional, so that speedy resolution is important; and they are a burden to the company charged with discrimination, so that conciliation is possible. These concepts lead to a system of counseling the client and meeting with the alleged offender, rather than assuming an adversarial position from the outset. The tasks of the low-level bureaucrat—the person who is the agency as the public sees it—were changed from form processing to personal complainer assistance. This was not a case of better management in the sense of making the old processing more "efficient." It was a new concept of what "to process" a complaint might mean. It did not require new personnel but, rather, new objectives with clearly related tasks. An information system was also adopted so that upper management could see where the bottlenecks occurred. As I understand it, the system has been quite successful in resolving more complaints with fewer resources.

In contrast, most areas of EEOC and antidiscrimination efforts of contract compliance agencies are a bureaucratic muddle. Exactly the kind of analysis presented here—questioning the concepts behind the daily tasks—is needed. I have refrained from suggesting answers, from providing an example of a theory which would lead to different bureaucratic tasks, so that my particular answers would not be confused with the necessity of framing the correct questions. It is a very general, obvious, but seldom practiced approach.

One could fruitfully have analyzed the Vietnam war this way: it's not that soldiers were asked to do impossible tasks, but that these tasks, even if done, could not have achieved a reasonable goal. It should not be too much to ask that Commerce, HUD, DOL, HEW, and independent agencies do the same. There theories may not always be correct, but at least, formulated and tested, we could learn something from the outcomes. It is safe to say that we can learn virtually nothing about whether community-based economic development can be federally promoted and, if so, how to do it, from OED's failure.

WRONG TIME, WRONG PLACE

We should recognize that there are programs which, however well-managed, face hopeless goals. That is not true of the Special Impact Program, which digs its own hole by giving miniscule grants (relative to the size area chosen) to skill-less agents on the basis of no known standards, to accomplish unachieveable objectives (profits) with no necessary relationship to the goal (economic development), and without knowing the results. It is not true of EEOC or the Office of Federal Contract Compliance Programs, where one could conceive of definitions and empirical tests of discrimination, though in over a decade these agencies have produced neither. It *is* true of youth employment programs sponsored by the Department of Labor and the U.S. Office of Education in HEW. This example is worth a word here so we can see that we should not waste efforts trying to get solid theoretical conceptions into programs where any intelligent theory would say the program is not even legislatively conceived to attack the problem.

DOL and HEW have been urged to coordinate because, on its face, there seems to be a conflict between programs which try to get teenagers into the workforce and programs which try to get them into school (see, for example, MacKinnon, 1978). Only two assumptions can justify this approach to youth unemployment: (a) there is a supply of jobs waiting for people with the right (attainable through these programs) skills, or (b) the supply of these trained people will increase the number of jobs created for them. Both assumptions require that the "market" which puts real capital in place does so to suit the labor supplied to it. Yet it was the insufficient or inappropriate (to current skills) placement of capital which created the problem in the first place. Thus the area of economic decision which creates the problem is assumed to function properly, while the population which suffers from the investment decisions is the target of ameliorative programs. There is no contradiction within the program (some youth can be trained, others educated). The contradiction occurs before the program.

"Rational" evaluators will look at the cost per youth of these programs and suggest that it would have been cheaper just to give the money to them. Such conclusions don't consider the conflict between the wage system (incentive to work) and the income transfer system (incentive not to work). The youth programs are not really designed to put youth to work. To do that, one would create an investment program. The youth programs are designed to get funds to youth and to social scientists, keep them busy, without calling it an income transfer program and further undermining the wage system. They may also provide a subsidy to capital, picking up some training costs.

IN SUMMARY

Bureaucrats are workers. In today's world of work, the tasks most workers perform are designed by management, presumably following a concept which relates individual tasks to accomplishment of management's objectives, the objectives themselves being directed toward some goal. To what extent the worker need agree with or even know the goal can be debated. But if his task is poorly designed to achieve the objective, and/or the objective is poorly designed to achieve the goals, then the bureaucrat may be surrounded by failure. One might think of the production workers who made the Edsel, for example. The public sees Edsel-like programs and often blames the functioning bureaucracy for the failure. However, some programs are *conceived* to fail. Others, though they could succeed, are *designed* to fail. Few, I think, are conceived and designed well, but managed badly; and even fewer are conceived, designed, and managed well but foiled by irresponsible workers beyond management's control. Granted, the solution to any problem only uncovers the next level of problems. Still, from my experience, I would look to the lack of conceptualization on the part of politically motivated and politically chosen top program management as the most important contributor to the failure of bureaucracy today.

NOTES

1. In Washington, a success is that which is called a success. Being successful means getting enough (and the right) people to call you successful. That is why the "highly successful Lummis," a CDC on the Lummi Indian Reservation in Washington State, are successful. They were successful in getting people to call them the "highly successful Lummis," which is the major operating goal of any government fundee.

2. I have begun the development of a theory which delineates the ways in which market "failure" can bring about poverty areas. The theory then asks which failures the community-based organization has some advantage in correcting. My theory says that OED expects CDCs to do just those things for which the CDC has no advantage, and does not reward those things the CDC may do well. If OED had a theory, mine would just be a different one; but OED has none at all (see Michelson, 1978).

For an analysis of bureaucratic maladies in some ways coincident with the one presented here but, I think, which fails to distinguish between differences in theory and the lack of theory, see Lilly and Miller (1977).

3. At the extreme, there was a machine gun raid on one faction by another in Roxbury. In Hancock County, Georgia, the CDC was (it was said) the political base of the black movement against minority white local government. One could say this CDC, also, was raided, though in this case the raid was "legal." Indictments of top staff were followed shortly by the death in a small plane crash of the director. On the other side are such obvious gestures as speeches at CDC functions by politicians who clearly would rather be somewhere else, but know they had better be there. Examples of more meaningful use of CDC power include getting first option on property claimed for tax default, provision of public services on demand by the CDC, and appointment of the CDC as the agent of the city in housing rehabilitation, CETA program management, and the like.

4. This is the purpose of Part A of Title VII of the Community Services Act, as it is currently on the books. See Federal Laws Title 42, Chapter 34, Subchapter VII, 2982.

5. See 45 CFR X, Part 1076. Briefly, poverty areas are seen as declining in a series of (unspecified) indicators, and "impact" is seen as arresting that decline. Only a scoundrel would point out that if one observed someone's declining pulse rate, "success" would come with death under this definition. The ultimate goal is "to achieve parity between the impact areas and the areas surrounding them, to correct the tremendous imbalance in institutional capacity, income, jobs and human resources," which may not be much of an accomplishment. However, neither of these standards is to be taken seriously, since neither a CDC nor the program is ever evaluated against them.

6. There are also public relations duties, such as cooling out Congress and providing information to potential agents.

7. These are the "Small Business Investment Corporation" and the "Minority Enterprise" SBIC, which are special programs of the Small Business Administration.

8. TEILACU—The East Los Angeles Community Union—was initiated by United Auto Workers funds, but has great expanded as a SIP-CDC.

9. This is easy to document. When at CCED I instituted a systematic data compilation based on CDC quarterly reports. Our inability to account for the funds the CDCs received, which is a kind of minimum check on the documents, was reported in writing to the director of OED.

10. Nothing in this article should be taken as praise for or defense of the analysts. They neither want nor expect—nor deserve—such sentiments from me.

11. Striking evidence of this involvement is the inability of the program to maintain a CDC within commuting distance of Washington, D.C. Two CDCs have been funded, PDP/PIC in the Northwest section of the city (near Howard University) and Anacostia Development Corporation in Anacostia, the poorest section of the city. There is ample evidence to show that the refusal of the analyst to let the CDC function at arm's length as the program's agent was primarily responsible for the failure within the SIP of both of these CDCs.

12. Michelson (1976) came to the general conclusion that the area is too large for the funds expended to have a noticeable impact.

13. After a planning grant year, the Dineh Cooperative on the Navajo reservation applied for grantee status. OED first said it would approve the grant only if they changed their proposed staffing. After many changes and resubmissions, eventually the original pattern was reinstated and the grant was approved.

14. Dineh's survival in the program can be explained by nothing else than OED's desperate desire to maintain an Indian presence. The failure of the Cheyenne CDC could

have been (and was) predicted. Control of the organization was in the hands of the wealthiest people on the reservation. Activity was directed, in traditional OED fashion, toward overall planning. Meanwhile, coal (the Tribe owns 6 billion tons of it) was lying uncovered (by Bureau of Indian Affairs bulldozers) but unused, while half the homes were heated by coal imported from Wyoming and half were heated by propane. The OED approach and selection criteria were hopelessly elaborate given the initial elementary problems.

15. Kentucky Highlands Investment Corporation is a good example of the former type, Pyramidwest Investment Corporation, the latter. Both of these organizations seem to be supremely capable of accomplishing what they set out to do. Both of them have a strong conceptual basis for their activities. Both have politically strong executive directors. Both changed from poverty program names to ones more business-sounding. Despite my admiration for both organizations, I have no idea if either furthers the aims of the program.

16. HUD often demands right of approval over contractors financed by HUD loans, and EDA sometimes retains the same right over the use of their grants. At best this process delays a project, which can add considerably to the cost. In addition, it can make the government agency liable for the work done, and the process itself can drive away private sector participants who are not interested in the bother.

17. Any agency which monitors should first develop a minimum review of agent actions, that required to fulfill the agency's legal responsibilities. I am questioning only the efficacy of monitoring above the minimum.

18. The phrase "venture autonomy" is common in this program. "Venture autonomy" would be the ability of a CDC to commit venture capital funds *without* specific approval from Washington. Although CDCs vary in their ability to function autonomously, and despite the formal existence of a "venture autonomy program" and a call for "maximum possible autonomy" in the regulations, there is no systematic mechanism to free CDCs of this oversight. One clever way around the venture autonomy problem is to receive permission to establish a "revolving loan fund." Only the fund requires approval, not actions of the fund—because the CDC (not the fund) is the agent. Its role is to establish the venture. Thus, a business loan from the CDC must be approved in Washington, but an equivalent loan from an approved loan fund requires no such approval.

19. The value of the plan, or the different values of different kinds of plans, has never been studied. There is no information on how many ventures specified in plans have been pursued to what extent (how many dropped for various reasons, how many started and failed, how many successful, and so forth). Nonetheless, all grantees are required to have such plans, though they are not held accountable to perform up to them.

20. See especially 45 CFR X, Section 1076.5-8(d).

21. The projections for five years after the date of the evaluation survey were compared with actual conditions at the projection date in *A Review of the Abt Associates' Evaluation of the Special Impact Program*, CCED, 1977.

REFERENCES

Abt Associates (1973) Evaluation of the Special Impact Program. Cambridge: Abt Books.

CASSIDY, R. (1978) "Can success kill a neighborhood?" Planning 44 (July).

Center for Community Economic Development (1977) A Review of the Abt Associates' Evaluation of the Special Impact Program.

LILLY, W., III and J. C. MILLER III (1977) "The new 'social regulation'." Public Interest (Spring): 49-61.

MacKINNON, P. A. (1978) The schooling industry versus the deschooling industry, or factors influencing policies in education/work programs." Presented at the American Educational Studies Association (November).

MICHELSON, S. (1978) "Community based development in urban areas," in B. Chinitz (ed.) Central City Economic Development. Cambridge: Abt Books.

——— (1976) "Projecting capital requirements." Center for Community Economic Development Newsletter (June/July).

Limiting Government Expenditure by Constitutional Amendment

AARON WILDAVSKY
University of California, Berkeley

DOING TOGETHER
WHAT WE CANNOT DO ALONE

In the season when hope springs eternal, April 1979, a proposed amendment to the Constitution that would limit the increase in federal expenditures to the proportionate rise in Gross National Product was introduced to the Congress of the United States.[1] It is a linked limit; each year's expenditure depends upon last year's expenditure, plus the percentage by which the output of the nation's goods and services has gone up. Hence, under the amendment, the size of the public sector could not grow faster than the size of the private sector. Should the political process produce a lower level of spending in any one year, spending in succeeding years, which depends on what has gone before, would similarly be smaller. Emergencies declared by two-thirds vote of Congress can raise the spending limit, but a majority vote is sufficient to decrease it. Spending can increase, but no faster than production. The idea is not to limit spending to some absolute amount, regardless of national productivity or new needs that cannot now be foreseen, but to relate public consumption to private production so the one does not eat up the other. A constitutional expenditure limit is a social contract establishing a division of resources between the private and public sectors.

Why do we need a spending limitation?

THE PRIVATE AND THE PUBLIC SECTORS

In the beginning, there was the private sector, and the public sector was so small it was scarcely noticeable. At the turn of this century, public spending at all levels was just under 7% of Gross National Product (GNP). Within that total, the states and localities spent just under twice as much as the federal government. Today federal spending has increased almost 10 times, from 2.4% to over 22% of GNP. And state and local spending is barely above half of the federal level. If money is power, relationships between citizens and government and between state and central government are not what they used to be. Public spending has been growing much faster than the economy. In 1900, one worker in 25 worked for government; now the figure is closer to one in 5. Projecting this trend over only the next two decades would bring total government expenditure to nearly two-thirds of GNP. The United States will have changed from a predominantly private to a preponderantly public country.

There may be those who want to turn the clock back to the days of yesteryear, but they are few and I am not among them. Government has assumed larger responsibilities for social welfare and national defense, without which the nation could not long continue. The question, for me at least, is not whether expenditures should take a deep dive, but rather whether they will continue their sharp ascent. I would much rather this did not happen.

Speaking personally, I think it would make life much less interesting. There will be less innovation; new ideas will languish. As the cost of regulation rises, so will the size of corporations who can afford to compete. There will be less variety; government guarantees collectivity not individuality. Though I do not expect the grey uniformity of Eastern Europe, I would expect the growing uniformity that is the unvarying result of bureaucratic rules. For me, diversity is a friend, but for government, even good government, diversity is dangerous.

For the country, big government is no bargain. Doing what comes naturally, big government will (with our consent, to be sure) eat us out of house and home. In a nation noted for the uneven development of its regions and peoples, policies that require selectivity will be based instead on homogeneity. Where race and class remain explosive issues, reducing growth in favor of giant government is unwise. Distribution of resources would smooth social relations. If competing for control over government, as vital and honorable as that is, becomes the only game in town, incumbents of institutional power have too great an incentive to rig the rules.

In terms of liberty, competition is the keystone. Just as science proceeds by refutation of hypotheses, and markets function by the ability to reject bids unacceptable to others, so democracy is about the ability to say "no." We may know what we're against, as is often observed, even if we don't know what we're for. Being against one's own government is almost a contradiction in terms. Yet if government is gigantic, opposition to it becomes at once essential and hopeless. Political passions will rise without moderation or melioration by the ability to retreat to private preserves.

There was a time, no later than the 1950s, when liberals lusted after federal expenditure to do good. If only there were billions for higher education, or for mass transportation, or for mental health, and on and on, what wonders would be performed! Now we know better. Government is an expensive and inadequate replacement for the family. Changing deep-seated behavior requires the cooperation of the convert and is difficult at any price. Those who used to argue that federal money would not bring federal effort to control education, as I did as a college student, have had their naiveté exposed. It is not that public policy is good for nothing, but that it is not good for everything. And the more that is done—the more large programs and the greater their interaction—the less we understand them. Thus it is reasonable for us to reconsider what has been done over the decades, with a view to deciding what we ought to want. A "wait and see" attitude should leave everyone relaxed. But reconsidering and revamping public policy cannot be carried on seriously while government is expanding on all cylinders and in every sector.

Reflection before expansion. Surely these sentiments are in tune with the times. Polls of public opinion show about three-quarters of the population opposed to growth of government, even if this means services are cut back (see *Nation's Business*, 1979: 19). Balanced budget amendments have been passed in 28 states. If lower spending is part of every politician's program, however, how come it never happens?

No knowledgeable person believes that it will be possible to halt, for more than a few years the inexorable increase in spending. A sense of hopelessness surrounds the issue. How did we get into this bind? Some say bureaucrats are serving their own ends. Other say politicians continue to promise and spend themselves into office. Still others see citizens snapping up the bait of public largesse. Citizens want less public spending, the cynics say, except when it comes to their favorite programs.

May I say as long and loud as I can that I emphatically do not subscribe to theories of bureaucratic conspiracy or manipulation to explain the growth of public expenditure. I wish to puncture the preposterous Parkinsonian proposition that bureaucrats expand their programs indefinitely by hoodwinking the population. Were these programs not deeply desired by strong social elements, they would not prosper. As Frank Levy told me, it is not the conspiracy theory, but the Pogo theory which is applicable here: *We have Seen the Enemy and They is Us.* The Pogo theory is that we-the-people (including citizens, politicians, and civil servants) are pushing expenditures up. This is a cooperative game. We do not like it—who said that people necessarily like what they do to themselves—but we do it.

Citizens, bureaucrats, and public officials are in the same bind. The direct benefits of specific spending legislation to them or to their constituents or clients are clear and palpable. The direct costs are diffused among tens of millions of taxpayers or 435 congressional districts or a myriad of other public and private activities about which one can know but little. Benefits are concentrated, costs are diffused. Participants are motivated to support programs that provide large direct benefits to themselves, oppose only those with large direct costs, and, in view of the great expense of information and activity, remain indifferent to the rest. Once the process is in high gear, so that there are many more large programs, the 3 motivations move together: As the scope of public sector activity increases, there is more support, opposition, and indifference. Specialized political activity increases (more support and opposition to programs offering direct benefits and costs), smoothed along by the possibilities for bargaining in areas of indifference. Many new programs are introduced, many old ones are enhanced, many are vetoed, but the rate of initiation is so high (direct benefits without direct costs are delectable) that every year more are added, and few, if any, are subtracted, because that would impose costs on others who could not easily be placated. There is progression, but is there progress? That depends. Every active participant experiences successes in promoting new programs and vetoing others. The total budget, however, is now much larger than when all participants started, a result universally regarded as undesirable. Though it is undesirable to reach the summit of absorption of the private into the public sector, it is unfeasible to march down the same mountain.

Any theory of the rapid growth of government should explain why it did not occur earlier. In the past, one could vote at low cost against a party which permitted the total budget to get out of line; the parties had the incentive and the power to control spending because every elected and appointed member risked losing his job if the sum of individual decisions led to overspending or poor governmental performance. Parties no longer have much leverage on individual members, individual members do not have much incentive to discipline other members, and, as a consequence, voters no longer have an incentive to vote against individual members to discipline the total budget.

A commitment to the balanced budget principle is another plausible explanation for slower past rates of increase in spending; so is the development of financial technology facilitating extraction of resources. The reforms of the progressive and Wilsonian eras—the growth of party primaries, the near-elimination of patronage, the attempt to create a career civil service under a merit system—simultaneously weakened political parties and insulated civil servants from party but not from policy pressures. In need of support, they organized themselves like everyone else—around issue networks spanning specific sectors of policy. Torn loose from past restraints on rising expenditure—a balanced budget ideology, political parties to enforce it, inability to raise and spend so much so fast—all actors in politics have begun to wonder whether this work of their own hands is what they meant to create. The parts are all so pleasant; it is only when they are put together that they begin to look like Dr. Frankenstein's monster. Once this monster is loosed on the world, there appears no ready way to domesticate it without destroying it (and its maker) as well.

Enter the expenditure limitation. What went up can now come down. Politicians do not have to argue that priorities are necessary (because they are) or that entitlements can not be eternal (because they can not) or that one's favorite program should not go first (because all sizable ones must be involved) or that caps are unthinkable (because everyone else will now insist that their open-ended character, whch implies taking from others, is what is unthinkable). Citizens and politicians can concentrate on a few favored programs to make up their priorities without worrying that the whole thing has gone out of control.

Expenditure limitation via constitutional amendment is a formal replacement for what once was an informal understanding. Why can't we recapture the old time religion (at least in regard to expenditure)? Why, if we acknowledge having done wrong, don't we trust ourselves to do right? If all this is so desirable, why can't we just do it? Why load the constitution down with our failure to act intelligently and responsibly?

If I thought the ordinary operation of the existing political process would lead to less expenditure, I would not be advocating a constitutional amendment limiting the rise in public spending to a proportionate increase in private production. If I thought democracy was doomed, if nothing could stop society from being absorbed into government, I would not bother. Why do I believe constitutional expenditure limitation will help us do together—prevent the public sector from growing at the expense of the private—what we are currently unable to do alone?

At a recent round table on budgeting, an experienced auditor rose up to say that the purpose of standards was to allow weak-minded auditors to stand up to pressure by saying "I can't do this." He was followed by a practitioner of budgeting who said that the prospects for reducing spending depended on three things: (1) the principle of equal sacrifice; (2) an inability to pass the buck; and (3) a gradual rather than precipitous reduction in expectations of service. All of these purposes would be accomplished by the amendment. Because there is a fixed ceiling that everyone knows will last a long time, constitutional limits prevent passing the buck; since spending is allowed to grow absolutely, being limited only relative to national product, there need only be a gradual reduction in expectations of services; because great growth in some programs will, by virtue of limitation, require a corresponding reduction in others, self-interest will help supervise equality of sacrifice.

ORDINARY DECISIONS AND
CONSTITUTIONAL RULES

There is a difference between making ordinary decisions and making constitutional rules to regulate daily choices in the light of how we expect them to turn out in total. The sum of our actions over time is not necessarily subject to the same considerations as a single action at a single time. We can (and do) want this or that expenditure now and still object to the total amount of spending to which our actions have contributed. Just because we want it does not mean we like it. Unlike other species, like lemmings plopping into the sea, mankind is doomed to observe its own disasters; we know we are doing it to us. So, for self-protection, like the dieting man who walks home without passing the bakery, we can safeguard ourselves against the temptation of eating so many desserts that we spoil the meal.

The sum of total spending we choose is smaller than the sum of individual items we choose to make it up. Deciding with a total in mind is different from deciding without. Unless we all work within the same total, at the same time, however, some of us stand to get more for our favorite programs. Unless we all slow spending simultaneously, therefore your forbearance will be my reward. In order to be free to pursue what we know is best, we must bind ourselves against our worst inclinations. Only then can the contradiction in blatant budgetary behavior—a *National Journal* (1979: 464-469) poll shows three-quarters of Congress agreeing that spending is too high, while simultaneously failing to support a presidential cut in the first money bill of the new session[2]—be overcome. It is only worthwhile for me to act in my best interest if I know you are also doing the same.

IRONIES OF EXPENDITURE LIMITATION

A nice irony of expenditure limitation is that it will lead to a 180-degree reversal of current political postures. Conservatives are used to arguing that social processes in which individuals are left to pursue their own interests (under agreed rules facilitating the flow of information and freedom of choice) will produce better results than central command. Markets, they believe, are smarter than hierarchies. Thus, conservatives contend that private enterprise provides a benevolent social intelligence which arrives at better outcomes without anyone directly deciding them.

Political processes are also interactive, involving bidding in elections and bargaining in between. In politics, like markets, good decisions are those on which there is agreement, not those deemed correct according to cogitation by a wise man sitting atop the relevant hierarchy. Yet the "invisible hand" which is supposed to guide markets must be missing in politics, for otherwise conservatives would not want to intervene, so to speak, with a constitutional club. For their part, liberals (in the pristine sense of the word signifying largesse and liberality, i.e., more spending), I predict, will postulate a hidden intelligence assuring optimal political outcomes. They must; otherwise, they would be unable to argue against those meddlesome social experimenters who would tamper with the wondrous work of the founding fathers. Left to their own devices, the liberals' position would be: The political process will arrive not only at individual items of expenditures but at expenditure totals that are on average more appropriate than if these decisions were prejudged by being fit into a procrustean constitutional limit.

The proponents of expenditure limitation argue the opposite: Individual expenditure decisions do not add up to a sum citizens would choose, were they given the choice. Each part of public expenditure is wanted; only the whole is unwanted. Bringing the two types of decisions together—totals over time and particular parts one at a time—is the essence of expenditure limitation.

THE AMENDMENT AND THE BUDGET

The amendment places a ceiling on spending but not a floor. Some of its sponsors hope that eventually expenditure will make up a significantly lower proportion of GNP than it does now. I doubt it. Whatever is known about spending suggests that ceilings also become floors. Too many people want too much from government to settle for less than they can get. Even conservative Congresses will discover that keeping constituents happy and reconciling diverse interests will be easier by spending up to (or just below) the limit. As soon as they realize that lowering spending one year shrinks the base for the next, they will be reluctant to tie themselves down.

Though the amendment does not mandate a balanced budget, by relating expenditure to national product, which in turn is related to revenues, it should achieve that result on a decade-by-decade basis. (If the amendment had been applied over the past decade, the budget would have been close to balance.) While balance over time is desirable, and I am sympathetic to those who want to bring revenues and expenditures closer together, I am not in favor of balanced budget amendments, because they are at once too rigid and too weak. Their rigidity prevents varying spending and taxation for countercyclical purposes. Their weakness lies in the permission they give for any level of spending, however high, so long as it is matched by revenues. I want to stop government growing larger than the rest of us, not to encourage government to take more from us.

What effects on economic management would there be from expenditure limitation? Slowing down the economy by decreasing spending and increasing taxation to create a surplus should create no new difficulty. Whatever was done yesterday can be done tomorrow. The difference would be that lower expenditure one year reduces the limit for the next, so that it becomes more difficult to increase spending. Going the other route, however, creating a budgetary deficit to stoke up the economy, cannot be done in quite the same way. Spending can be pushed to the limit but not beyond. This means that in a severe situation, tax reduction to create a deficit must bear the brunt of "priming the pump." The question is whether raising or lowering taxes should be the mainstay of budgetary policy in attempting to manage the economy. Aside from a depression, which could be countered by spending permitted under the emergency provisions, I believe that spending is counterproductive for smoothing out economic fluctuations.

ADVOCACY AND SKEPTICISM

The amendment is not a mere technical improvement in budgeting. It does more than limit expenditures. The amendment is a budget of budgets. If it did not affect outcomes—who gets how much for what—there would be no reason to bother. Grand choices are up for grabs, so it is prudent to proceed with care.

I am an advocate, but I have also tried to be a skeptic. Many difficult questions must be answered before any reasonable person would want to support an amendment to limit federal expenditure. Is it desirable to amend the Constitution to limit federal spending? Why not rely on the political process? Why limit flexibility of future generations? Why read an economic doctrine into the Constitution? Why tamper with a procedural document that has achieved widespread acceptance pre-cisely because it does not take sides on public policy? These are good questions which I believe can be reasonably answered. They raise fundamental issues about how the American political system has been transformed by the rise of big government, and what, if anything, should be done about it.

Even if it were desirable, the amendment might not be workable. Would a constitutional amendment limiting federal expenditure to its existing amount plus the percentage increase in dollar gross national product, we ask, be efficacious? A skeptical suspension of judgment is in order. Getting around the amendment—by increasing tax expenditure (reducing taxes if the money is spent for particular purposes), by imposing costs on the private sector (such as mandating health insurance or environmental protection), or by guaranteeing credit (already at astronomical levels)—might lead the nation to spend more in stupider ways than before. If increases in the gross national product can be expanded by sleight of hand, or receipts subtracted from outlays, or other devices used to circumvent its intent, expenditure limitation may be another wonderful idea whose time will never come.

Even if an amendment was workable, it might not be desirable. Any constitutional amendment should make most citizens better off, not just a favored few. Should the amendment be shown to favor the rich over the poor, white against black, or, more generally, the have-much over the have-little, it could not command our respect. The place to begin is not with the amendment itself but with the nation's experience with big government. For if we found it so satisfying, there would be no need to guarantee ourselves less of a good thing. It is also well to remember that this experience is recent—barely twenty years old—so it is not surprising that neither the nation nor its government knew all there was to know about public policy at the beginning. By surrounding liberal social policies with conservative spending constraints, constitutional expenditure limitation shows that we are beginning to learn.

WHY AMENDING THE CONSTITUTION IS ESSENTIAL TO ACHIEVING SELF-CONTROL THROUGH SELF-LIMITATION OF EXPENDITURE

Just as there are many ways of breaking windows but only a few of making glass, so there are many more reasons not to put preferences into a constitutional amendment. It is so permanent. It is so inflexible. And it may also be unfair to social groups that are already disadvantaged. So, let us consider the alternatives.

It is a settled principle of prudence that something that can be done in the ordinary way, without involving fundamental features of state or special procedures, would be better. My argument is that no proposal for improving the process of public expenditures will keep public expenditure from continuously growing larger in relation to the private sector.

Some people say that exhortation will exorcize the ghost of spending past. By this I mean such efforts to improve the process of decision-making as requiring projections of expenditure five years into the future; requiring recertification of programs every five years (otherwise known as sunset legislation); or calculating costs and benefits every year for every program from the ground up as if there were no past, called zero-base budgeting. Exhortation is involved, because all that is required by law is to go through the motions. For instance, multiyear projections have been mandatory for twenty years, without making a difference (presumably decision makers were to shrink back when they were faced with the bad news) and without most people even knowing they exist. All the law can do is get projections made; it cannot make them accurate or, more importantly, relevant. To do that, in return for making accurate estimates, it would be necessary not only to impose an obligation but to give a reward; i.e., agencies could receive assurance that if the present program is approved, future expenditures will be forthcoming.[3] They give accuracy and get stability. If they are asked to stick out their necks only to have them cut off, no one is going to play this one-sided game . . . unless, of course, there is no alternative.

"Sunset laws" are but pale reflections of real expenditure limitation. These laws, passed in a number of states and proposed in Congress, require that agencies expire after a number of years, instead of continuing indefinitely, unless continuation is voted. Because sunset legislation does not get at the causes of continuance but only at the outward appearance, it fails to affect anything but small and defenseless units. Termination, as Robert Behn (1977) has written, requires a terminator. It requires political attack and political defense. None of this is forthcoming. The assumption that government grows because no one looks is absurd. It is worse than foolish, because it deflects attention from deep-seated difficulties on the grounds that they are due to inattention. Actually, attention is focused on all agencies that matter by those who are affected by what they do. Since there are so many agencies and so many more programs, the whole exercise becomes pro forma. Because no advice or incentive is given on how to overcome entrenched interests, "sunset appreciation for beginners" is a lousy course. Why should legislators who spend all their waking hours establishing new programs and defending old ones suddenly take the pledge? Expenditure limitation pits agencies and programs against each other: Sunset laws enable them to say they have all given one another the stamp of approval.

A common claim made for zero-base budgeting and sunset legislation is that they "force" or "compel" consideration of the ultimate desirability of expenditures and of the priorities among them. Not so. All that is mandatory is going through the motions. For one thing, no one can figure out what the world would be like if things were different. For another, the type of action implied—elimination of agencies and programs and drastic reduction in expenditure—runs counter to the everyday actions of all the decision makers. In fact, more new programs are legislated and old ones expanded after these procedures are instituted than are eliminated or reduced. The point is that with no incentives to alter customary behavior, there is no reason to believe that spending behavior will change. And it hasn't.

It could be argued that indexing taxes against inflation would, by reducing the federal tax take, decrease the room for spending maneuvers without producing unacceptably high deficits. Or reducing tax rates in general could be said to have much the same effect. Imagine, however, that external events or internal miscalculation drive actual and proposed expenditures up. The unemployed are out of income, North Yemen is under attack, and so on. Who believes, contrary to all recent experience, that there will be resistance to these pressures? No way. Instead, either larger deficits will be justified (namely, balancing the budget at full employment) or higher taxes will be imposed. True, indexing taxes will make the free ride of inflation—higher revenues without having to raise taxes—more expensive. But this is one-sided: Efforts to index taxation will surely be accompanied by enhanced efforts to index expenditures; why should widows and orphans (or national defense for that matter) be treated worse than high-income taxpayers? The end result is likely to be a compromise—indexing both income taxes and a substantial proportion of expenditure—amounting to a return to the status quo ante (if everything is indexed, no one changes relative position).

IS ITEM-BY-ITEM INTELLIGENT?

Up until now, I have not specifically stated the most obvious and direct alternative to a constitutional expenditure limitation—acting intelligently on major items of expenditure. If you and I believe that expenditures are too high, this argument goes, we should specify which ones should be cut and how much. From this standpoint, a general injunction to keep within expenditure limits, without dealing with individual programs, is the height of irresponsibility. As Jude Wanniski (1979) wrote in the *Wall Street Journal*:

> The trouble with a constitutional amendment requiring a balanced budget [the stricture holds against expenditure limitation as well] is that it doesn't tell us how to do it, nor do its proponents confront the issue in these terms. Surely most of those aboard the bandwagon, if asked, would tell us they would slash federal spending. But then the public opinion polls tell us that more than 95 percent of the American people want federal spending reduced.
>
> This bit of information, though, is also of no value. Each individual citizen wants spending cut according to a list of priorities. Some would cut defense spending, some social spending. Urban citizens could cut rural spending, and vice versa. It's the South against the North, the West against the East, sunbelt versus snowbelt, and so forth. But these priorities are already reflected in the voting patterns of the Congress, and still the budget is out of balance and has been for decades.

Somehow, he seems to feel that if what we are doing does not work, we should do nothing else. But the question Wanniski raises is crucial. Why a constitutional amendment if it escapes instead of grasps responsibility? Why an amendment if ordinary action is more efficacious?

If you want to cut expenditures, you must cut programs—these words have much to commend them; I know, I have used them myself. Improving efficiency, reducing overlap or duplication, and perfecting procedures may be valuable as far as they go, but they ordinarily do not involve substantial sums that quickly cumulate into large savings. You only fool yourself if you think nibbling at the edges is a substitute for the main meal. I have suggested and will now state directly: Investigating individual items is misleading as a general guide to expenditure decision-making.

It is all so seductively simple that it is almost sad. Decide each case on its merits, and you will have a meritorious outcome. Adding one decision to another, all on their merits, however, turns out to be at once too much and not enough. Total expenditures are too much, and each expenditure, however meritorious it might be considered by itself, receives insufficient consideration compared to the others. This must be so, not only because we are so often disappointed with the consequences, but also because the widespread agreement that total spending is too high must mean that some items are included that should have been excluded. Either we conclude that wrong results must be right, because the procedures that produce them appear reasonable, or that there is something not quite correct in what we are doing.

Doesn't everyone do it this way—you do your best on each choice and then trust the best has been done? Not really. In the home or in business, there is an expenditure constraint beyond which one cannot go. Not so in government, which prints its own money or can invade previously private preserves. Our complaint has not been that government spends all national income, for there is assuredly an outside limit for this, but that it takes too much.

CRITERIA FOR A CONSTITUTIONAL AMENDMENT

As good a statement as any on criteria for including rules for decision in a constitution is set forth by James Buchanan and Richard Wagner (1977: 176), who favor a balanced budget amendment. They write:

> There are several qualities that any such rule must possess if it is to be effective. First of all, it must be relatively simple and straightforward, capable of being understood by members of the public. Highly sophisticated rules that might be fully understood only by an economists' priesthood can hardly qualify in this count alone. Secondly, an effective rule must be capable of offering clear criteria for adherence and for violation. Both the politicians and the public must be able readily to discern when the rule is being broken. Finally, and most importantly, the fiscal rule must reflect and express values held by the citizenry, for then adherence to the precepts of the rule may, to some extent, be regarded as sacrosanct. These basic qualities add up to a requirement that any effective budgetary rule must be understood to "make sense" to the ordinary voter.

The amendment appears to meet the first two requirements. It is simple and it is clear. But would it fit comfortably with the values of the American people? The easy answer, unfortunately too facile by far, is that this is exactly what the effort to amend the constitution is about. The hard part lies in the realization that an amendment may survive the process of ratification and yet, to revert to an earlier form of expression, be found alien to the genius of the people.

Answering the question really calls for a prediction: Will the spending proclivities of the population prove long-lasting, while the sobersided saving syndrome withers away? Or will restriction be revealed as rewarding, so that the institutional embodiment of expenditure limitation becomes integrated into the political personality of American life? Making these predictions is tantamount to answering the question in question: Why amend the constitution to limit federal expenditures?

THE RATIONALE:
CHANGING RESULTANTS INTO DECISIONS

This is the rationale for a constitutional amendment: Not only a particular public policy at a particular time is being negotiated, but rather a social contract into which no one will enter without some assurance it will last. The relative shares of the public and private sectors are fixed, so that the private is protected from diminution and the public guaranteed the availability of its part of the national product. If the alleged advantages are to be obtained, sacrifices must be symmetrical; I will sacrifice today because I know your turn will come tomorrow. We must know that we are in this together to make it worthwhile to do at all. Since "everybody is for it [cutting the federal budget] in general," as Vice-President Walter Mondale (1979) observed recently, "as long as it doesn't affect them specifically," we all must know, to paraphrase Franklin, that we are going to hang separately before we will be willing to hang together.

The rationale may be restated to reveal the steps involved in its reasoning. The people and their government, separately and collectively, make decisions that add up to larger expenditures than they think appropriate. Rather than choose a number that must be divorced from reality, they prefer a relationship to national product, so that the public and private sectors can join in this social contract: self-control through self-limitation of expenditures.

A constitutional amendment is being considered precisely because it is not an ordinary but an extraordinary rule, a rule, so to speak, that governs other rules. Such a rule is necessary, because a social contract dividing the relative shares of the public and private sectors requires a solemn formulation and a secure resting place; without the expectation that the rules will remain the same, few will play the expenditure game. A grand rule is also necessary in order to reflect public opinion accurately. If substantial spending is desired by strong and lasting majorities, the rules of the political game permit this opinion to be registered in budgetary decision. But an opposite opinion, reflecting a desire to slow down spending, does not have an equal opportunity to manifest itself in the budget. Without the amendment, there is no way for slow spenders to get together to enforce equal sacrifice so that the general rule becomes part of the calculus involved in individual spending decisions.

Most of the decisions that affect our lives are not directly decided by anyone. The distribution of income, the size of families, the location of residences are not direct decisions but indirect resultants of a variety of public and private choices—from pay scales in industry to welfare provisions by government, from tuition rates in college aid to dependent children, from zoning laws to highways to the cost of air conditioning. Changing a resultant into a decision is of the highest importance, because it implies not one but a whole host of choices. After World War II, for instance, when it was decided that unemployment was not inevitable but manipulable, public policy was never the same. A decision to fix the relative proportions of the public and private sectors would mean that many matters would never again be dealt with in the same way.

A constitutional expenditure constraint tied to the level of national product need not necessitate wholesale rejection of past accommodations and would positively improve ability to make calculations. Comprehensive and simultaneous calculation of resources and objectives, every program compared to every other, is beyond human ken. It requires far more knowledge than anyone is likely to possess now and in the foreseeable future. It implies an instantaneous radical restructuring of expenditure priorities that is undesirable (and probably unfeasible) in a democracy. Too much too soon. The amendment slows down spending. Simplifying calculation is a means to the end of improved decision, not an end in itself. If all we wanted to do was to simplify choice, constraints could be complete, leaving us totally determined, a stuck record bleating out to eternity. It is not no choice but better choice we want.

FORCED TO BE FREE?

Here we have the modern resurgence of an ancient dilemma: Can mankind force itself to be free? Can there be freedom in restraint? Knowing our own weaknesses, may we decide in advance to bind ourselves against them? So Ulysses chained himself to the mast so as not to be seduced by the Sirens. Unlike the crewmen, who plugged their ears so as not to be tempted at all, an alternative not permitted to modern self-conscious man, Ulysses allowed himself to hear and yet guarded himself against his all-too-human nature. All this may seem disproportionate when talking about an ordinary activity like budgeting, but it is concerned with the public virtue and the public economy, of which spending is already a third or more of what we do.

Budgeting is continuous. The problem is that the cumulation of choices over time adds up to too much. The solution to this problem is to face the legislature, and therefore those who work through it, with a rule that already takes into account consequences over time. By directly deciding a limit that would last long enough to make its costs widely acceptable in terms of its benefits, a constitutional cap on spending supplies its own support. Unless I am much mistaken, this capacity to make the future part of the present is precisely the purpose of constitutional provisions.

Restriction may be liberation. The poor bureaucrat knows that his behavior, intended to be individually rational, will likely end up as collectively irrational. But with whom can he share his guilty secret? Now, after expenditure limitation, our carefree civil servant can be consumed with clientele interest, yet remain confident that his own behavior will not bust the budget. In his own interest, he will defend his own program and attack others that prevent it from expanding. But he will be saved from his worst self.

Citizens may feel more secure. Politicians may discover they can resist unwanted pressures. Bureaucrats may be relieved at losing their bad-guy image. Equity may be pursued by lower and progressive tax rates, by targeting existing programs to the poor, and by squeezing out subsidies to the better-off elements in society. Too sanguine? All right, then, future expenditures will be as inequitable as past ones, except that they will be smaller than they would have been. Presidents and appropriations committees will play more important roles. There is something to be said for being different, for showing that the doctrine of "American exceptionalism" still applies, for being the unusual modern industrial democracy that slows the rise of spending and limits the relative size of the public sector.

NOTES

1. The sponsors were Senators John Heinz (Republican of Pennsylvania) and Richard Stone (Democrat of Florida), and the exact date was April 5th. The amendment was patterned after an amendment prepared under the auspices of the National Tax Limitation Committee. The only difference is that the Heinz-Stone amendment leaves enforcement up to a congressional enabling statute.

2. "If we cannot now do the job," says the Chairman of the House Budget Committee, Robert N. Giaimo, "then the American people, led by the balance-the-budget people, will impose a discipline on us that we refuse to impose on ourselves" (*National Journal*, 1979: 464). All of us know better; this is where we came in. The question addressed by constitutional expenditure limitation is how to get out of this box.

3. This was the bargain behind the disastrous Public Expenditure Survey Committee (PESC) in Britain. See Heclo and Wildavsky (1979).

REFERENCES

BEHN, ROBERT (1977) "The false dawn of the sunset laws." Public Interest 49 (Fall): 103-118.

BUCHANAN, J. M. and R. E. WAGNER (1977) Democracy in Deficit: The Political Legacy of Lord Keynes. New York: Academic.

HECLO, H. and A. WILDAVSKY (1979) The Private Government of Public Money. London: Macmillan.

MONDALE, W. (1979) Comment in New York Times (March 2): A-11.

Nation's Business (1979) March 19.

National Journal (1979) "Lobbying Over the 1980 Budget—Can Congress Say NO?" March 24: 464-469.

WANNISKI, J. (1979) Wall Street Journal (March 5).

Government and the Economy

Collective Inefficiencies

WILLIAM C. MITCHELL
University of Oregon

My theme is the allocative inefficiency of the modern democratic
state. I will begin with a consideration of some well-known govern-
mentally induced inefficiencies in the market, then consider the
provision of public goods, and complete the discussion with some
observations on the difficulties of correcting these inefficiencies.
Part of the analysis provides a springboard for understanding a new
development in public choice, namely, the rise of the "bureaucratic
state" or, in the language of Rothbart (1970) and Tullock (1974: ch. 3),
the "exploitative state."

Finally, it is argued that a reduction in state activities rather than
bureaucratic reform—however ingenious—is a more certain means
to major efficiency gains. Reforms aimed at salary adjustments, work
loads and office conditions, paper-processing, and formal structures
are focused on symptoms of bureaucracy rather than the fundamental
sources of waste. Those who wish to effect substantial benefits are
better advised to forget waste *in* government and concentrate on
waste *from* governmental activities that might better be performed
by markets. This chapter deals with the more basic source of inefficiency. Much of the analysis is based on the assumption that government and the democratic polity function differently, and necessarily
so, from business enterprise and the market economy. Efficient or
not, government is an essential institution in civilized societies. Such
a broad-scale recognition does not, however, inform us on just what
governments ought to do.

MARKET INTERVENTION:
REAL LOSSES, ILLUSORY GAINS

While governments affect the private market in countless ways, the major ones are price controls, taxes on transactions, quotas of production or consumption, and subsidies. Each of these interventions into trade has the highly probable effect of reducing the obtainable efficiencies of market-clearing prices. Unless some compensatory action is taken by government, welfare losses are incurred. The distributive effects of these losses and whatever gains may be produced by the intervention are also important, but especially in explaining the political popularity of such measures.

Taxes on transactions, whether imposed on buyers or sellers, surely reduce consumer and producer surpluses and perhaps benefit those designated as beneficiaries of public expenditure. Some of the losses are deadweight—suffered, i.e., by both producer and consumer with no offsetting benefits. Since taxes on transactions involve a transfer from both consumers and producers to government, we can well understand the attractiveness of such policies to officials. To put the matter bluntly, transfers can be employed to "buy" votes and improve the material well-being of office holders.

While quota restrictions operate in a somewhat different manner, the ultimate efficiency effects are similar to those of taxes. Again the distributive consequences vary according to whose behavior is being controlled. A production quota entails a transfer from consumer to producer, while a consumer quota (rationing) involves a transfer from the producer to the consumer. And like taxation on transactions, both quota systems reduce overall efficiency, because they restrict output and reduce the volume of trade.

Marketing quotas so beloved by certain industries become expensive to maintain, since the value of such scarce possessions as a license to operate a cab or liquor store lead to extraordinary capitalized values and rents. The only ones to gain immediately are those privileged enough to obtain the scarce permit and those who traffic in illegal ventures and goods. Needless to say, these legal privileges are not rationed on the basis of market contributions or efficiency, but political clout, indebtedness, and even blackmail.

Subsidies are not usually considered as "intervention" in the market, but they do, in fact, alter the allocation of resources and the distribution of income. Worse, many of them produce perverse results.

With more than $120 billion in subsidies spent annually by the federal government alone, we should hardly be surprised to discover inefficiency and exploitation. Many activities would probably take place even without the subsidy. And many activities would doubtless be subsidized by private persons and organizations in the absence of governmental support. Then, too, subsidizing an activity has the dual effect of increasing the costs of production, yet lowering prices for the higher-income consumers of the activity. In short, subsidies not only constitute a major market intervention but a very expensive one for the taxpayers and most consumers.

Price supports, subsidies, output restrictions, and market quotas, whether or not deliberately enacted by government to increase the welfare of a few producers, are highly successful at achieving that end, but at inordinate cost to society. A recent investigation contends that the milk price support program of 1949-1975 cost consumers $10.4 billion, over $400 million per year (Heien, 1977). And worse, such policies prevent or delay appropriate supply and demand adjustments by the market. Interventionist policies frequently prolong the agony of those the policies were supposed to assist. Agricultural output restrictions do not improve the lot of the marginal farmer to find a better job might. While the many marginal farmers continue to suffer, a few wealth absentee agriculturalists profit. More importantly, the politicians who enact these measures and bureaucrats who administer the controls manage to become more powerful, spend more of the taxpayer's money, and pose as benefactors of "the people."

Governments have been known to set maximum prices at which goods and serivces may be bought and sold. Such practices are typically justified as consumer protection and warranted under certain emergency conditions. Wartime provides such circumstances, but increasingly governments have discovered special conditions as more or less permanent features of modern life. In any event, the ceilings are set below the market price. When the maximum price is set below the market price, a shortage develops, for more is demanded than will be supplied at that fixed price. But two important results need be summarized here: (1) Income is transferred from producer to consumers, since the amount spent is less than would be spent in the absence of controls; (2) price controls fail to resolve the basic problem of distribution, i.e., which consumers will get how much of the scarce goods. Since price is no longer the chief allocator, various nonprice practices must be employed to resolve the increased competition among consumers. Thus, scarcity is handled by queuing and its inconveniences, barter, pure favoritism, and, of course, violence. Black markets may also be expected, because consumers with excess funds will attempt to bribe sellers and will, in fact, succeed. Of course, black market prices will be considerably higher than the controlled price and probably higher than the equilibrium price of a free market. What could be more inefficient?

While market interventions can always be justified on the basis of some simple equity argument, we cannot readily defend them as contributions to efficiency. Why, then, are interventions so popular? Why is the plea and power of the economist's analysis so easily ignored in the political arena? Are citizens unaware of the increased prices they must pay? Of the unwanted surpluses of agricultural commodities? Of the immobilities of resources? Of the high cost of subsidies? Are not producers aware of their own incentives to circumvent output restrictions? The reason for all the "unreason" is not really difficult to fathom.

Selective market intervention is a preferred strategy among politicians, because it is also the preferred choice among certain influential voters. Voters do not live in a world of gross national products, nor a world of the public interest, in which the great aggregates of investment and consumption are meaningful daily experiences. A voter does not ask: What can I do for the GNP? Instead, the voter lives in a world of particular markets, his or her own salary or wage, and prices found in markets in which they transact frequent business. Because income concerns appear to dominate most of the time, public policies that insure or promise increases in income are apt to be popular. Government purchases, policies fostering artificial scarcities, and increased prices can all accomplish that end. Unfortunately, we still know little about governmental choice among these policy instruments.

On the other hand, the interests of consumers in lower prices and higher quality are not to be underestimated, as we have learned from the successes of Ralph Nader. The late Harry G. Johnson (1975: 207) once wrote that men vote jobs and women vote prices. Price controls on commodities of significance to buyers are politically popular; witness the longevity of rent control in New York City and recurring calls throughout history for price control. While these controls will produce dual perversities (increased demand and decreased supply), the immediate beneficial effects of the control are readily apparent to the strapped consumer/voter. The consumer/voter can hardly be faulted for behaving as economists predict and usually defend, i.e., as a utility-maximizer choosing within a restricted opportunity or feasibility set. Politicians have no trouble understanding the electoral implications. Accordingly, the politician deals with particular industries, particular commodities, particular costs, particular prices, particular forms of control, and not with the macroeconomic aggregates so treasured by Keynesian economists. The literature of public choice surely cannot be regarded as an ally by Keynesians. Governmental choices are not based on the complexities of the macroeconomics textbook but the simple imperatives of the ballot box.

The major imperative of the ballot box is the redistribution of wealth and income. And the major consequence is a misallocation of resources or a tragic lessening of total welfare—a result few voters would knowingly support. But the logic of elections, divorced and therefore distorted private costs and benefits, and log-rolling all contribute to the undesired collective outcome.

GOVERNMENTAL SUPPLIES OF "PUBLIC" GOODS

As our illustrations have shown, interventionist policies are a major but hardly the sole source of exchange inefficiencies. We must examine the provision of collective goods—the ultimate rationale for the formation of states and extension of governmental activity. Public goods, i.e., those goods possessing the characteristics of nonrivalrous consumption and nonexclusion, do afford rational grounds for collective provision, including *private* collective as well as public provision.

The failure of markets to generate optimum quantities of public goods is so familiar that the theory need not be summarized. Less well known is the theory of collective effort to compensate for market failure, i.e., difficulties governments encounter in deciding the "correct" supplies of public goods. Formally, the optimum quantity of public goods is achieved where marginal social benefits equal marginal social costs. At this point, the marginal cost equals the sum of the marginal utilities of all individuals. But a most difficult problem arises: If individuals are to be taxed in proportion to benefits received, they would have a powerful incentive to conceal and understate their true preferences. Since true preferences are not disclosed, the government would have an extremely difficult task in determining the optimal amount.

If the government were to allocate taxes on other bases than marginal benefits received by individual citizens, few citizens would be satisfied with whatever amount of the goods was produced; in short, some would complain because too many goods are being produced at the given tax-prices, while others would protest an insufficiency. This is so because citizens, unlike consumers in the market, cannot adjust their consumption in accordance with uniform market prices and their own tastes and income. Once a decision has been made by government to provide a certain quantity of the goods, the same amount is available to all. Given differing tastes yet equal consumption of public goods, the only way that government could equate individual marginal utilities and tax prices would be to charge different citizens different taxes for the same goods. But if this is done, we are back to our original point re preferences: Citizens could not be induced to reveal their true preferences for the goods. Without that information, the government is unable to decide on individual tax payments and the appropriate supply of the goods. In short, no efficient solution exists! Whatever amount is supplied will be too much for some citizens and too little for others.

Since (fortunately, as libertarians remind us) few goods are genuinely public, private markets can be established to equate supplied and demands. Most alleged public goods are simply private goods with varying externalities—externalities that can often be efficiently handled by a reallocation of property rights among private property-holders. In this context, it is most important not to confuse public goods and common property. Public goods once produced are shared equally and independently of one's contribution to their provision. Accordingly, the marginal cost of adding another user is zero. On the other hand, common property is distinguished from a public good by the fact that one user's utility is affected by the uses made of the property by others. In short, while consumption of public goods is non-rivalrous, common property is rivalrous. The so-called "tragedy of the commons" can make sense only if based upon this distinction. The policy significance of this important distinction is simple: If a good is basically private in nature, we can use the market, and if the good is being held in common, we can improve upon its efficient use by instituting private property rights and obligations. An account of transaction costs among property-holders must be taken, but the same must also be done when considering public solutions to externality and public goods problems.

At the risk of offending professors and students alike, I venture to suggest that education is not primarily a public good. It can be readily and efficiently marketed: Skeptics might explain the existence of private schools teaching language, dance, cooking, flying, auto mechanics, and so on. Skeptics might also explain the survival of the Ivy League! Education does not have to be supplied by government; if it is, it need not be so highly subsidized. We can all observe the dismaying spectacle of local and state governments providing "free" education in unwanted kinds, quantities, and qualities. Most transportation, medical care, parks, insurance, and even police protection are provided by private organizations or firms at a price to the consumer. And if W. Allen Wallis (1976: ch. 30), President of Rochester University, is correct, the supply of each of these services would be greater with open markets alone, than with both markets and government acting as suppliers, as is currently the case. Wallis also contends that the quality of the service would be improved under private provision.

His theory runs as follows: Competing politicians have a choice among three policy options: (a) to eliminate or reduce a governmental service; (b) to offer a new service; or (c) to offer an established private service but paid for by the government. If the private service is something that is both costly and in widespread demand, politicians will select that activity for their platform. Medical care fits the bill perfectly. Wallis argues that the supply for private services decreases while the actual supply for publicly financed services increases, but its increase is less than the optional private supply. Consumers spend less on private services but pay the same or more in the way of taxes. Politicians are in turn leery of raising taxes, because the taxpayers do not see their added taxes going toward the direct financing of medical services. Eventually, the service is taken over by the so-called "professionals" and treated as their own property to be administered in their own self-interests rather than those of the doctors or the patients. Inferior service and other thwarted expectations lead to a greater demand, especially among upper-income groups, for additional and superior private provision. This in turn leads to a return to greater private provision as it has with police protection, postal services, and increasingly, education.

Publicly provided private goods generate every known type of inefficiency and inequity. We should hardly be surprised whenever costs and benefits cannot be internalized. If the political system were able to apportion taxes in accordance with benefits received, it would in effect be emulating the market. But since this rarely occurs, we can conclude that voting and log-rolling will indeed provide services but in a highly inefficient manner.

In view of all these difficulties, why the great demand for still more governmental provision of still more services and goods? One reason is the perfectly sound one that many goods possess significant public properties. More importantly, the public good argument about market failure is employed as a highly persuasive and convenient political rationale to conceal the use of public funds for indirect income transfers to those who would benefit from the service at less than cost, as well as those who would benefit by supplying the service or its components. Beneficiaries, politicians, and administrators alike treat public funds as though they were costless. Accordingly, we are entitled to all we can get; those who exercise self-restraint are considered fools.

FISCAL TACTICS AND ILLUSIONS

Governments use their taxing and spending powers to "buy" votes. That is why the power of the purse is so jealously guarded by all governments. Most voters can be "bought" by governmental actions favorable to them and/or unfavorable to others. Because this is so, governments, including the conservative, prefer the more flexible fiscal policy instruments over those of monetary policy in which distributive discretion is more carefully circumscribed by law. Freedom of action may impose responsibilities, but like individuals, governments seem to prefer the possibility of discretionary action. And furthermore, governments should not be viewed as helpless victims of circumstance, for they have a power unknown to the individual—that of authoritatively shaping their own environments. Governments have a wide capacity to act; fewer constraints stand in their way. The primary informational problem of a government is not restricted to anticipating exogenous change but rather estimating the more remote and less obvious consequences of its own actions. In any event, governments not only make budgetary decisions but attempt to shape the information and biases of voters concerning these decisions. Unhappily, governments are not above concealment, the dissemination of misleading and even false information, strategically timed policy announcements, symbolic stances, and budgetary gimmickry. We must accept the elemental fact that governments find it highly desirable to create and exaggerate a demand for their product when none had previously existed. Ironically, Galbraith's theory of artificially created wants in the market is more plausible in the public than the private sector.

These contentions can be illustrated in an ad hoc manner. On the spending side, we may assume that governments will advertise and indeed adopt only those programs whose ostensible benefits can be made to appear highly visible, here and now. Then too, citizen choice between the government and private products can be biased because the public benefits are made to sound tangible. The old adage "what you don't know won't hurt you" has some truth, at least in the short run.

Since nothing is more disturbing to a bureaucrat and bureau than to be asked to do nothing, the strategic-minded bureaucrat seeks to maximize his budget by taking advantage of ignorance among sponsoring legislators as well as voters (see Niskanen, 1971). Pseudodemand curves are easily advanced and defended by articulate spokesmen "on the Hill." In the first place, politics does not offer sensitive means for estimating public demand. Given that uncertainty, the bureaucrat is able to provide the hoped-for "pseudocertainty" and to do so under the guise of fulfilling unmet societal needs. If there are none (an unlikely prospect), due to previous efficient operation of the bureau, the public can still be duped by the claim that the proper level of service is determined not by equating MB and MC, but by equating total benefits and total costs.

The spurious demand curve for public services can be easily defended by claiming all sorts of positive externalities and intangible social returns. Recreational benefits are a favorite form of the latter, while the scientific advances of space exploration are a much used example of the former. The intangibles also have the virtue of being unmeasurable. And what is unmeasurable has a certain virtue or vogue among some educated elements of the population.

On the revenue or cost side, we may note even more imaginative, clever, and often duplicitous efforts on the part of governments. Many of these were first pointed out by the Italian economist Puviani at the turn of the century (see Buchanan, 1967: ch. 10). Ironically, many of the same ruses are still employed by far more democratic states than then existed.

The cost of public services can be misrepresented in different ways. The most obvious is to underestimate costs. Or a government may maintain that the costs are constant rather than increasing and thereby justify larger projects. Or total costs can be understated by using lower discount rates and/or ignoring social or external costs associated with each project.

Perhaps more important than governmental underestimation of public program costs is the extensive "deception" practiced on the individual taxpayer. Here we find an entire repertoire including payroll deductions, progressive rates accompanied by loopholes, indirect and hidden taxes (excises, mortgage payments that include automatic property tax deductions), biased referenda (double negative proposals), and financing by inflation. These tax ruses can do more than confuse; they seriously understate the personal impacts of the costs of government.

Then, too, governmental accounting baffles all—including accountants and economists. The use of multiple budgets (administrative budget, cash budget, income and product budgets, full employment budget) permit a government to conceal unpopular fiscal choices and popularize the apparent vote-getters whenever electoral necessity seems to dictate. The means by which governments count the unemployed, estimate the wealth and income of the nation, and present fiscal and monetary policy are technical matters with enormous policy and electoral implications. Since many public expenditures are based on changes in economic indicators, the definitions of key terms and measurements are critical in who gets how much. The strategic use of these concepts and data is now a well-practiced art. Appointed officials have been fired for not taking political difficulties or considerations into strategic account, and civil servants have suddenly found themselves transferred to some "Siberian" outpost for embarrassing superiors. Presidents have been known to present dishonest budgets so as to inconvenience an incoming President of a rival party. Recent mayors of New York City have had continuous opportunity and incentive to practice every known fiscal gimmick in history. Perhaps someday, someone wise to fiscal strategies and knowledgeable in accounting and public choice will document the sorry history. (That day may have arrived; see Auletta, 1979).

Politicians and bureaucrats may be expected to represent themselves in such ways as to claim credit for favorable economic outcomes and avoid blame for disagreeable ones. Thus, we should not be surprised if they employ multiple measures of policy outcomes which enable them to devise and present favorable interpretations of events. We should also expect them to take advantage of any favorable events regardless of cause and responsibility. And of course, we should not be surprised if they emphasize the potency of their offices, policy instruments, and leadership during "good times" and their limited responsibility for the bad when it occurs.

POLICY CYCLES

As with certain built-in cycles and biases of a market economy, one may detect certain repetitive phenomena occurring in the electoral life-cycles of governments. Recent research, stimulated by the early work of Michal Kalecki (1943) strongly suggests that "policy cycles" may be readily discerned over the electoral period. (The current state of the art is summarized and added to by Tufte, 1978.) A policy that expands the economy before an election to reduce unemployment and contracts the economy after the election to curtail inflation will presumably attract more voters than a policy that maintains constant rates of both over the electoral span or term of office. Many readers are doubtless familiar with the so-called "ratchet effect" of governments coping with both inflation and unemployment. Dealing with two "bads" produces predictable overresponses as the politicians attempt to minimize vote losses from too much unemployment and then too much inflation, and so on in sequence. We also know that governments have a powerful tendency to announce new benefits, benefit increases, or benefits to new recipients just before elections and to delay the impacts of new taxes, tax rate increases, and inclusion of new tax-payers until after the elections. The history of social security in this country offers convincing evidence (Mitchell, 1977).

CORRECTING ALLOCATIVE "ERRORS"

The argument thus far has emphasized certain difficulties in collective choice and how politicians and bureaucrats can take advantage of them. Attention has also been paid to a political incentive stucture that systematically directs political actors away from efficient decisions and toward activities and policies designed to further the interests of government. The politician's dream easily becomes an economist's nightmare.

Let us consider mechanisms and incentives for the correction of errors in economic policy, i.e., inefficiencies that are endogenous, ubiquitous, inevitable, and known. To be sure, market errors are frequent and inevitable, although usually of lesser magnitude than those committed in the political arena, especially those by the government itself. Whenever resources are wrongly committed in the market, an opportunity is presented for another entrepreneur to rectify the mistake; such entrepreneurs have an incentive in the form of an unexpected gain or profit. Those who made the mistake pay the price not only in the form of failure to make a profit but bankruptcy. Resources may now be directed to other more profitable uses, and waste is thereby reduced. None of this happens in a rapid, pristine, pleasant manner; it is as sloppy as most other social change and costly for those who declare bankruptcies or see the firm they founded "taken-over," or persons dismissed in an executive reshuffle. But at least the opportunities and the incentives to reallocate are there and are effective.

Contrast the situation in the political arena. I begin with an hyperbole: Whoever heard of a government project going bankrupt and another, more profitable project adopted? Or, more realistically, how long does it take to make simple, obvious policy reforms *after* error is detected and acknowledged? Neither political science nor economics provides us with the solid empirical evidence needed to answer the question, but widespread professional wisdom suggests that reform is lengthy and exceedingly costly. Years, decades, and generations are often required to effect significant alterations of policy and administrative practice.

While political scientists have long noted these shortcomings of democratic choice, they have not paid equal attention to the more generalized possibility that democracies can overreact to error in *both* directions, i.e., offer "too much" or "too little" and "too soon" or "too late." Much of the macroeconomic debate of the past forty years has focused on these four possibilities, with Keynesians contending that past governments have opted for too little, too late, and the opposition arguing that government usually overcorrects for errors by too much intervention (often the wrong kind) too soon. Another way of stating the matter is to say the polity lacks a "hidden hand" or at least a sensitive mechanism to produce the right actions at the right time. Since public officials, unlike businessmen, can neither gain from the long-term benefits of their decisions nor lose from long-term costs, they have less incentive to be right in the economic sense.

Even if economists and social scientists, more generally, knew more than they do about the right timing of the right actions, we would still be faced with the basic dilemmas of collective choice—

dilemmas produced by differing rules of the aggregative game. Reformers must recognize that while institutional tinkering can improve political choices, no amount of democratic reform can repeal the intrinsic difficulty of collective choice—that individual preferences differ yet must be aggregated into a single decision. While imaginative, the market-inspired reforms of Buchanan, Friedman, and Niskanen must confront not only the inherent difficulties of collective choice and governmental biases but of political acceptance under existing electoral rules. While the hope is not reassuring on either account, certain current constitutional amendment proposals to limit spending have the attractive quality of relevance, i.e., of being directed at the fundamental sources of inefficiency—spending and revenue-gathering by government. If governmental spending can be limited as proposed by Buchanan, Friedman, Niskanen, and others, a new politics will emerge—one in which potential beneficiaries of political largesse will have to compete more and coalesce less for larger relative shares of a slower-growing budget. Such competition should have a salutary effect on the kinds of rationale that interest groups must advance in justification of their claims. External costs and benefits of political allocations cannot be ignored or treated with cavalier indifference. How politicians, bureaucrats, interest groups, and voters will adjust to a politics of limitation (zero-sum games?) after two centuries of essentially positive-sum fiscal games could be one of the more exciting analytical challenges for a new generation of social scientists. Of course, we are still confronted with only a small possibility of constitutional change.

The reason for all this allocative "unreason" is a simple extension of our basic thesis: The potential gains to be made from efficiency moves are too widely dispersed to incite the kind of entrepreneurial response the market obtains, while the threatened losses current beneficiaries may experience are much more direct, visible, and substantial. The latter group will obviously have an incentive to perpetuate its minority privileges—better known these days "entitlements." Because efficiency is a public good, very few citizens or leaders have any meaningful stake in working for its achievement; accordingly, the constituency for inefficiency is both more numerous and powerful. The collectivization of choice and the separation of cost and benefit decisions insure no other outcome. We must recognize that good economics and good politics are antithetical.

Fairness compels us to recognize that the *detection* of error or the misallocation of resources and its *correction* are less costly in the marketplace than the polity. The price system not only announces the existence of incorrect allocations but makes correction abundantly profitable. As stated above, it is eminently worthwhile to ferret out inefficiency. Thus we see entrepreneurs constantly seeking out new ideas, new products, new consumer tastes to develop, new resources, and new means of production. Governments do not display similar energy, inventiveness, or success.[1] It is particularly difficult for any kind of institution providing collective goods to be efficient. Furthermore, the very task of providing these goods tends to make institutions inefficient, whereas the provision of private goods through a market has the opposite effect.

SUMMARY

The polity is inherently inferior to the free market in the efficient provision of most goods and services. The inefficiencies are by definition costly, for they diminish what is most valuable and thereby put more valued resources into the hands of those who value them less as well as into less valued uses. To allocate resources without markets and prices is not only highly complex and costly, but an extraordinarily wasteful task with arbitrary and unstable outcomes. Policies are made on case-by-case considerations in which the power of competing organized interests decide the issues. Administered supplies and prices are not based on recognized market principles but on the electoral necessities of the politicians and the budget maximization goals of bureaucrats. The rationing process of government cannot be other than arbitrary, inconsistent, temporary, and inefficient. And worse, citizens devote less of their scarce time and other resources to productive uses and more to waging conflict in political arenas. Slow economic growth rates may be better explained by these political factors than the usual economic variables.

Finally, if not inherently exploitative, the political process at least encourages one citizen to exploit another and affords ample opportunities for politicians and bureaucrats to exploit the citizenry. I cannot think of a better reason for a minimal state.

NOTE

1. Milton Friedman (1978) wrote about these matters as they pertain to the IRS and Federal Reserve Board.

REFERENCES

AULETTA, K. (1979) The Streets Were Paved With Gold. New York: Random House.
BUCHANAN, J. M. (1967) "The fiscal illusion," in J. M. Buchanan (ed.) Public Finance in Democratic Process. Chapel Hill: Univ. of North Carolina Press.
FRIEDMAN, M. (1978) "Inertia and Fed." Newsweek (July 24): 70.
HEIEN, D. (1977) "The cost of the U.S. dairy price support program: 1949-74." Rev. of Economics and Statistics 59 (February): 1-8.
JOHNSON, H. G. (1975) "The problem of inflation," in H. G. Johnson (ed.) On Economic and Society. Chicago: Univ. of Chicago Press.
KALECKI, M. (1943) "Political aspects of full employment." Pol. Q. 14 (October/December): 322-331.
MITCHELL, W. C. (1977) The Popularity of Social Security: A Paradox in Public Choice. Washington, DC: American Enterprise Institute for Public Policy Research.
NISKANEN, W. A., Jr. (1971) Bureaucracy and Representative Government. Chicago: Aldine-Atherton.
ROTHBART, M. N. (1970) Power and Market: Government and the Economy. Menlo Park, CA: Institute for Humane Studies.
TUFTE, E. R. (1978) Political Control of the Economy. Princeton, NJ: Princeton Univ. Press.
TULLOCK, G. (1974) The Social Dilemma. Blacksburg, VA: University Publications.
WALLIS, W. A. (1976) The Overgoverned Society. New York: Macmillan.

Process and Outcome in Regulatory Decision-Making

GIANDOMENICO MAJONE
Yale University

Today regulatory bodies find themselves in the eye of a storm of criticism and distrust. Two main approaches have emerged as possible solutions of the "crisis of regulation." The first, strongly advocated by economists, is deregulation. The second, favored especially by legal scholars, relies on procedural innovations to improve the ways in which agencies examine the evidence, analyze a wide range of alternatives, and take conflicting opinions and interests into account in their determinations. These different approaches reflect deep differences in disciplinary perspectives. Economists have been largely concerned with the efficiency of the outcomes of regulatory policies. Deregulation (either in the sense of a return to control by the market, or in the sense of greater reliance on market-oriented mechanisms like pollution charges) is justified by the inefficiency of regulation when measured by the standards of an economic optimum. Following a different tradition, legal scholars have been less impressed by the evidence of "regulatory failure" and have focused their attention on process rather than outcome.

Evaluating process by outcome has an obvious intuitive appeal, but presupposes the existence of an objective and unambiguous criterion of evaluation. When agreement on the correctness or fairness of a decision cannot be assumed a priori, when the factual and value premises are controversial, the process of reaching the decision has more than instrumental value. This obvious fact has been too often forgotten in the past. Regulators have sought legitimacy for their decisions by wrapping them in a cloak of scientific respectability. For a number of reasons to be discussed below, it has been found convenient to assume that conclusions could be directly derived from the scientific analyses made by qualified experts.

The cognitive complexity of the problems arising in pollution control and risk evaluation, to mention only two important areas of regulation, has dispelled the pristine faith in the power of expertise. It is now abundantly clear that the knowledge base is generally so inadequate that issues can be fully explored only by means of a dialectic process in which disagreement is openly recognized. How to use conflicting opinions in a constructive way is probably the major problem facing regulators today. It is, quite obviously, a problem in procedural design and a new challenge for policy analysis.

THE IDEOLOGY OF EXPERTISE

Faith in the power of expertise is an engine of social regulation—technical expertise which neither legislators of "lay" courts nor bureaucratic generalists presumably possess—has been a traditional source of legitimation for administrative agencies. For writers of the New Deal era like Merle Fainsod, regulatory commissions emerged and became instruments of governance for industry precisely because Congress and the courts proved unable to satisfy the "great functional imperative" of specialization. Administrative agencies "commended themselves because they offered the possibility of achieving expertness in the treatment of special problems, relative freedom from the exigencies of party politics in their consideration, and expeditiousness in their disposition" (Fainsod, 1940: 313). Among the important reasons for the establishment of regulatory commissions mentioned by Cushman (1937) is the greater ease in recruiting experts for an independent agency than for executive departments.[1] Landis (1966: 23, 25-26) finds an even closer relationship: "The demand for expertness, for a continuity of concern, naturally leads to the creation of authorities limited in their sphere of action to the new tasks that government may conclude to undertake." And conversely, in Say's law fashion, the supply of regulation creates its own demand of expertise:

> With the rise of regulation, the need for expertness became dominant; for the art of regulating an industry requires knowledge of details of its operation, ability to shift requirements as the condition of the industry may dictate, the pursuit of energetic measures upon the appearance of an emergency, and the power through enforcement to realize conclusions as to policy [Landis, 1966 [1938]: 23, 25-26].

To be sure, the New Deal advocates of regulation knew that, as Fainsod put it, the expertness of the administration is not always above suspicion. But they rejected any suggestion that the quality of regulatory decisions could be improved by "mere" procedural means. Issues of fact should be handled by experts, using whatever methods appear to be most appropriate; administrative findings of fact are to be regarded as final. Judicial review of the evidence used in reaching a decision would be a serious threat to "the very virtue of specialized knowledge which constitutes one of the chief justifications for the establishment of commissions" (Fainsod, 1940: 318).[2]

Idealization of the administrative agency as the embodiment of Weberian *Zweckrationalität* have been replaced by contemporary discontent with the regulatory process. But today's critics share the attitude of yesterday's advocates toward procedural constraints. Procedures—it is said—often make impossible any firm or consistent pursuit of the public interest (Caves, 1970: 145). Regulatory commissions adhere to cumbersome procedures instead of speeding them through informal action (see, for example, Wilcox, 1968). Equally revealing of the prevailing attitude is the fact that the various theories of economic regulation have hardly paid any attention to evidence concerning the procedures employed in regulatory decision-making (Posner, 1974: 350).

Actually, the opinion, so common among political scientists and economists, that regulatory agencies are procedure-ridden is largely based on weak and impressionistic evidence. Legal scholars point out that in the past many agencies have paid scant attention to procedural matters at all, while others "followed homemade schemes that departed widely from the judicial-type procedures that the rooted tradition regarded as the finest fruit of centuries of Anglo-American legal experience" (Freedman, 1975: 1042).[3] The Federal Administrative Procedure Act introduced some uniformity into the variegated procedural styles followed by the different agencies. But even the 1970 Clean Air Amendments, for example (though they represent "a remarkable effort on the part of Congress to constrain the administrative discretion of a major regulatory agency" (Stewart, 1977: 722), often fail to make clear whether the Environmental Protection Agency (EPA) should follow a trial-type hearing or a notice-and-comment rule-making procedure in taking various actions. And even today, cross-examination of experts is the exception rather than the rule among major federal regulatory bodies (Miller, 1977).

This is not to deny that there are cases where the zeal for procedure overwhelms substance, but rather to suggest that an attitude of indifference or scorn toward questions of process is not conducive to a balanced assessment of the benefits and costs of alternative procedural arrangements. There is, in fact, a close connection between such an attitude and the ideology of expertise. The basic function of the ideology is that of providing comfort and reassurance in the face of the crucial uncertainties of policy-making. It enables Congress to assume that once the policy objectives have been stated, the administrative agencies can determine the appropriate means for their accomplishment on a strictly scientific basis.[4] It allows the agencies to create the impression that regulatory decisions follow directly from the facts and analyses provided by technical experts, even when the conceptual basis of those decisions is uncertain and controversial (Nelkin, 1975). Finally, the courts, too, have found the ideology useful in allocating institutional responsibility between the judiciary and the agencies—crediting to administrative expertise what they did not justify in terms of reasonableness (Freeman, 1975).[5] Procedural constraints can only reduce the effectiveness of the ideology.

Perhaps the belief in the possibility of discovering technically correct solutions for a wide range of important policy problems has served a historically useful function. It is doubtful that this belief can still fulfill a useful function today. Under conditions of increasing cognitive and social complexity not only the ideology, but the very notion of expertise must be either abandoned or drastically revised. As the following discussion shows, the rationality of regulatory decision-making leaves much to be desired. I shall argue that this is not because of the lack of a rigorous methodology by which optimal decisions could be derived from the available evidence, but because of the lack of procedures reflecting the ambiguity inherent in the data, theories, and values on which decisions are based.

THE UNCERTAIN LOGIC OF
REGULATORY DECISION-MAKING

In this section I review the intellectual content of different classes of regulatory decisions, beginning with rate regulation. In order to determine the rate level for a regulated firm, the agency must ascertain the firm's costs in a test year and the rate base, and then decide upon a "fair" rate of return on investment. In determining the rate base property can be evaluated on the basis either of the original costs actually incurred, or of reproduction or replacement costs. In a series of decisions beginning around the end of last century, the Supreme Court indicated that "dominant effect" must normally be recognized to reproduction costs, but without indicating what the appropriate weight should be, or which principles should be used in making the determination (see for example, the classic essay by Frankfurter and Hart, 1970: 1-17). Since 1944, when the Court declared that the method of valuation was to be left to the discretion of the commissions, regulators have tended increasingly to base their valuations not on reproduction, but on historical or sunk costs. This, economists have repeatedly pointed out, violates the basic principle that "bygones are forever bygones" and should not affect current decisions.[6] Nonetheless, a reasonable case can be made for the use of sunk costs from the point of view of equity, if not of economic efficiency. If the investor is denied windfall gains by a ceiling on earnings, he should also be granted some protection against windfall losses. Thus the earnings an investor in a regulated firm is offered should not depend on the values which subsequent random events have assigned to his investment, but should be based on his past investment outlays, suitably corrected for depreciation and changes in the price level (Baumol, 1970: 193).

The determination of the "fair" rate of return on equity capital is equally beset with conceptual and practical difficulties. First, there is the problem of determining a level of earnings that is high enough to enable the regulated firms to attract new capital. There are no definite rules for ascertaining the level of earnings required for this purpose. The agencies and the parties at interest usually proceed by analogies and comparisons. But the comparisons are either circular—because they refer to other regulated industries—or irrelevant—because they compare a regulated firm with firms that are not monopolistic and are engaged in dissimilar business (Posner, 1974). Second, the rate of return should be fair to past investors. The definition favored by the courts— earnings are fair if they are equal to those obtainable in other industries with comparable risks—has limited operational usefulness because of the difficulty noted above of establishing meaningful comparisons. Also, the level of earnings needed to attract new capital is likely to be different from that required by fairness to past investors: the two criteria are logically independent. In practice, commissions and courts use "judgmental" rates of return that can range from less than 6% to 8% and more. Unfortunately, the rationale of these determinations remains obscure since the underlying reasoning is not usually disclosed.

There are many other problems—from determination of the rate structure to the allocation of joint costs among different services—that admit only conventional or arbitrary solutions. Understandably, economists complain that the regulatory process lacks sound conceptual foundations. But the general principles they propose are of limited usefulness to the regulators. For example, the principle of marginal-cost pricing has limited usefulness when uncertainty, competing policy goals, market imperfections, or "second-best" problems are present.

As my second example I consider environmental standards-setting. It is usual to distinguish two stages in the standards-setting process. In the first stage qualitative environmental goals are translated into numerically stated criteria or ambient standards such as "Sulfur dioxide content of air should not exceed 0.05 ppm for 350 days per year or 1 ppm at any time," or "Average coliform concentration not greater than one organism per 100 milliliters." In the second stage effluent standards are set to limit the amount of pollution that can be discharged at any given source to levels that are compatible with the stated quality criteria, for example, "No plant may discharge effluent containing more than 60,000 pounds of BOD a day."[7]

How are the ambient standards defined? In theory, biomedical science would tell the standards setters what effects on health can be expected from various concentrations of pollutants. Given this information and the environmental goal, maximum permissible limits of waste discharge could then be calculated. For a few noxious substances the amount of harm usually associated with different dosages is known and defensible standards (e.g., for drinking water) can be set accordingly. But for most pollutants that are either known or suspected to be damaging to health, firm knowledge about the amount of damage done by given concentrations under various environmental conditions is simply not available. Official reports often attempt to conceal fundamental uncertainties in the scientific base behind large amounts of irrelevant or poor data. For example, the first criteria for sulfur oxides (SO_x) established by the National Air Pollution Control Administration (NAPCA) in 1967 were allegedly supported by over 300 studies on the effects of SO_x on man, animals, plants, and materials. But the value of these studies as evidence was rather limited. The reports differed greatly in quality and relevance; the summaries prepared by the staff of NAPCA drew conclusions which were not justified by the studies them-selves; the recommended standard was actually based on only two or three studies of dubious quality; finally, the logic of NAPCA's decision could not be tested since the derivation of the standard from the goal of protecting the most susceptible segments of the population had not been made explicit (Davies, 1970: 163-169). Eventually the SO_x standard was challenged in court (Kennecott Copper Corp. v. EPA, 1972) as unsup-ported by evidence of adverse effects at the prescribed concentrations. The court decided to remand the case for a fuller explanation and, as a result, EPA withdrew the standard.

The usual procedure for setting effluent standards consists in cal-culating the percentage reduction necessary to get from existing levels of pollution to the desired ambient standard, and then applying the same percentage reduction to existing emissions. This seems to be a purely mechanical process—a task that can be safely entrusted to technicians. But in reality, how many assumptions and value judgments are implicit in the calculations! How good are the original data? Which one of several equally plausible models describes most adequately the effects of individual sources of pollution? How should one deal with the many uncertainties affecting the risk associated with given levels of concen-tration of pollutants? Should polluters be required to reduce their emissions equally in physical terms—the usual practice—or in propor-tions corresponding to equal financial effort?

Regulatory agencies are now required to take the cost of regulation explicitly into account—to perform a "regulatory analysis."[8] But the cost of abating pollution varies significantly from industry to industry, from firm to firm, from location to location. If ambient standards are to be met efficiently, such cost differentials must be taken into account in setting effluent standards. The resulting system of emission standards will almost certainly differ from systems satisfying one or the other formulation of the equity principle.[9] How the trade-off between effi-ciency and equity is perceived and resolved will ultimately depend not on explicit formulas but on basic regulatory philosophies.

To the extent that they have not rejected environmental standards in favor of price-like mechanisms such as pollution charges, economists have advocated the use of cost-benefit analysis in standards-setting. They argue that since setting a standard is equivalent to imputing a monetary value to life, health, or well-being, the rationality as well as the efficiency of the process would be greatly improved by making the valuation explicit. In this view, cost-benefit calculations can not only specify the optimal standard (at the point where the marginal cost of treatment just equals the marginal damage caused by pollution), but also effectively dispel the mystique that so often enshrouds the process of standards-setting. Unfortunately, the practical and conceptual problems of actually calculating the benefits and costs of a standard are staggering. Neither treatment costs nor damage costs are known with any degree of precision. Treatment costs vary greatly between firms, municipalities, and households. Ecological damage varies not only with the type and level of activity, but also with the location of the polluting unit, general environmental conditions, strength of interactions, and so on. Additional problems arise in connection with persistent pollutants like cadmium, mercury, and chlorinated hydrocarbons. Here the most serious threat is represented by an essentially nonreducible stock, rather than by the flow, of pollution, and marginal calculations of the type used by cost-benefit analysts are ill-suited to such cases. Marginal calculations are also inappropriate in ecologically unstable situations, where the assimilative capacity of the environment would be soon unable to cope with the levels of pollution permitted by static cost-benefit considerations (for a technical discussion of these and related issues, see Pearce, 1976).

Finally, an explicit comparison of benefits and costs requires that monetary values be attached to the health effects of pollution—at best an uncertain and highly subjective judgment. The fact that a valuation of life and limb is implicit in the definition of any health-related standard does not in any way simplify the task. The economist's argument is correct: setting a standard necessarily entails making an implicit estimate of a cost-benefit ratio, based on whatever data and information are available. But this methodological clarification is not very helpful when treatment costs and damage functions cannot be known within reasonable limits. In this situation an overall estimate of the cost-benefit ratio is perhaps more reliable than a set of separate assessments of the different factors appearing in the numerator and the denominator of the ratio.

Determining socially acceptable levels of risk for toxic and carcinogenic substances presents problems that are, if possible, even more awesome than those discussed so far. Again, there are a few cases where the preponderance of the evidence is such that a decision is clearly indicated. Sometimes the existence of safe and easily available substitutes greatly simplifies the regulatory task. In most cases, however, it is highly uncertain whether the possible risks of using a substance outweigh the benefits, or conversely. This uncertainty is reflected in the existence of different and conflicting conceptual bases for the determination of acceptable levels of risk. For example, a section of the 1958 Food Additives Amendment known as the Delaney clause states that "no additive shall be deemed safe if it is found to induce cancer when ingested by man or animal, or if it is found, after tests which are appropriate for the evaluation of the safety of food additives, to induce cancer in man or animal." Regarded by many consumer advocates as a powerful decision tool for the regulator, the Delaney clause in fact poses serious problems of interpretation and application. It does not tell the regulator what are "appropriate tests" and what evidence is to be considered sufficient to establish that a given chemical can induce cancer, while forbidding him to weigh the risks, however small, against the potential benefits, however large.

The statutes regulating the use of pesticides and toxic substances, and even of carcinogens, as long as they do not enter the food supply as additives, do not follow the no-risk approach embodied in the Delany clause, but require that regulatory decisions be based on an "administrative" weighing of risks and benefits. This obviously leaves room for a wide variety of procedures and methodological choices. Concepts like "acceptable risk doses," "acceptable daily intake," "virtual safety," and "no observed effect level" (NOEL) leave ample room for discretionary choices and rules of thumb. Consider, for example, how the EPA's Office of Toxic Substances set chemical plant effluent standards for benzidine, a carcinogen:

> For benzidine, officials in the agency's Office of Toxic Substances began by selecting a risk that seemed acceptable—a chance of one in a million that people drinking water contaminated with benzidine would develop cancer—and then calculated a "dose" or exposure limit that would pose a risk of cancer no greater than this. The Environmental Protection Agency based its calculations on small-scale rat experiments done in the late 1950s that showed benzidine to be a carcinogen in mammals. To account for the differences between rats and men, and for a number of other imponderables, the Environmental Protection Agency threw in a safety factor of 100 and ended up with a standard that—if formally adopted—would allow dye manufacturers to dispose of no more than a pound of benzidine a day in a moderately large river flowing at 10,000 cubic feet per second [Gillette, 1974, cited by Lowrance, 1976: 136].

The technical core of such toxicological procedures is a dose-response model establishing a relationship between different dose levels and the probability of a lifetime response. But the relationship can be represented by many different functions and a firm scientific basis for choosing a particular functional representation is lacking. However, such a choice can have a major effect on the determination of the virtually safe dose.[10] As statistician Cornfield (1977: 698) writes, "All present safety evaluation procedures, whether involving the use of NOEL's, or of some favored nonthreshold dose-response function with a "virtually safe" level, must be regarded as mathematical formalisms whose correspondence with the realities of low-dose effect is, and may long remain, largely conjectural."

Additional evidence on the difficulty of either proving or disproving the validity of a particular dose-response model is provided by the heated debate that followed the "direct frontal attack" by Gofman and Tamplin on the radiation standard of 0.17 rem per year for the general population (Gofman and Tamplin, 1971). While most of the scientists involved in setting radiation standards rejected the conclusions of Gofman and Tamplin, they found it difficult to disprove specific points. On the other hand, the main argument in favor of a linear dose-response model—the model favored by Gofman and Tamplin—is not scientific, but has to do with the wisdom of conservative procedures in the face of scientific uncertainty. Essentially they argued that since carcinogenesis and the genetic or somatic effects of radiation are so poorly understood, conservative assumptions are needed in order to protect the public safety.

But where should one stop along the scale of increasingly conservative procedures? An outright ban is more conservative than a virtually safe dose derived from a linear model; this in turn, is more conservative than a threshold model. Similarly, in deciding whether a substance induces cancer in man or animal, why be satisfied with a statistical significance level of, say, 0.0001 when even safer levels could be chosen? Why consider the distribution of responses in particularly sensitive or susceptible segments of the population instead of adopting the response of the most sensitive individual in the population as reference point (Cornfield, 1977: 695-696)? As a principle of choice, conservatism in risk assessment violates the logic of decision-making under uncertainty. From the perspective of a decision theorist, conservatism in the assessment of risk compromises the rationality of the regulatory process since it focuses attention on extreme events and most unfavorable outcomes instead of considering the entire range of uncertainty and the benefits as well as the risk of the different alternatives. Decision theory suggests a way of balancing risks and benefits in a consistent way—by calculating the expected utility of each alternative. Unfortunately, the theory offers no suggestions as to how probabilities, utilities, and consequences are to be estimated when the data are ambiguous, theories are poorly tested, and expert opinion is contradictory. A regulator facing such problems needs good rules of evidence rather than optimal decision rules.

WHEN THE EXPERTS DISAGREE

Obtaining and processing expert opinion in areas like nuclear power, environmental protection, and public health and safety has proved to be a much more difficult problem than the early advocates of governmental regulation could imagine. Expert A disagrees with the conclusions of expert B but finds it difficult or impossible to disprove specific points in B's arguments. The same data, differently interpreted, lead to divergent policy recommendations. Factual arguments become practically inseparable from considerations having to do with the plausibility of the opponent's assumptions, his or her selection of the evidence, or choice of methodology. And because there seems to be no objective way of checking the conclusions of a technical analysis, the credibility of the author becomes as important as his or her competence. Hence, ad personam argument and other rhetorical devices: blank denials of the claims of the opponent, sweeping generalizations, arguing from different premises, presenting as firm conclusions what others regard as tentative hypotheses (see, for example, Mazur, 1973).

Many people fear that the failure of scientists and engineers to reach a consensus on technical issues with important policy implications could have a devastating effect both on regulatory decision-making and on the public image of science. While policy makers are concerned that the ambiguity of the expert advice they receive may undermine the legitimacy of their decisions, researchers raised in the traditional ethos of science fear that the principles of scientific method are being contaminated by the increasingly adversary atmosphere of the policy process.[11] Actually, closer analysis of recent controversies shows that the issues over which expert disagreement is most serious are, in Alvin Weinberg's terminology, trans-scientific rather than strictly scientific or technical. Trans-scientific issues are questions of fact that can be stated in the language of science but are, in principle or in practice, unanswerable by science (Weinberg, 1972).

One of Weinberg's examples is the determination of the health effects of low-level radiation. It has been calculated that in order to determine by direct experimentation, at the 95% confidence level, whether a level of X-rays radiation of 150 millirems would increase the spontaneous mutation in mice by 1/2 percent, would require about 8 billion mice. Time and resource constraints make such an experiment all but infeasible. Similarly, the choice of a particular dose-response function must be treated at present as a trans-scientific question. The same is true of calculations attempting to determine the probability of extremely unlikely events like catastrophic reactor accidents—as far as any direct verification of the calculations is concerned—and of the issue of when animal data alone form a sufficient basis for standards-setting (good examples of the latter issue can be found in Shapley, 1977). Much policy-oriented research is large-scale, heavily computerized, and often uses sophisticated techniques developed ad hoc for a particular study. This is another important source of trans-scientific questions, since severe problems in obtaining the original data or in checking the methods make it extremely difficult for independent scientists either to confirm or to refute the conclusions of such studies.[12]

The increasing frequency of trans-scientific disputes is closely related to the expansion of the area where science, technology, and public policy intersect. Not only are facts and values much more difficult to separate in policy-oriented research than in traditional scientific work. The status of the facts themselves changes when their quality or their value as evidence is called in question. Nor can disciplinary standards and traditions be relied on to provide the necessary quality controls for research projects involving a variety of disciplines and specializations of different degrees of maturity. Thus it is not surprising that the style of debate and the role of the expert in areas of public policy involving trans-scientific issues are quite different from the situation where a generally accepted set of criteria and well-established rules of professional etiquette provide control, guidance, and legitimacy. In trans-scientific debate arguments replace proofs, conclusions must be persuasive as well as logically adequate, and the line separating the expert from the nonexpert becomes evanescent. But while these features of the policy debate pose new problems to the policy analyst and the scientific advisor, they do not in themselves threaten either the efficiency and legitimacy of the policy process, or the integrity of science. The real problem facing regulatory bodies today is not the existence of conflicting expert opinions, but the inability of existing procedures to channel disagreement toward constructive purposes.

THE SEARCH FOR NEW PROCEDURES

At the heart of the current debate about ways of improving the quality of regulatory decision-making lies the question of the appropriateness of adversary procedures as a method of dealing with controversial technical aspects of public policy. Weinberg (1972: 216) has characterized quite well the two extreme positions:

> To one trained in the law, a rather formal and somewhat stylized adversary procedure might seem to be a reasonable institutional arrangement for arriving at truth—whether it be legal, trans-scientific or scientific. But to the scientist, adversary procedures seem inappropriate and alien to his tradition. To be sure, such procedures are useful in establishing the credibility of witnesses. . . . In science, however, the issue is not a witness's credibility; it is his specific competence—that is his ability to recognize and know scientific truth—and this is not reliably established by an adversary procedure conducted by lawyers rather than scientists.

Scientists who reject the idea that the adversary process may help in discovering scientific or technical truth, or even in throwing some light on such subtle issues, have favored the use of high-level advisory panels or special commissions "constituted from the best and most responsible members of the scientific community" (McGill, 1977: 25). These elite groups of consultants would evaluate the scientific evidence, draw conclusions and, if necessary, suggest to the agency questions that require further investigation. This is essentially a process of peer review, operating with the same criteria that are normally used by scientists to evaluate academic research. Generally speaking, the system has not worked very well in the context of policy-making. On the one hand, the reports of high-level advisory bodies tend to be consensus documents that avoid dissenting opinions in order not to detract from the aura of objectivity of the report and thus reduce its political effectiveness (Primack and von Hippel, 1974). On the other hand, scientists with a special expertise in a given area are likely to have predetermined opinions and vested interests in the way issues arising in that area are settled. This seems to disqualify the specialists as impartial judges, and yet they could certainly play very useful roles as advocates. Proponents of the science court attempt to resolve this dilemma by means of an adversary proceedings with the experts as advocates and judgments left to established experts in areas adjacent to the dispute. In this way, it is hoped, a situation is created in which:

> The adversaries direct their best arguments at each other and at a panel of sophisticated scientific judges rather than at the general public. The disputants themselves

are in the best position to display the strengths of their own views and to probe the weak points of opposing positions. In turn, scientifically sophisticated outsiders are best able to juxtapose the opposing arguments, determine whether these are genuine or only apparent disagreements, and suggest further studies which may resolve the differences [Task Force of the Presidential Advisory Group, 1976: 653].

The proposed science court would only examine, and decide upon, questions of scientific fact, where by scientific fact is meant "a result, or more frequently the anticipated result, of an experiment or an observation of nature." After the evidence has been presented, questioned, and defended, the panel of judges issues a report in which the points of agreement among the advocates are noted, and judgments over disputed statements of fact are given. The report may also suggest specific research projects to clarify points that remain unsettled.

Critics of the proposal have rightly stressed the difficulty (and also the undesirability) of separating the scientific from the political and value elements of policy issues encompassing both (Casper, 1976 and Nelkin, 1977). But the more basic issue is whether adversary hearings are a useful mechanism for dealing with the sort of factual statements that would fit the narrow definition given above. In the words of the Task Force's (1976: 193) proposal, "This definition excludes statements such as 'if X occurs, then Y *may* occur.' Such a statement is valid even if the probability of the occurrence of Y is infinitesimally small, so the experiment required to refute the statement is impossible. An acceptable version of the statement must specify a finite probability which could be refuted by a possible experiment."

Does this mean that the court would not consider issues involving the probability of extremely unlikely events—precisely the issues of greatest importance to safety regulators? Experts can fruitfully discuss the reasonableness of an estimated probability of a catastrophic reactor accident—say, 10^{-7}/reactor/year, to use one of Weinberg's examples. But they cannot check the estimate experimentally, for instance by building 1,000 reactors and operating them for 10,000 years. And if such trans-scientific questions do not come within the purview of the Science Court, why use a quasi-judicial procedure?

If the question is unambiguously scientific, then the procedures of science rather than the procedures of law are required for arriving at the truth. Where the questions raised cannot be answered from existing scientific knowledge or from research which could be carried out reasonably rapidly and without disproportionate expense, then the answers must be trans-scientific and the adversary procedure seems therefore the best alternative [Weinberg, 1972: 215].

The advantages of the adversary procedure are those of partisan discussion with respect to cooperative discussion (Lindblom, 1965: 220-222). The procedure creates a situation in which it is unnecessary to presuppose objectivity, fairness, or shared values, since each party has the full responsibility and opportunity to reveal defects in the rival's arguments. Unlike the consensus-seeking mechanism of advisory bodies, the adversary system provides powerful incentives for the adversaries to present the strongest arguments in favor of their respective positions. Unlike the traditional system of legislative hearings, where opposing witnesses often fail to speak to each other's conclusions and where differences in assumptions are often mistaken for disagreements about facts, adversary procedures are specifically designed to bring out unstated assumptions, differing interpretations, and gaps in logic or in the factual evidence.

But these advantages are paid for in terms of strict procedural requirements that can impose considerable costs and delays in decision-making. For this reason, the courts have been rather cautious in urging regulatory agencies to adopt full-fledged adversary proceedings. In the area of environmental regulation, for example, they have developed "paper-hearing" procedures that combine many of the advantages of a trial-type adversary process (without oral testimony and cross-examination) while avoiding undue delay and costs. The Federal Administrative Procedure Act (APA) provides two basic procedures for regulatory decision-making: trial-type or quasi-judicial hearings for formal adjudication, and "notice-and-comment" requirements for informal rule-making. In trial-type hearings the agency and the parties at interest can introduce direct and rebuttal evidence through oral testimony and have the opportunity for cross-examination. Moreover, the agency's decision must be based on the evidence developed at the hearing and usually takes the form of an opinion. The statutory requirements for informal rule-making are more limited. The agency must publish in the *Federal Register* the substance of the proposed regulation and receive comments from interested persons prior to the final adoption. There is no trial-type hearing and the decision is not "on the record," since the agency is not required to base its decision solely on the written comments submitted but may take into consideration any information which it finds relevant to the case (Stewart, 1977: 729).

Now, many regulatory decisions fit under the APA definitions of both rules and orders, so that agencies have traditionally enjoyed a considerable amount of freedom in choosing between the two types of pro-

cedure. Understandably, the historical trend has been toward the aban-
donment of the full machinery of adjudication (not only of cross-examination and oral testimony, but also of the requirement that a decision be
explained in terms of a record to which all parties had an opportunity
to contribute) in favor of more informal procedures. However, these
procedures have often become *too* informal to provide sufficient incentives for the agency officials to probe deeply into the complex and often
ambiguous nature of the technical information at their disposal, or to
permit a critical review of the quality of their decisions (Pedersen,
1975).[13] When the scientific and technical basis of regulation is as uncertain as our previous discussion indicates, it would be absurd to require
that decisions be supported by "proof" in the strict sense of the word.
But cognitive uncertainty, far from justifying carelessness in choosing
among alternative data, theories, and methodologies, in fact demands
strong procedural controls to make sure that the implications of those
choices are explored from a variety of viewpoints. This is the main objective of the "paper hearings" recently devised by the federal courts to
improve the quality of decision-making at EPA and at other regulatory
agencies (Stewart, 1977: 733). The substance of the new procedural
requirements has been summarized by Pedersen (1975: 75-76, notes
omitted):

> First, both the essential factual data on which the rule is based and the methodology
> used in reasoning from the data to the proposed standard must be disclosed
> for comment at the time a rule is proposed. . . . Second, the agency's discussion
> of the basis and purpose of its rule—generally contained in the "preambles" to
> the notices of proposed and final rule-making and in the accompanying technical
> support documents—must detail the steps of the agency's reasoning and its factual
> basis. Third, significant comments received during the public comment period
> must be answered at the time of final promulgation. However, comments must
> meet a standard of detail equal to that required of the agency in promulgating
> its rule before they will be considered significant. Fourth, only objections to
> the regulations which were raised with some specificity during the public comment
> period, and to which the agency thus had an opportunity to respond, may be raised
> during judicial review.

These requirements are only a first step toward a procedural reform
that could have a major impact on regulatory processes. Much remains
to be done in this direction,[14] but some evidence of significant improvements in the quality of decision-making is already available (Pedersen,
1975: 73-74; Stewart, 1977: 731-732).[15] Data and technical studies
are collected and organized more systematically; outside criticism is
explicitly taken into account so that policies reflect a broader range

of considerations and interests; the various subunits of an agency are motivated to coordinate their assessments, methodologies, and conclusions. It also seems likely that the new procedures will increase the influence of the people who, because of their special knowledge, are more directly involved in rule-making.

In this section I have discussed several proposals aimed at improving the quality of regulatory decision-making. The purpose has been not to provide a detailed comparison of their advantages and shortcomings, but to explore their broader significance. And this significance, we can see now, is to be found in the insight that as regulatory decisions are increasingly based on arguments and judgments about competing benefits and risks rather than on conclusive facts, procedural rationality—the effectiveness of the procedures used to choose actions—becomes at least as important as substantive or instrumental (means-end) rationality.

PROCEDURAL RATIONALITY

The policy sciences have traditionally concerned themselves with the problem of choosing the best means for the achievement of exogenously determined ends. The basic conceptual categories of the policy analyst—goals, alternatives, consequences, impacts, effectiveness, choice—clearly reveal his deep commitment to a teleological conception of policy-making. According to this conception, as formulated by Rawls (1973: 24), "those institutions and actions are right which of the available alternatives produce the most good, or at least as much good as any of the other institutions and acts open as real possibilities." Rawls adds: "Teleological theories have a deep intuitive appeal since they seem to embody the idea of rationality. It is natural to think that rationality is maximizing something. . . . Indeed, it is tempting to suppose that it is self-evident that things should be arranged so as to lead to the most good." Hence the preoccupation with methods of analysis and evaluation that emphasize outcome rather than process, and the interest in what decisions are made, rather than in how they are made (Simon, 1978: 2, 10).[16] Hence also the lack of a methodological equivalent of the legal notion of "reasoned decision."

This indifference toward procedures and the formal layout of arguments becomes understandable with the assumption that there exists a one best way of making a decision. If the correctness or fairness of the outcome can be determined unambiguously the manner in which the decision is made is largely immaterial; only results count. But when the factual and value premises are moot, when no independent criterion for the right result exists, the process or procedure of decision-making acquires special significance. This is the basic insight on which the classical theories of judicial, legislative, and administrative procedures are based (Barker, 1958; Luhmann, 1975). Even in the policy sciences the explicit recognition of uncertainty forces a certain change of perspective. Under conditions of uncertainty different alternatives correspond to different probabilistic distributions of consequences so that it is no longer possible to determine unambiguously what the optimal decision is. Consequently, the theory of decision-making under uncertainty replaces the optimality criterion of instrumental rationality by the weaker notion of internal consistency. The rational decision-maker is no longer an optimizer. All that is required now is that his or her choice be consistent with his or her subjective evaluations of probability and utility.

This new formulation shifts the focus of analytic attention toward process, but only in a modest way as can be seen by contrasting the decision-theoretic treatment of alternatives with the approach of a fully-developed procedure like adversary proceedings. Decision theory conceptualizes a decision problem by introducing a list $d_1, d_2, \ldots, d_m$ of m exclusive and exhaustive possible decisions and a second list $E_1, E_2, \ldots, E_n$ of n (equally exclusive and exhaustive) uncertain events. The problem is to select a single item from the first list without knowing which member of the second list will occur. The theory is silent about how the alternatives are to be generated and how the uncertainty is to be structured. Notice, however, that since each d_i represents a possible solution of the same decision problem all the alternatives are functionally related as different means to the given end. Also, they are all bounded by the same constraints and their consequences are evaluated in terms of the same set of uncertain events. In short, the theory has little to say about the design of the decision process and can only handle processes whose components are sufficiently homogeneous.

On the other hand, radically different alternatives are not only tolerated, but actively encouraged in adversary proceeding. An adversary process develops through a sequence of contradictory statements representing contrasting interests and incongruent interpretations of reality. Conflicting viewpoints are not eliminated in the name of logical consistency, or by subordinating them to a common goal. Inferior alternatives are not automatically discarded (as are "dominated" alternatives in decision theory) for, as the ancient dialecticians knew, in order to keep a discussion going it is often necessary to "make the weaker case the stronger." Thus, by keeping as many possibilities open for as long as possible an adversary process can generate radical criticism and truly different alternatives. The result—a cooperative search for truth starting from initially divergent positions—is beyond the capabilities of more direct methods of problem-solving. In the words of Parsons (1966: 27), "Only on the basis of procedural primacy can the system cope with a wide variety of changing circumstances and types of cases without prior commitment to specific solutions."

We have seen that regulatory policies involve issues of great cognitive complexity for which no satisfactory methods of resolution yet exist or may ever be found. This does not justify the currently popular slogan of regulatory failure, or the inference that deregulation is the only reasonable alternative to the present system. In the field of environmental regulation, for example, recent evidence indicates a substantial reduction in the discharge of conventional water pollutants as measured by BOD and total suspended solids. Since the Clean Air Act was passed in 1970, sulfur dioxide levels have dropped about 27%, carbon monoxide has decreased by 20%, and particulates have decreased by 12%. Analytic technology has advanced to the point that it is now possible to detect the presence of a chemical pollutant in parts per trillion (Train, 1978). Even the record of industrial regulation is not as uniformly bad as some critics seem to suggest. Along with the well-publicized failures of agencies like the Federal Trade Commission, the unbiased observer cannot fail to notice the solid performance of other bodies, for example the Securities and Exchange Commission (Freedman, 1975). The truth of the matter is that the performances of federal regulatory agencies vary too widely to justify any generalized assumption of a crisis in the administrative process.

A satisfactory theory of regulation must recognize and explain such differences in performance. But it should also accept the fact that when policy problems exceed a certain threshold of complexity, evaluation of results must be supplemented by evaluation of process. Absent an unambiguous criterion for the right outcome, substantive rationality cannot be judged independently of procedural rationality.

This chapter has focused on process, more precisely on certain aspects of process related to the use of scientific and technical knowledge in decision-making. The analysis has shown that many regulatory decisions leave much to be desired in terms of procedural rationality. First, the procedures used in processing and evaluating information do not reflect the basic uncertainties and ambiguities inherent in the cognitive basis. And, second, the derivation of conclusions is not sufficiently organized and transparent to permit a detailed factual probing of the intellectual merits of the decision. A number of proposals have been mentioned that attempt, in various ways, to improve the quality of the regulatory process in both directions. The differences among these proposals are not as important as the common recognition of the need for procedural improvements. Implicit in most proposals is also a rejection of the ideology of expertise in favor of a dialectical approach capable of bringing into the open critical unresolved issues of policy.

The experience of the "paper hearing" procedures developed at EPA under the Clean Air Act is particularly instructive, for it shows that regulatory decision-making can be significantly improved by careful procedural design. The requirement of an open record that includes the factual and methodological bases of the agency's conclusions, as well as outside criticism and responses to such criticism, is a powerful incentive to more careful agency deliberations. The need to improve the intellectual quality of agency deliberations is not, however, the only reason why questions of process are so important today. Particularly when the factual evidence is highly uncertain, it is essential that affected interests be willing to accept the outcomes of the administrative process even before their substantive contents have been determined. By ensuring the representation of conflicting opinions and the examination of a wide range of alternatives, well-designed procedures can greatly improve not only the rationality but also the legitimacy of regulatory decisions.

NOTES

1. Cushman (1937) is cited by Fainsod (1940: 312).

2. According to Landis (1966: 142), "The positive reason for declining judicial review over administrative findings of fact is the belief that the expertness of the administrative, if guarded by adequate procedures, can be trusted to determine these issues as capably as judges. If so, it is only delay that results from insistence upon independent judicial examination of the administrative's conclusion." But Landis is aware of the variable quality of decision-making in different administrative agencies: "If the extent of judicial review is being shaped, as I believe, by reference to an appreciation of the quality of expertness for decision that the administrative may possess, important consequences follow. The constitution of the administrative and the procedure employed by it become of great importance. . . . Different agencies receive different treatment from the courts."

3. Even today the overwhelming mass of administrative adjudication is informal; see, for example, Lorch (1969: ch. 6).

4. Thus the 1970 Clean Air Amendments direct EPA to use scientific evidence to determine threshold values for different types of pollutants, even though the existence of threshold for the health effects of carcinogens, mutagens, and radiation has never been firmly established. In the present stage of scientific knowledge, the notion of a threshold value is little more than "a politically convenient fiction which permits the law to appear to require pollution damage to be reduced to zero" (see Kneese and Schultze, 1975: 51). Similarly, the 1963 Clean Air Act instructs the Secretary of HEW to "compile and publish criteria reflecting accurately the latest scientific knowledge," although biomedical knowledge is barely sufficient to detect the presence of adverse health effects of different air pollutants, let alone measure them.

5. In the past the courts and legal commentators have often maintained that a regulatory agency can rely on its expertise in promulgating rules even when that expertise is not reflected in any record (see Pedersen, 1975: 61).

6. Typical of the attitude of most professional economists is Stigler's (1966: 104) caustic remark that "[h]istorical costs have powerful sway over untutored minds. The Internal Revenue Service insists that corporations' assets be so valued. The public utility commissions consider historical costs a relevant or even decisive item in setting rates."

7. This is a simplified description of the standards-setting process. In some cases emission standards are not directly related to quality criteria but are made to depend on factors like "best practicable technology" (BPT standards) or "best available technology" (BAT standards). In other cases the law fails to differentiate clearly between criteria and effluent standards, or to establish strong links between them. The emission limits on newly constructed stationary sources under the 1970 Clean Air Amendments and the 1965 Water Quality Act exemplify the two situations.

8. Executive Order 12044 issued by President Carter in March 1978 requires a "regulatory analysis" setting forth a careful comparison of alternatives and their economic consequences for all proposed regulations likely to have an effect of $100 million or more on the economy annually, or lead to a substantial increase in costs or prices in particular industries, regions, or levels of government.

9. The same problem would of course arise with a system of effluent or pollution charges—a system which in principle would minimize the social cost of satisfying a given environmental standard.

10. More than a 100,000-fold effect, according to the Food and Drug Administration Committee on Safety Evaluation.

11. For a characteristic expression of such fears see McGill (1977: 2-25). Adversary arguments have their place in the courtroom, but scientific disputes are resolved neither by disputation nor by appealing to lay judges, but by "the objective analysis of experimental results by our best scientific minds." Of course, rejection of argumentation as a method of discovering truth in favor either of experimentation (Bacon) or of logicomathematical deduction (Descartes) is an important aspect of the Western scientific tradition. No one has expressed this distaste for argumentation better than Descartes himself in a well-known passage of his *Regulae ad Directionem Ingenii:* "Every time two men make a contrary judgment about the same matter, it is certain that one of them is mistaken. What is more, neither of them possesses the truth, for if one of them had a clear and precise view of the truth, he would be able to expound it to his opponent so as to force the latter's conviction."

12. See the editorial by Comar (1978). Similar problems arise in other policy areas where large-scale, computer-based models play a significant role (see, for example, Lee 1973).

13. See also note 4.

14. For instance, Pedersen and other legal analysts have pointed out the danger that the formal record may come to include much information that is not really needed to understand the reasons of an agency's decision, while excluding important documents.

15. Professor Stewart (1977) stresses the significance of these procedural developments in inducing EPA to pay greater attention to the economic and social costs of environmental regulation. See also additional references cited in Pedersen (1975) and Stewart (1977).

16. "[E]conomics has largely been preoccupied with the *results* of rational choice rather than the process of choice."

REFERENCES

BARKER, E. (1958) [1942] Reflections on Government. New York: Oxford Univ. Press.

BAUMOL, W. J. (1970) "Reasonable rules for rate regulation: plausible policies for an imperfect world," pp. 187-206 in P. W. MacAvoy (ed.) The Crisis of the Regulatory Commissions. New York: W. W. Norton.

CASPER, B. M. (1976) "Technology policy and democracy." Science 194 (Ocotober): 29-35.

CAVES, R. E. (1970) "Performance, structure, and the goals of civil aeronautics board regulation," in P. W. MacAvoy (ed.) The Crisis of the Regulatory Commissions. New York: W. W. Norton.

COMAR, C. (1978) "Bad science and social penalties." Science 200 (June 16).

CORNFIELD, J. (1977) "Carcinogenic risk assessment." Science 198 (November): 693-699.

CUSHMAN, R. E. (1937) "The problem of the industrial regulatory commissions," in President's Committee on Administrative Management, Report with Special Studies. Washington, D.C.

DAVIES, J. C., III (1970) The Politics of Pollution. New York: Pegasus.

FAINSOD, M. (1940) "Some reflections on the nature of the regulatory process." Public Policy.

FRANKFURTER, F. and H. M. HART, Jr. (1970) "Rate regulation," pp. 1-17 in P. W. MacAvoy (ed.) The Crisis of the Regulatory Commissions. New York: W. W. Norton.

FREEMAN, J. O. (1975) "Crisis and legitimacy in the administrative process." Stanford Law Rev. 27 (April): 1041-1076.

GILLETTE, R. (1974) "Cancer and the environment II: groping for new remedies." Science 186: 242-245.

GOFMAN, J. and A. TAMPLIN (1971) Poisoned Power. Emmaus, PA: Rodale.

KNEESE, A. V. and C. L. SCHULTZE (1975) Pollution, Prices, and Public Policy. Washington, DC: Brookings Institution.

LANDIS, J. M. (1966) [1938] The Administrative Process. New Haven, CT: Yale Univ. Press.

LEE, D. B., Jr. (1973) "Requiem for large-scale models." Amer. Institute of Planners J.: 163-178.

LINDBLOM, C. E. (1965) The Intelligence of Democracy. New York: Free Press.

LORCH, R. S. (1969) Democratic Process and Administrative Law. Detroit: Wayne State Univ. Press.

LOWRANCE, W. W. (1976) Of Acceptable Risk. Los Altos, CA: William Kaufman.

LUHMANN, N. (1975) Legitimation durch Verfahren. Neuwied: Luchterhand.

McGILL, W. J. (1977) "Adversary legal process vs. scientific research." Columbia Today (Winter): 2-25.

MAZUR, A. (1973) "Disputes between experts." 11 Minerva.

MILLER, J. C., III (1977) "Regulators and experts." Regulation (November/December).

NELKIN, D. (1977) "Thoughts on the proposed science court." Newsletter on Science, Technology, and Human Values 18 (January): 20-31.

——— (1975) "The political impact of technical expertise." Social Studies of Sci. 5: 35-54.

PARSONS, T. (1966) Societies, Evolutionary and Comparative Perspectives. Englewood Cliffs, NJ: Prentice Hall.

PEARCE, C. (1976) "The limits of cost-benefit analysis as a guide to environmental policy." Kyklos 29, Fasc. 1: 97-112.

PEDERSEN, W. F., Jr. (1975) "Formal records and informal rule making." Yale Law J. 85: 38-88.

POSNER, R. A. (1974) "Theories of economic regulation." Bell J. of Economics and Management Sci. 5 (Autumn): 335-358.

PRIMACK, J. and F. VON HIPPEL (1974) Advice and Dissent—Scientists in the Political Arena. New York: Basic Books.

RAWLS, J. (1973) A Theory of Justice. New York: Oxford Univ. Press.

SHAPLEY, D. (1977) "Occupational cancer: government challenged in beryllium proceeding." Science 198 (December): 898-901.

SIMON, H. A. (1978) "Rationality as process and as product of thought." Amer. Economic Association Proceeding 68 (May): 1-16.

STEWART. R. B. (1977) "The development of administrative and quasi-constitutional law in judicial review of environmental decisionmaking: lessons from the Clean Air Act." Iowa Law Rev. 62: 713-769.

STIGLER, G. J. (1966) The Theory of Price. London: Macmillian.

Task Force of the Presidential Advisory Group on Anticipated Advances in Science and Technology (1976) "The science court experiment." Sci. 193 (August): 653-656.

TRAIN, R. E. (1978) "The environment today." Science 201 (July): 320-324.

WEINBERG, A. M. (1972) "Science and trans-science." 10 Minerva (April): 209-222.

WILCOX, C. (1968) "Regulation of industry," in D. L. Sills (ed.) International Encyclopedia of the Social Sciences 13. New York: Macmillan and Free Press.

Problems and Procedures in the Regulation of Technological Risk

DOROTHY NELKIN
MICHAEL POLLAK
Cornell University

The public bureaucracies responsible for regulating complex technologies are increasingly challenged by scientists calling public attention to the risks of technology-based projects, and by citizen groups demanding greater accountability and participation in technical policy decisions. Indeed, decisions about science and technology, long considered the domain of expertise, are more and more the targets of political controversy. And the persistence of conflict—over nuclear power plant siting, airport expansion, food additives, toxic substances, chemical carcinogens; the list is long and growing—indicates that existing procedures for mediating among competing interests and resolving political conflicts are far from adequate.

Until recently, the risks of technology have mainly been perceived as a technical problem, not a political issue, a problem to be relegated to expertise, not to public debate. But controversies have politicized the issue of risk, called attention to the interests and the questions of power involved. Several features of these disputes have contributed to this politicization and to the difficulties of bureaucratic decision-making.

First is the nature of the risks that are characteristic of many new technologies. These risks are often "invisible" and vaguely understood.

Authors' Note: *Data on the United States was developed with funding from the NSF-NEH EVIST Program; the European data was developed with a grant from the German Marshall Fund. This article was first prepared for a conference on technological risk organized by the European Commission, Berlin, April 1979.*

How does one know if a lethal gene has been produced by recombinant DNA research? Or if a nuclear waste storage facility is adequately protected against radiation leakage? Often it is the fear of an unlikely but possibly devastating catastrophe (e.g., a nuclear accident) that sustains conflict. Problems of regulation derive from inherent ambiguities in the data about risk that permit conflicting technical interpretations. Scientists' disagreement and their public disputes reveal their limited ability to predict the environmental and health effects of certain technologies. This is particularly upsetting to those responsible for making decisions. For how are regulatory authorities and legislators to make judgments when faced not only with diverse political interests but also with conflicting evidence and polarized expert opinion? How can decisions be made about the acceptability of risk given the confusion among facts, their interpretation, and their subjective evaluation?

A related feature of recent technological disputes is the vague and shifting boundary between the technical and political discourse. Questions of risk can be defined in technical or political terms; even if scientific consensus exists, finding an acceptable level of risk requires weighing costs and benefits and balancing competing priorities.

Finally, concerns about risks are often translated into questions about political authority and the legitimacy of decision-making procedures. This reflects a far broader characteristic of modern industrial societies—the declining trust in decision-making authority and expertise. The credibility of scientific expertise as a reliable basis for decision-making is suspect: Public bureaucracies, accustomed to relying on expertise, find that their technical assessment of risk bears little relationship to public attitudes. Other factors, including the acceptability of the decision-making process, intervene to affect the public assessment of controversial projects.

These three features of disputes over science and technology have shaped efforts to resolve them—to find means to establish rules of evidence, to assess the adequacy and competence of information, and above all, to assure the procedural conditions that will bring public acceptance of specific projects and restore confidence in decision-making authorities. This chapter will first describe some of these efforts in the United States and Western Europe, and then analyze their limits in the context of the expectations of opposition groups.

EXPERIMENTS IN CONFLICT RESOLUTION

Experiments in conflict resolution follow from the assumption that appropriate procedures to evaluate risk will lead to public acceptance of controversial technologies. However, ideas about what procedures are appropriate vary considerably depending on how the problem of risk is defined. It is mainly a problem arising from insufficient technical evidence? Then the goal is one of ascertaining "scientific truth," and this leads to a structure based on scientific advice. However, where controversy is defined rather in terms of the public's acceptance of risk, a more participatory or consultative system is developed to advise decision makers about the terms of public acceptability. Often the problem of acceptability is defined in terms of information; it is assumed that people fear risks because they are poorly informed. The task is then to educate the public. But if concern about risk is defined as a political problem of trust in expertise, then participatory procedures seek to involve the public in defining the salient information as a basis for greater influence. These four definitions of the problem of risk underlie differences in the procedures created to resolve conflict, and we have organized our discussion accordingly. Indeed, some experiments are primarily intended to advise decision makers about scientific opinion and about public concerns. (See Table 1.) Others are intended to inform the public and are dissociated from the decision-making process. (See Table 2.) Some of these advisory and information procedures are organized around an elite, that is, scientists and officials from large representative associations or governmental institutions. Others are more participatory, including civil servants and a broader public constituency.

ADVISORY MODELS: ELITIST

Among the more well-publicized and controversial proposals to resolve technological disputes in the United States is the "Science Court," a quasi-judicial procedure in which scientists with different views on issues such as nuclear safety or the effect of high-voltage transmission lines would argue before "impartial scientific judges" (Task Force of the Presidential Advisory Group, 1976: 653). In this

TABLE 1
CONSENSUS PROCEDURES: ADVISORY MODELS

Type	Who Participates	General Intention
Elitist		
1. Based on Scientific Authority		
Science Court (United States)	Scientists	An adversary procedure to establish a consensus on "scientific truth."
Energy Campaign (Austria)	Scientists	An adversary procedure to establish consensus on which problems remain controversial within a scientific community
2. Based on Consensus Among Elites		
Advisory Commissions of Science Ministry (Germany)	Scientists Representatives of Major Institutions	A comprehensive discussion of a project or problem area.
Regional Concertation (France)	Local Dignitaries State Officials Engineers	To reach local agreement in order to implement national policies which affect the local environment.
Royal Commissions (England)	Experts and Officials	Comprehensive discussion to achieve agreement on a controversial issue.

Table 1 (Continued)

Type	Who Participates	General Intention
Participatory		
Public Inquiries Windscale Inquiry (England) Berger Commission (Canada) Policy Intentions (Holland)	Scientists Interested Public	Comprehensive discussion of a project or broad problem area to raise public awareness.
Complaint Investigations Declaration d'Utilite Publique (France) Atom Law (Germany)	Civil Servants Interested Public Scientists	To formulate objections and claims based on individual or collective rights and to correct decisions.
Citizen Advisory Groups (United States)	Community Groups	To allow local community to influence a specific decision affecting local interests.
Environmental Mediation (United States)	Environmental Groups Project Developers	To allow face-to-face confrontation over specific project and to settle disputes.
Referenda (United States, Austria, Switzerland, Holland)	Voting Public	To arbitrate a controversial decision by direct vote on an issue.

TABLE 2
CONSENSUS PROCEDURES: INFORMATION MODELS

Type	Who Participates	General Intention
Elitist		
Conseil d'Information sur l'Energie Electronucleaire (France)	Scientists High Officials Representatives of Ecology Associations	Oversee all information by public agencies and recommend what should be publicized.
Ad Hoc Groups: Groupe de Bellerive (International) Reflection Groups (Holland) Council for Science and Society (England)	Scientists Enlightened Power Elites	To enlighten decision-making and to generate discussion and publicize information about policy.
Participatory		
Study Circles (Sweden) Burgerdialog (Germany)	Large Voluntary Associations and Their Constituency Scientists Public at Large	Broad debate over a problem area to raise public awareness

proposed forum, debate would be limited to questions of fact: judges are to give opinions only on factual matters, leaving social value questions for the political arena. But the opinion of the Science Court is expected to have enough authority to provide a basis for policy decisions. Democratic control of technology, claim Science Court proponents, follows from establishing "the truth among conflicting claims of scientists." This concept has seeded a crop of similar proposals for a "Technical Review Board" (see Ackerman, 1974: 156 ff.), a "Technological Magistrature" (Bugliarelli, 1978: 34-37), and a new profession of "Certified Public Scientists" (Glick, 1976: 189-190). All these proposed institutions would provide neutral judgments to help settle disputes. They assume that scientists, through adversary procedures, can reach agreement on specific questions of risk, and that this will lead to public consensus. Similar positivist assumptions motivated the experimental "energy campaign" in Austria, where the government set up structured public debates among scientists with opposing positions on the government's nuclear policy (Nelkin and Pollak, 1977). The purpose, however, was not to verify points of agreement, but rather to highlight the controversial dimensions of the nuclear program and to clarify areas of persistent disagreement.

Other efforts to enhance the public acceptability of decisions involve, in addition to scientists, the leaders of major associations and state and regional officials. France developed a system of "regional concertation" to facilitate industrial siting decisions (Colson, 1977: 114 ff.). For example, in 1976, seeking to win acceptance of nuclear siting plans, Electricité de France (EDF) circulated dossiers providing technical data on 34 potential nuclear sites to the regional assemblies. They were to examine the dossiers and reach an informed agreement about the acceptability of the sites.

In the German political context, consensus on controversial projects is sought by including leaders of key institutions in advisory committees; in 1975, for example, the Ministry of Science and Technology employed 927 consultant experts from research, industry, unions, and other interest groups. But 80% of these experts represented scientific and industrial interests, suggesting that harmony within the sector is perceived as the crucial component of political consensus (*Bericht der Kommission,* 1976: 473).

ADVISORY MODELS: PARTICIPATORY

The declining influence of the citizen in an expertise-based society is a pervasive concern in many disputes, and most procedural reforms try to involve the citizen more directly in the formulation of policy. This is the rationale behind public inquiries, advisory councils, and mediation procedures.

Public inquiries serve as a forum for comprehensive discussion of specific projects and as a channel for the expression of a range of opinions. But the spectrum of opinions normally considered by an inquiry varies. At one extreme, the Canadian Berger Commission, created to assess the Mackenzie Valley Pipeline controversy, was extraordinarily open to nontechnical participation (Gamble, 1978). Intervener groups were given financial support to develop their case. The commission heard everyone from fishermen to legislators and considered political testimony as important as technical information. However, such an open procedure is unusual. In most commissions, the agenda is limited, dominated by scientists, and pervaded by the belief that factual evidence should carry more weight than subjective concerns.

This was the case in the Windscale public inquiry into the British plan for THORP, a thermal-oxide reprocessing plant (Wynne, 1978). Hundreds of individual organizations testified at this one-hundred-day inquiry which was to assess the conflicting arguments in order to evaluate the "facts" of government policy. With no source of funding, objectors had great difficulties in developing a coherent and coordinated position to counter the arguments of British Nuclear Fuels Ltd. Judge Parker, left to interpret conflicting evidence, recommended construction of the reprocessing plant.

In the Netherlands, the government organized an elaborate public policy inquiry system on the principle that the public must be consulted on all decisions affecting the environment. Government plans are preceded by the publication of "policy intentions" dealing with political and philosophical questions: the objectives of growth, the goals of particular projects, and their likely impacts (Nelkin and Pollak, 1977). These are widely distributed for public comment. A representative group analyzes the reactions and the appropriate ministry must answer the criticism and justify the policy. The entire dossier developed through this process serves as a basis for a parliamentary decision.

Other inquiries are essentially inquests into public objections and complaints about specific projects. This is the purpose of the French Declaration d'Utilité Publique (DUP) and certain provisions of the German Atom Law. To build a nuclear power plant in France, Electricité de France (EDF) must undertake an inquiry through a "DUP" procedure (Colson, 1977). Originally developed as a channel for objections to the practice of eminent domain, the DUP has recently become a forum for the expression of concerns about environmental risk and personal safety. In the DUP process, all people living within five kilometers from a proposed nuclear site have access to a technical dossier from six to eight weeks, during which time they can voice their objections. The prefect appoints an investigating commissioner, usually a local dignitary or a retired civil servant, who collects and evaluates the complaints and EDF's response. Using this evidence, he recommends whether the project should be given public utility status. To date, no commissioner has ever denied an EDF application.

Under the German Atom Law, electricity companies wishing to build a nuclear plant must apply to the land administration for a construction permit and hold a public hearing. Documents are available for public inspection for a month, and anyone affected by a project is entitled to object; the courts have accepted claims from people within one hundred kilometers from the plant site (Nagel and von Moltke: 31 ff.). But the hearing is restricted to discussion of nuclear safety; other environmental issues and economic and social concerns are considered irrelevant, a restriction that often limits meaningful lay participation.

Several kinds of participatory procedures have developed in the United States in response to controversies. In 1976 a citizen review board formed in Cambridge, Massachusetts, to advise the Cambridge City Council on a policy for allowing recombinant DNA research in the city. This was organized on the following principle:

> Decisions regarding the appropriate course between the risks and benefits of potentially dangerous scientific inquiry must not be adjudicated within the inner circles of the scientific establishment . . . a lay citizens group can face a technical scientific matter of general and deep public concern, educate itself appropriately to the task and reach a fair decision [Sullivan, 1976; Cambridge Experimentation Review Board, 1976].

For four months, the review board discussed complex questions about the risks of DNA research and, with a modification requiring local monitoring, approved the research under the federal guidelines set down by the National Institute of Health. A similar citizen review structure has been proposed by a study group at the Oak Ridge National Laboratory to resolve nuclear siting disputes.

Also in the United States, a number of conflict-resolving procedures utilize techniques of social research to provide advice to decision makers about actual public preferences in controversial areas. In 1970, the

Forest Service employed an instrument called "code-involve" to uncover public attitudes about its proposed use of DDT to protect Douglas Firs. Code-involve is a computerized content analysis system designed to transfer information from very diverse sources (editorials, letters, petitions) into a condensed form useful for policy review. This technique can tap a wider spectrum of attitudes than may emerge through other procedures such as public hearings, and theoretically allows the problems to be defined by the public. However, like opinion polls and similar techniques to uncover public preferences, code-involve is surrogate for direct participation. Moreover, since there are no provisions to generate a public reaction, it is only useful in cases where significant debate has already generated large quantities of controversial written comment.

Mediation is the largest proposed elixir for environmental disputes in the United States. This process is based on voluntary participation by the contesting parties, who meet face to face in discussions with a third party to facilitate the arbitration of disputes.[1] Mediation procedures have helped to reach settlements in several environmental disputes, for example over highway routing and strip mining policies.

Finally, referenda are a growing feature of the political landscape. In the United States, thousands of referenda take place each year on questions ranging from local property taxes to airport expansion or nuclear power plant development. Now 21 states have petition procedures for placing issues on the ballot; 23 states permit direct legislation through voting, and 38 permit voters to review laws passed by the legislature. Thus referenda allow citizens to initiate legislation or to repeal existing laws. Significantly, technological decisions are increasingly appearing on ballots in Europe as well as the United States; Austria, Switzerland, and Holland have all held referenda on nuclear power. While posing significant problems of representation, adequate information, and cooptation, the growing popularity of the referendum suggests the interest in dealing with controversial technical questions in a more participatory framework.

INFORMATION MODELS: ELITIST

Access to information about controversial projects is a necessary precondition of conflict resolution, but information can serve several ends. Some hope that access to information will enhance trust in administrative decisions; others look to greater access in order to influence such decisions. Information is usually controlled by an "inner circle" of scientists and officials, but some experiments have been organized to involve broad segments of the public in defining salient issues.

In France, public information about nuclear power prior to 1974 consisted mostly of promotional material; EDF distributed comic strips to school children and glossy brochures to adults. As countergroups responded with a "war of words," it was clear that promotional material increased polarization; therefore in 1975 EDF cut back its public relations campaign and established a "Groupe d'Information Nucléaire" and a documents center for nuclear information. Then in 1977 the government established a Counseil d'Information sur l'Energie Electronucléaire made of the scientists, high officials, and representatives from ecology groups. Its purpose is oversight: It reviews the information on nuclear power disseminated by the government to the public, evaluates its quality and completeness, and recommends what should be publicized.

Another way to expand information is through establishing ad hoc groups that can rise above the polarization characteristic of so many disputes. Most such groups are not officially linked to government; they seek a membership satisfying both public opinion and governmental authorities and an image as responsible and respected sources of public information. For example, the Groupe de Bellerive, an international council "for reflection and evaluation," formed out of concern about the violent opposition to nuclear power in Europe. Its purpose is to bring together "minds both enlightened and recognized as such (scientists but also jurists, technicians but also philosophers, economists but also the politically aware, leading bureaucrats but also those elected by the people), capable of analyzing complex problems and forming independent judgments."

The British Council for Science and Society, organized in 1973, assesses new developments in science and technology for their potential social impacts. It includes scientists, lawyers, and philosophers who meet to consider contemporary problems and to stimulate informed public discussion.

Similarly ad hoc reflection groups often meet in the Netherlands to discuss controversial policy issues. In 1974, for example, a reflection group of scientists, parliamentarians, industrialists, and journalists examined the social and economic dimensions of the nuclear program and called for a five-year reflection period to rethink the basis of national planning. With no formal decision-making authority, all such groups exercise influence mainly by trying to create an informed citizenry and attracting the attention of the media.

INFORMATION MODELS: PARTICIPATORY

In 1974, disturbed by the antinuclear movement, the Swedish government initiated an experiment in public education in the field of energy. Using a system of study groups managed by the principal popular organizations and political parties, the government financed a program to inform broad segments of the public about energy and nuclear power (Nelkin and Pollak, 1977). The program involved some 8000 study circles, each with about 10 members who met together to discuss those energy-related questions they felt to be most important. It was fully expected that greater information would create more favorable attitudes toward government policy. Yet reports from these groups suggest continued uncertainty and ambivalence—a lack of consensus that was evident when the Center Party successfully used its antinuclear position to displace the Social Democrats in the 1975 elections.

The Burgerdialog in Germany, first organized in 1974, represents a similar effort to involve broad sectors of the public in an information program. Organizations such as churches, unions, and adult education groups are funded to organize discussion groups and meetings which include speakers both for and against nuclear power. The goal is "to strengthen confidence in the ability of the democratic process to function, especially in the controversy over nuclear energy, and to restore confidence wherever it may be undermined" (International Atomic Energy Agency, 1976; see also Nelkin, 1978: 59 ff.). This information effort is distinct from the decision-making process; it is intended less to ascertain public opinion than to inform citizens about the necessity for nuclear energy and convince them that risk is minimal. The "dialogue" has thus frequently become a monologue, and it has clearly failed to create consensus over nuclear policy.

PROBLEMS OF PROCEDURAL ACCEPTABILITY

We have described a variety of procedures intended to avoid or to resolve the controversies that obstruct so many decisions about science and technology. Most of these procedures rest on a traditional "welfare model," in which risks are defined as *problems* to be dealt with, mainly by experts. It is assumed that if a problem is solved by a respected group of elites or the best available scientific opinion, this will enhance the legitimacy of public authorities. And it is assumed that if the public is adequately informed, this will result in consensus. These hopes are often dashed: Conflict and mistrust persist, and the procedures themselves are often debunked. Neither public participation nor enlightened representation appear to assure systematically the acceptability of controversial technologies. For protest groups see the issue of risk not as a problem to be solved, but as a controversial question requiring dialogue and negotiation.

What then must one do to enhance legitimacy? What kind of procedures would be acceptable to critical groups? To explore these issues, we turn to five questions that are frequently asked by opposition groups.

How are the boundaries of the problem defined? Who participates in the experiment? Who conducts the procedure? What is the distribution of technical expertise? Is there really a choice?

DEFINITION OF THE PROBLEM

A first principle of negotiation over controversial policies is that there be mutual recognition of the real source of conflict. Is opposition to a technology really based on concern about risk, or is this a surrogate for more fundamental social concerns? Too often, highly political issues are defined as technical; questions about the impact of a technology on community values are translated into arguments about the degree of risk involved. It is somehow assumed that agreement about technical issues will help to resolve questions of political choice.

This definitional bias is most obvious in experiments such as the Science Court, which, in trying to differentiate facts from values, ignore the value interpretation that enters even into the collection of data. In the social and institutional context of science and technology today, it is highly anachronistic to seek resolution of conflicts through scientific expertise. Moreover, even if technical consensus could be established, this may have little effect on public attitudes. Technical consensus may narrow the range of choices, but procedures that bypass underlying value concerns will have little effect on the resolution of disputes.

Yet commissions and inquiries also tend to give disproportionate weight to technical evidence over subjective concerns. The wide publicity given to the Canadian Berger Commission hearings suggests that their careful balancing of technical and nontechnical criteria was relatively unusual. For example, the German hearings required by the Atom Law restrict discussion to the technical dimensions of nuclear risk, avoiding the economic and social issues that are often the primary concern of the nuclear opposition. Even the broadly participatory citizens review in Cambridge was limited to an agenda set by academic scientists that defined the DNA issue narrowly in terms of short-range health hazards and adequate safety measures. Questions of long-range risks or of ethics were put aside.

Similar definitional problems impede the efforts to open public access to information. How does one select the materials to be released to the public? Information on sensitive topics such as the extent of police controls over nuclear facilities or evacuation plans in case of accidents are often excluded from circulation, despite, or perhaps because of, their political importance as a basis for nuclear opposition.

WHO PARTICIPATES?

A second principle of negotiation is that participation must include appropriate interests. In most procedures, two criteria are used to establish the right of participation: "affected interests" and "representativeness." The interests affected by a project are often defined by geographic proximity to a project, but this varies. The German nuclear inquiries have no geographic limits to participation in public hearings; the French restrict participation to those in a five kilometer radius from a proposed site. The limits that are placed on public involvement may predetermine the assessment of risk, as those living near the site of a controversial facility may use different criteria to evaluate the technology than those further away. For example, the employment and economic benefits expected by those living near a nuclear site may clash with the more abstract environmental concerns of those in adjacent communities. Conversely, neighbors of a nuclear facility may feel that the unjustly bear the risks of a project intended to benefit a wider region.

The notion of who is representative and therefore entitled to participate in decision-making procedures also varies. In Sweden, study circles were broadly participative, but organized by a relatively small group of trusted representative elites, the leaders of major associations and political parties. In France, with its comparatively limited tradition of voluntary association, representatives are often defined as civil servants or local elected officials. In the United States, participation is often more direct, as in the Cambridge Citizens Review Board.

In some inquiries, the question of who should be involved is avoided by the use of a public referendum. Local governments in France, for example, have often organized referenda on nuclear power plant siting. These, however, serve only as a source of information; they are neither decisive nor do they necessarily create consensus, for they fail to account for the intensity of opposition from small but actively critical groups.

Problems in defining appropriate participation also limit the usefulness of mediation procedures. Mediation works best when two major protagonists share a minimum common interest that will lead to a mutually satisfactory compromise. In technological controversies, antagonist groups are not necessarily well defined, nor do they necessarily share the values that will compel a compromise.

WHO RUNS THE SHOW?

A major source of criticism of consensus procedures focuses on their management—the choice of commissioners and of various supervising and consulting agencies. In Germany, the civil servants in charge of public hearings often serve at the same time on the administrative boards of the firms applying for permits. For example, the Minister of Economics, politically responsible for the nuclear inquiry procedure in Wyhl, was also the acting vice-chairman of the board of directors in the electric utility. The large state-run Institute for Reactor Safety consulted in the German licensing process had formed out of the first generation of enthusiastic German nuclear experts. Nuclear critics feel such groups are biased and prone to underestimate information that comes from outside the nuclear establishment.

In France, the commissioners who evaluate the public inquiry procedures are also suspect. Often retired civil servants, they lack the technical competence to judge the details of EDF's studies. Yet they maintain a monopoly of information in the DUP nuclear siting procedures.

DISTRIBUTION OF EXPERTISE

Because disputes are so often translated into technical terms, resolution of conflicts requires a reasonable distribution of expertise. Indeed, expertise is a crucial political resource, and if parties in conflict are to have any sense of political efficacy, they must have access to technical advice. In major inquiries, such as Windscale, the lack of technical resources among intervener groups seriously undermined their ability to present an effective counterargument. The French program for regional concertation has been criticized as a "phantom consultation" because regional councils lacked the expertise to evaluate EDF technical dossiers on the nuclear sites. Thus they could only respond in terms of traditional political alignments.

Inadequate distribution of expertise allows control of information. The Conseil d'Information in France can only respond to the information made available by public authorities. It cannot generate its own data nor insist that information be released. Thus, while leaders of ecology associates agree that the Conseil is an important concept, they believe it is "a bluff"—simply another way to subdue opposition.

In the German nuclear inquiries, only those documents that are part of the formal application to construct a plant are officially open to the public. Internal administrative evaluations are available on request but only at the discretion of the administration.

Control over information and its distribution is an important procedural consideration, for the selection of the technical data available for discussion may predetermine final decisions. Aware of the political implications of expertise, ad hoc "science for the people" groups have organized in many countries. They include Science for the People in the United States, the Wetenschapswinkels or "science shops" in the Netherlands, the Health Hazards groups in England, and Groupe de Scientifique d'Information sur Electronucléaire (GSIEN) in France. They distribute expertise to environmental and antinuclear groups lacking ability to generate the information required to challenge policies affecting their interests.

IS THERE REALLY A CHOICE?

In 1977 a public inquiry for a nuclear plant opened at Le Pellerin where local resistence had long been evident. The mayors of 7 out of 12 communes in the region had refused to use their offices for the inquiry, and documents had been stolen and burned in two city halls. The prefect was forced to open an "annex to the city hall" under police protection (*La Gazette Nucléaire* 17: 8 ff.). The population agreed to boycott the official inquiry; of the few people who did participate, 95 approved the project, 750 opposed it. About 80% to 95% of the population in each of several municipalities signed antinuclear petitions; one had 30,000 signatures. But the outcome of the inquiry was as unexpected as the whole procedure: The inquiry commissioners declared themselves incompetent to judge the issue, but nevertheless concluded in favor of the project.

This is an extreme example, but it suggests the low tolerance for disagreement in the public inquiry procedure. Most are simply structured discussions over predetermined policy with few real options. The financial and administrative investments involved in specific technologies are simply too great to allow a real margin of choice. Thus, when the first opposition to the nuclear plan appeared in Whyl, Germany, the Prime Minister of the Land said, prior to the licensing procedures: "There can be no doubt that Whyl will be constructed" (Wustenhagen, 1975: 61). In the case of a plant in Esensham, Germany, regional officials acknowledged that secret negotiations with the nuclear industry had taken place for more than a year prior to the official application for a construction license. And in several cases, Electricité de France began preparatory work on a construction before the end of inquiry procedures.

The limits of choice are evident in the very specific and short-term questions approached by most forums, except for those "reflection groups" specifically organized to consider the long-term effects of technology. Of all the advisory models, only the Dutch "policy intentions" seek to incorporate public opinion at an early stage when policy objectives are first articulated. Most are directed toward seeking informed consent rather than expanding democratic choice. Determination to implement preconceived decisions leads officials to ignore, to debunk, or simply to be unaware of opposition. And this results in the transfer of conflict from the hearings to the courts, and often to the streets.

CONCLUSIONS

Governments in most Western countries share a common set of political problems—how to reconcile technological systems with social values, how to develop sufficient consensus about controversial technologies to permit continued growth, how to clarify citizen interests and produce the political support necessary to make authoritative and acceptable decisions. The inadequacy of existing institutions to deal with this problem has inspired many experimental procedures designed to achieve consensus through better distribution of information and greater opportunities for public input into the decision-making process. These experiments open up a range of possibilities for institutional change and suggest a set of criteria that they provide no systematic solutions.

Comparative policy studies often approach common problems by seeking a "best solution" that can be transferred to other contexts. Our analysis is not to be interpreted in this way, for we find that the structure of these experiments—the definitions of "appropriate" procedures— varies, reflecting national political styles and expectations about the role of government, about participation, and about who represents the collective will. The approach to solving conflicts in a political context of consensus and compromise will differ from that in an adversary context: Holland, with its tradition of cleavage reflecting religious and regional differences, has had long experience in accommodating competing interests. It can be expected to develop quite different procedures from Sweden. The French tradition of open ideological factions within a centralized political and administrative structure calls for different conflict-resolving procedures than Germany, where consensus through internal negotiation within major party and union organization is expected. The structure of experiments and the assumptions about who should participate in programs seeking public involvement reflect basic political differences and cannot be simply transferred without consider- able adjustment. Indeed, transferring means of conflict resolution can pose problems not unlike those of technology transfer.

What can be generalized is not the structure of the experiments but the conditions that will allow dissenting groups to articulate effectively with administrative agencies: a careful definition of the agenda that gives due weight to social and political concerns, the appropriate involvement of affected interests, an unbiased management, a fair distribution of expertise, and a real margin of choice. In fact, these conditions are not likely to produce consensus, but they may reduce mistrust and hostility toward political and administrative institutions in order at least to allow detente. Our conclusion, however, is that detente is a more appropriate and realistic goal. Resolving conflicts is not necessarily always desirable. And seeking consensus is like wanting

100% risk-free technology—hardly a feasible objective. One of the more important effects of recent disputes is an awareness that decisions about technological risk are not simply matters of sufficient technical evidence and adequate information. They embody highly controversial political and social values, requiring institutions and procedures that will allow an open and balanced dialogue and enhance the constructive sense of collective responsibility necessary for legitimate and acceptable decisions.

NOTE

1. See, for example, a proposal by the American Arbitration Association in Strauss (1977). See also Hammond and Edelman (1976).

REFERENCES

ACKERMAN, B. (1974) The Uncertain Search for Environmental Quality. New York: Macmillan.

Bericht der Kommission fur Wirtschaftlichen und Sozialen Wandel (1976) Bonn: Author.

BUGLIARELLI, G. (1978) "A technological Magistrature." Bull. of the Atomic Scientist (January): 34-37.

Cambridge Experimentation Review Board (1976) Guidelines for the Use of Recombinant DNA Molecule Technology in the City of Cambridge, Submitted to the Commissioner of Health and Hospitals. Cambridge, MA: Author.

COLSON, J.-P. (1977) Le Nucléaire sans les Francais. Paris: Maspero.

GAMBLE, D. J. (1978) "The Berger inquiry." Science 199 (March): 946-951.

GLICK, J. C. (1976) "Reflections and speculations on the regulation of molecular genetic research," in M. Lappe and R. Morison (eds.) Ethical and Scientific Issues Posed by Human Uses of Molecular Genetics. Annals of the New York Academy of Sciences 265. New York: New York Academy of Science.

HAMMOND, K. R. and L. EDELMAN (1976) "Science, values and human judgment." Science 194 (October): 389-396.

International Atomic Energy Agency (1976) Unpublished document.

La Gazete Nucléaire (1978) May.

NAGEL, S. and K. VON MOLTKE (n.d.) "Citizen participation in planning decisions of public authorities." (mimeo)

NELKIN, D. (1978) Technological Decisions and Democracy. Beverly Hills, CA: Sage.

——— and M. POLLAK (1977) "The politics of participation and the nuclear debate in Sweden, the Netherlands and Austria." Public Policy 25 (Summer): 331-357.

STRAUSS, D. B. (1977) "Mediating environmental, energy and economic tradeoffs."
    AAAS Symposium on Environmental Mediation Cases, Denver, Colorado, February
    20-25.
SULLIVAN J. (1976) Letter to the City Council of Cambridge (August 6).
Task Force of the Presidential Advisory Group on Anticipated Advances in Science and
    Technology (1976) "The Science Court experiment." Science 193 (August 20).
WUSTENHAGEN, H. H. (1975) Burger Gegen Kernkraftwerke. Reinbek: Rowohlt.
WYNNE, B. (1978) "Nuclear debate at the crossroads." New Scientist (August 3): 349-360.

The Political Economy· of American Bureaucracy

SUSAN S. FAINSTEIN
NORMAN I. FAINSTEIN
Rutgers University

The deficiencies of governmental bureaucracy in the United States are rooted in the institutional and class context within which the state functions, in other words, the political economy of capitalism. For this reason, diagnoses that blame universal problems of large organizations or idiosyncracies and irrationalities of American public administration for poor governmental performance distort the real situation. The dominant ideology of advanced capitalism, which stresses the evils of state intervention, colors perceptions of the bureaucratic phenomenon. The attack on the state diverts attention from class privilege and enormous concentrations of private power in the economy. But perhaps even more importantly, it continually propagandizes the idea that state administration is opposed to private business, harassing it at every opportunity and wasting the labor of American citizens through unproductive bureaucrats and bungling interventions. While problems of governmental performance and accountability are real enough, they need to be seen within the totality of the public and private sectors. From this systemic perspective, public failure is frequently produced by private success; government agencies are ineffective because their missions are impossible; and the least controversial bureaucracies are those which smoothly serve the particular interests of capitalism and its dominant class. The task, then, is to reinterpret the shortcomings of

Authors' Note: *The authors wish to thank Paul Adams, George Sternlieb, and especially Robert Beauregard for their comments on earlier drafts of this article.*

bureaucratic performance and accountability within the parameters set by the distribution of power under capitalism.

In doing so, this chapter adopts a Marxist structuralist approach, which, while rooting the failures of American public bureaucracy in capitalism, does not discard liberal democratic values. Thus, it necessarily rejects both centralized state socialism and the conservative solution of market hegemony. The discussion begins by summarizing the Marxist interpretation of state administration; it examines the conservative attack on liberal expectations; it identifies the structurally based cause for alleged bureaucratic malfunction and lack of accountability; then it redefines the bureaucratic problem within the context of American capitalism.

BUREAUCRACY AND CAPITALISM

Positive liberalism, developed theoretically at the turn of the century and incorporated in New Deal and War on Poverty programs, calls for governmental activity to fill in gaps left by private initiative. The liberal hope is that the harshness of the capitalist market system can be tempered through humane public action. Within this context, the intentions of the state are generally regarded as beneficent, even if its capacity to produce intended results is found wanting.[1]

While liberals have sought to blame governmental malfunction on institutional shortcomings, contemporary Marxist critics have attributed the failings of state interventionism to fundamental contradictions within the political economy. O'Connor (1973) traces fiscal crisis to the demands placed on the state by monopoly capital, which requires government to assume the burden of fostering economic growth (capital accumulation), educating and maintaining the labor force, and coopting rebellion through the provision of welfare. At the same time, capitalists privately appropriate the return on publicly subsidized investment, leaving the government with insufficient funds to carry out its functions. O'Connor's analysis derives from Marx's characterization of the state as the executive committee of the bourgeoisie, carrying out the collective interests of the property-owning class. Most state expenditure, despite loose employment of the term "welfare state," subsidizes capitalists. The extent to which the state spends money directly to benefit the populace depends on the degree to which the masses threaten ruling-class interests, forcing the government to respond so as to retain its legitimacy. Miliband (1969) examines the political relationships of capitalist society and asserts that even when socialists capture the government, they cannot act in ways opposed to capitalist interests. Rather, they are bound by the hold which the economic elite has over the entire society—its ideological domination and its ability to threaten economic collapse. In Offe's (1975: 126) words, the "very decision-making power [of the capitalist state] *depends* (like every other social relationship in capitalist society) upon the presence and continuity of the accumulation process" (italics in original).

Contemporary Marxist analysts thus make three major points about the capitalist "welfare" state: (1) Its intervention is largely devoted to enhancing the process of capital accumulation rather than directly increasing the welfare of the masses; (2) it provides social benefits only as they are necessary for capitalist legitimation; (3) it is the servant rather than the master of the capitalist class. Massive state bureaucracies therefore arise in response to capitalist needs for nominally depoliticized structures to administer the common interests of the class as a whole.

Conservative opposition to liberal interventionism employs vastly different categories.[2] Rather than questioning the outcomes of bureaucratic activities (who benefits?), conservatives examine inputs (who directs the process? how much does government regulation cost?) and outputs (aggregate benefits). They agree that the interventionist state cannot succeed in its objectives, but do not blame this result on its capture by the economically dominant class. Instead, they see government as counterproductive in its efforts to regulate the economy; moreover, its attempts at assuring social welfare foster parasitism within both its bureaucratic ranks and its dependent clienteles. Implicit in this critique is the characterization of bureaucracy as a Frankenstein's monster, reified and uncontrollable, operating according to its own autonomous logic rather than rooted in the social structure. State administration is a monstrosity forever trampling on individual liberty. Far from being a way to defend capitalist privilege, the state spawns a new ruling class. Increased socialization of the economy can only mean replication of the Soviet model and the destruction of democratic pluralism and freedom of choice.

Accordingly, the conservative solutions to the problem of bureaucracy under capitalism are privatization and deregulation. Doubts about the responsiveness of the state sector express themselves through proposals for a negative income tax to substitute for state services or educational vouchers to replace centralized public school systems. This mistrust of state administration reflects a Weberian pessimism over social progress under state auspices.

The elements which Weber identified as endemic to bureaucracies—secrecy, lifetime tenure, rigidity—mean that the translation of broad social goals into actual governmental operations is distorted (Gerth and Mills, 1958: 196-204). Organizational maintenance displaces goal attainment as the main activity of bureaucrats (Merton, 1957). The Weberian argument, which underlies most modern sociological analyses, traces bureaucratic functioning to social interests, but it looks only at a narrow range of interests—those directly involved with the bureaucratic organization itself. As a result, it is not so much inaccurate—within its confines it is in fact quite valid—as it is misleading. It is misleading in two respects: first, in its selective factual discussion, which excludes private sector causes and failures; and second, in its definition of categories for analysis.

PUBLIC-PRIVATE COMPARISONS

The contention that public bureaucracies are not accountable to outside forces is both theoretically deducible and empirically verifiable within the boundaries of a discussion that looks at the public sector in isolation. Theoretically, it can be seen that bureaucratic clients have few sanctions over their caretakers and regulators, while politically appointed heads of bureaucracies are restricted from exerting substantial control by the unlimited tenure, expertise, and control over information of their subordinates. The testimony of disgruntled clients and ineffective agency heads corroborates these points.

But using these findings to condemn the public sector means avoiding appropriate comparisons with private bureaucracies. Large businesses, for example the oil companies, are not controlled at the top by representatives of the public nor at the bottom by their clienteles. Moreover, they are accorded rights of privacy not granted the government. In theory, private industry is accountable to its customers through the market. Yet in practice, the ability of individuals to choose alternative sources to replace unsatisfactory suppliers is hardly greater in the oligopolistic private sector than in the public domain. The only meaningful choice that remains in either area is boycott—people can opt to go without gasoline or food stamps. The consequences of such a decision, however, are far greater to the consumer than the provider. Where demand is inelastic and supply constrained, consumer sovereignty is a myth regardless of who owns the means of production.

Similarly, corruption within the public bureaucracies is usually discussed without examination of business practices. If public officials prostitute themselves, private businesses buy their services. Moreover, most of the rules for those in government service regarding competitive bidding, lack of favoritism, and refusal to accept emoluments are either nonexistent or unenforced in the corporate world. The hidden tax of corruption affects the public regardless of whether it is paying its costs to the Internal Revenue Service or a privately owned utility company.

Escalating administrative costs for programs are another example of selective use of facts to denigrate public but not private sector operations. The heads of large corporations routinely earn ten times as much as their government counterparts. The theory of the market is that consumers will force companies to reduce their costs by choosing a cheaper alternative. The fact of the matter is that public oversight keeps down the salaries of government officials, while consumer preference has no such effect on corporate management. The private entrepreneur who makes a fortune is applauded for his initiative; the public servant is castigated for his rapaciousness.

The seemingly uncontrollable growth of government has paralleled a corresponding expansion of the monopoly sector of private industry. Large organizations dwarf the individual, regardless of ownership. "Voice" (Hirschman, 1970) has some effect when applied to government—witness the triumphs of the tax revolt—but not when directed against private monopolies except as it evokes government regulation. Neither Marxists nor public choice theorists have presented a convincing alternative to organizational giganticism in an economy based on large-scale production. Enraged citizens have largely blamed government for their misery, not because it is less, but precisely because it is *more* controllable than business, and because the dominance of capitalist ideology diverts critical analysis from the hegemony of privately controlled organizations.

The differing standards used to judge public and private performance make comparisons of efficiency and effectiveness problematic. The state serves important latent functions which are distorted by commonly used evaluative criteria. Thus, if the government acts as employer of last resort, absorbing the unemployed created by private industry in its drive to cut labor costs, then the low productivity of the public service needs to be seen as a price of capitalism rather than of government alone. Likewise, excessive government expenditure on public works fuels private profit and is generated by capitalist pressure. Ultimately, the translation of cost savings by private industry into profit contributes no more to the general welfare than does government "waste," less so if that waste is widely distributed.

For bureaucracies with a primarily lower-class clientele, the popular criterion for success is a trend toward disappearance rather than good service or growth. Thus, welfare bureaucracies are rarely attacked for inefficiency in distributing checks; rather they are called to account for permitting the rolls to increase. Presumably the best welfare agency would distribute no benefits at all. Now that welfare clienteles are demobilized, the welfare bureaucracies are again more responsive to taxpayer and business groups, the "welfare problem" has been mitigated; the rolls have been cut, and inflation has been permitted to reduce real benefit levels.

The facts of poor public performance therefore seem less self-evident when examined in a context that includes the private sector. But our argument goes further than this. The very way in which the conservative critique is phrased begs certain questions; it is inherently nondialectical and segmented. By seeing public and private as antinomies, the conservative argument attacks the public sector rather than seeing it as a consequence of the political economy of advanced capitalism. Public and private function and malfunction are intimately related, and major reforms of either sector require systemic change in the nature of political control over the economy.

A REDEFINITION OF THE CATEGORIES
OF ANALYSIS: EFFECTIVENESS

The fact of capitalism has enormous implications for the operation of governmental bureaucracies. Put bluntly, it means that when government acts in the public interest, it maintains and strengthens business institutions and class inequality. Because everyone's life depends on business, responsible governments must create situations conducive to corporate success. In doing so, they divert tax revenues raised from the majority of citizens—the real tax rate is, after all, barely progressive—to the benefit of corporations and their owners. Nationally, defense spending, investment tax credits, and depreciation allowances reward business for pursing profitability. At the local level, debt, especially bonded debt sold by municipal governments to private owners of capital, provies direct benefits to capitalists: First, they receive a low-risk (and labor-free) return on investment; and second, they profit from public expenditures for economic development which facilitate capital accumulation. On the public side of the balance sheet, however, debt service comes to take over an ever larger chunk of operating budgets. The result is revenue-starved municipal service agencies with declining performance, fiscal stress, and taxpayers' revolts. Washington can print money, so nationally the outcome is inflation and consequent efforts to hold down social expenditures benefiting the lower classes.

Consider an example or two. During the late 1950s, downtown corporations and hotels supported the efforts of the San Francisco Redevelopment Agency to renew a "blighted" neighborhood south of Market Street in order to construct a high convention facility—Yerba Buena Center (Hartman, 1974). The direct beneficiaries in the first instance would be the tourist industry and business generally. The city government would be a secondary beneficiary through increased property tax revenue. Thousands of lower-income people were displaced, as were hundreds of small businesses. Since there would be revenue-producing facilities in Yerba Buena (a hotel, garages, and so on), the Redevelopment Agency was able to float bonds without public referendum. Ten years later, Yerba Buena Center still is not producing any revenue, but its financial obligations are being met with municipal and federal resources. Even when the center begins to function, it almost certainly will create a continual drain on the municipal budget, as a second and equally typical case illustrates.

The New York Yankees threatened to leave town unless their stadium was refurbished. "Under duress," the city agreed to expend about $28 million of its capital budget on the job and to grant the Yankees a lease on very favorable terms. To abbreviate the story, a decade or so later New York City is servicing a debt of $125 million, and the Yankees are making very large profits indeed. Multiply the Yerba Buenas and Yankee Stadiums a hundredfold, and you have a major cause of urban fiscal crisis. The very governments which have continually sought to subsidize business are then charged with inefficient performance by the business class. Municipal bankruptcy is attributed to the high wages and low outputs of working- and middle-class employees or to excessive kindness toward the poor. And the superior performance of private bureaucracies is trumpeted to the citizenry.

Conversely, when public administration takes on missions contrary to capitalist interests, it becomes mired in conflict and suffers withdrawals of support from corporations and economically powerful groups. The possibilities of good bureaucratic performance are severely restricted by arrangements which are defined as outside the sphere of the state. Governmental agencies are structurally related to private business so as to be constrained by at least one of three factors: (1) Private profit is enhanced (if not directly created) by public debt or by tax revenues derived disproportionately from the working and middle classes; (2) the private sector monopolizes profitable activities; public agencies are left with tasks which produce no financial rewards and are difficult to accomplish, such as housing the poor, educating the masses, and cleaning the streets; and (3) their effectiveness is hampered severely by private control over the means of production, i.e., by private control over most of the really important decisions which directly determine social structure and quality of life, including what is to be produced, where, and at what wage rate.

The tasks of public agencies are made more difficult by private control of the means of production. The image comes to mind of the postman carrying heavy advertisements while ITT transmits computer telecommunications. To the extent that public operations are relatively labor intensive, they are inevitably susceptible to breakdowns of human organization. Even beyond this, governmental bureaucracies rarely have the ability to control an entire process of production. Thus, the public schools train children for economic success, yet have no control over the requirements of private employers. The Department of Energy is supposed to insure an adequate supply of gasoline, but it cannot even command accurate data from the oil companies, much less itself extract petroleum from the ground and process it. The Department of Housing and Urban Development (HUD) can subsidize low-income housing, but it can neither build units itself nor divert private investment from middle-class suburban development. In each case, the public bureaucracy is inefficient and ineffective. But its problems are foreordained by the conditions under which public agencies operate.

The environments of bureaucracies are defined not only by administrative and legal structures, but also by classes and interest groups, by political milieus of consensus or conflict, by missions which serve the rich and powerful or the poor and weak. Just as inequality and conflict are the "other side" of capitalist economic structures, so too are they central elements in the bureaucratic context. From a Marxist structuralist perspective, the mission, resources, and performance of state administration are the outcomes of political struggle, defined more or less directly by class conflict. The performance of various state agencies will be affected by which class interests they serve and by how well those interests are mobilized. State agencies routinely serve the need of capital, but only serve the lower class when pressured from below.

Agencies with lower-class constituencies will be regularly assaulted by upper-class groups for their inefficiency, ineffectiveness, and conflictual operation. Of course, this very attack, combined with lack of cooperation, contributes to agency failure.

We suggest that the relative effectiveness of state bureaucracies will increase as agency activity *corresponds* to upper-class interest. So too will praise for such agencies by powerful political elements. Thus, some bureaucracies will be routinely supported, while others will suffer the continual sniping which further hampers their performance. A brief list of the conditions which make for a "supportive" class environment might look like this:

(1) The agency *does not* carry out activities which, if undertaken by business, can produce a profit;
(2) *does* increase profitability of capital in general;
(3) *does* increase profitability for particular, well-organized fractions of capital;
(4) *does not* redistribute material benefits toward the lower classes;
(5) *does* contribute to social control;
(6) *is not* accountable to lower-class constituencies.

While most cases will be mixed in terms of these six criteria, they do help us differentiate between the environments of, say, the Army Corps of Engineers and the Office of Economic Opportunity (OEO), or the Federal Housing Administration and the Model Cities Administration. Only political struggle is likely to produce agencies in major violation of the conditions of correspondence. Some past victories over private capital may, however, in a new historical period result in bureaucracies which become more acceptable to the upper classes as their benefits become increasingly obvious. Consider public power and Social Security Public power was and still is bitterly opposed by private utilities for its violation of our first condition. But in the West, public power agencies have also come to meet the second and third by giving industry the benefits of cheap power. Social Security was initially opposed by business because it had redistributive potential. But the program became shaped so as to facilitate social control without being strongly redistributive and without violating the first and sixth conditions. The lesson of the Social Security Administration, in contrast, for instance, to OEO, is that government agencies which assist the poor must also not threaten capital if they are to operate at all well, or even survive longer than the period of mobilization in which they were born.

The relative importance of the several conditions in affecting bureaucratic functioning depends on the overall state of mobilization and consciousness of the classes in capitalist society. Northern European capitalist states differ from the United States in their much greater degree of state planning, in their broader "welfare" activities (e.g., health care and housing), and in the overall higher legitimacy of public administration in the eyes of corporate management (Fainstein and Fainstein, 1978). These differences result in part from European acceptance of a larger realm of public production and of the subordination of particular capitalist interests to those of the whole class, as defined by the state administration itself. The greater viability of Northern European welfare bureaucracies, however, also derives from the far greater strength of working-class parties there than here. The acceptability to the upper classes of redistribution (the fourth condition) depends on a payoff in social control (the fifth condition). Where the lower classes are poorly organized (as in the United States), they can be controlled without redistribution. The point here is that public bureaucratic performance is both a major factor in ideological conflict and is strongly affected by the interplay between agency mission on the one hand and the balance of forces within and between classes on the other.

LACK OF ACCOUNTABILITY

Accountability, defined as the ability of individuals or groups to monitor and control bureaucratic performance, involves different considerations from effectiveness. In general, the agencies which routinely serve capitalist interests are infrequently criticized as unaccountable, and these include much of the state administration. Put another way, because the Federal Reserve Board and the Department of Commerce act in the public interest as defined by the business class and its dominant ideology, procedural issues about how such agencies are governed do not customarily arise. Indeed, bureaucracies which represent the interests of capital are frequently unaccountable to the electorate. As Friedland et al. (1977) show, economic development agencies, port authorities, pension funds, and the like—bureaucracies which command vast capital resources—are, segmented off from the political process, made invisible. So these agencies, at all levels of government, are not part of the accountability problem for the upper classes. Nor are they under much attack from below, since they are effectively obscured by administrative arrangements: Their actual importance and the interests they serve are mystified by the dominant ideology. Agencies which directly serve the interests of capital (called "the economy") are perceived as outside politics and thus outside contests of accountability. No one, in fact, is preoccupied with the activities of these agencies except those interests which can profit directly from their activities.

The accountability problems of state bureaucracies which are not obscured and depoliticized stem from the basic contradictions between democracy and capitalism. On the one hand, the state is legitimated as reflecting the public interest defined by electoral majorities (albeit through a complex process of representation). On the other hand, the state is fully committed to economic growth at home and security abroad. It must attain these objectives within the context of corporate organization of production and class hierarchy. Moreover, economic growth is required if the upper classes are to maintain their privilege and the lower classes to remain peaceful. Therefore, the state must further capitalist accumulation and must define the public interests as coincident with the interests of capital and the upper classes. In other words, the state must benefit upper-class minorities, while appearing to be controlled by working-and middle-class majorities.

A very important way in which this feat gets accomplished is through the relative autonomy within the state of the administrative apparatus. Legislative debate can center about what the people want, while the state administration looks after what capital needs. In the process, bureaucracies inevitably make policy. While in rare instances (for example, OEO), these bureaucracies interpret legislative intent in favor of the lower classes, by far the more usual situation is to go the other way, to put into practice what legislators hesitate to put into words. Thus, the FBI is officially established to fight criminals and enemy spies but in operation it also acts to intimidate political radicals. State public utility commissions officially intended to control the industry become vehicles for protecting profits. Redevelopment agencies, charged with eliminating slums and blight, end up displacing the poor into even worse neighborhoods.

In each case, when mass mobilization of some egregious event demystifies the operations of the agency in question, politicians declare an accountability problem. The FBI is said to be too independent of the Department of Justice; the utility commission should have a gubernatorial appointment representing public interest groups; redevelopment agencies are required to provide structures for citizen participation. The fault is with the bureaucracy, not with the intrinsic character of the state. The politicians symbolically slap administrative hands and reaffirm the democratic character of government. Accountability problems become pathologies in a healthy democratic body politic. When they are spotted, they are blamed on the bureaucratic phenomenon and duly exorcised. Legitimacy is reestablished.

Another publicly defined accountability problem is that Washington bureaucrats are "too remote" from the electorate, while local government is more easily controlled and responsive. Here again, the definition of the problem must be understood as ideology which obscures or safely redefines the actual situation. The ideology of localism has its roots in the business class and is expressed through conservative attacks on big government and faceless Washington bureaucrats. Business concern over runaway Washington, however, focuses on welfare programs and regulatory activities, not defense spending, central banking, and loan guarantees. Moreoer, the distribution of power within the federal system benefits business. Corporations need a strong central government with flexible revenue resources and the capacity to regulate the national economy. At the same time, local governments and thousands of separate jurisdictions permit the upper classes to encapsulate themselves in homogeneous residential areas, thereby escaping the social costs of the lower classes; and local jurisdictions permit corporate flight from onerous taxation or labor organization. Federalism produces a general system of local mercantilism from which business benefits immensely.

Conservatives, particularly in the corporate sector, further object that Washington bureaucracies engulf them with oceans of red tape, requiring endless documentation, thereby adding needlessly to business costs. Here again, some of the objection must be understood as actually based in the substantive programs in question. It is not just red tape but *red* tape when the government tries to control pollution or requires minority employment. Yet there certainly is actual basis for claiming that Washington administrative agencies require disproportionately great amounts of paper work, often for no apparent purpose. The irony here is that Washington red tape proliferates precisely because of the state structure in which the central government cannot direct economic production and does not even control the means of public administration. Facing two markets—one of the business and the other of local governments—Washington agencies attempt to implement programs at a distance through the carrot of subsidy and the stick of regulation. Each approach is associated with red tape in the application for funds, monitoring of performance, and proof of compliance. Thus, the very weakness of the central government—an objective of conservatives—

contributes to some of the annoying requirements of its administrative agencies, which must depend on regulation as a substitute for operational authority.

Over all then, governmental bureaucracies *are* accountable, if not to the citizens of democratic theory, then to the corporate interests of capitalist practice. While bureaucratic accountability, like bureaucratic performance, does indeed constitute a universal problem of governance, the real problem of the American state system is not unaccountable bureaucracies, but the class to which they are routinely accountable. The problem lies not so much in bureaucracy itself as in the political economy of American capitalism.

DEMOCRATIC CONTROL OF BUREAUCRACY: IS THERE A SOLUTION?

Questions of performance ultimately reduce themselves to questions of control. Social organizations crystallize sets of human relationships based on ownership of resources and psychologically rooted patterns of domination and subordination.[3] If organizations function below their theoretical capacity, it is because they are commanded by internal or external constituencies which are not their manifest beneficiaries. For example, if garbage collectors spend half their day drinking coffee instead of gathering trash, then the work schedule is controlled by them rather than the householders whose refuse is neglected. If utility rates rise because a generator breaks down, then the companies rather than the customers control the regulatory commission. Under the current system of American capitalism, public bureaucracies serve the interests of the economically dominant class, but they must also mediate tensions placed upon the state apparatus by other social groupings mobilized as voters, bureaucatic clients, politicians, and bureaucrats themselves. In the absence of private economic privilege, the other bases of identification become more significant in determining who has power.

Those of us who critize the present system from the left are vulnerable to the rejoinder that we can offer no alternative arrangement which solves the problem of bureaucratic control. Elimination of private ownership gives rise to new sources of domination. Its demise means that the state apparatus itself becomes the principal resource in the drive for social power. Our reasoning does not deny the problems of state domination under socialism; they are mentioned here both to indicate the weak-nesses of the Marxist utopia (although not its critique) and to suggest directions for overcoming these problems. In brief, the obstacles to transcending the situation of domination by the governing class through the state apparatus can be summed up under two categories, one universal, and one peculiar to the socialist analysis.

The universal difficulty. Even if it can be shown that under capitalism bureaucracy is an instrument of class power, the end of capitalism will not eliminate social hierarchy or domination. Dahrendorf (1959) persuasively contends that divisions exist between the haves and have-nots regardless of whether the stakes are financial or positional. As long as the social setting contains good and bad jobs, access to scarce goods or lack of it, positions of authority and subordination, individuals will seek not only to capture the top places, but to cement their hold on them and pass them on to their progeny.

The Marxist paradigm disregards the psychological motives which sustain manipulation and suppression. As a result, it is unsatisfactory without modification as an explanation for modes of domination based on gender or status. While Marxism proposes a social transformation which would terminate class-based oppression, it too easily reduces other unequal relationships to a material basis. A complex analysis of bureaucracy must examine the disposition of social surplus under alternative social arrangements and explore ways of designing institu-tional structures so that bureaucratic cadres or political officials cannot use their positions to expropriate what justly belongs to others.[4]

The socialist difficulty. All political-economic systems contain arrangements for social sorting, and no advanced economy is without extreme differences in power. The problem, however, reaches a particularly acute form where the state controls the economy, thereby creating a monolithic system fusing political and economic institutions and justifying the hegemony of the ruling group through a powerful ideology of communal interest. Even though under capitalism the state acts on behalf of the capitalist class, it does not totally belong to that class, at least in the United States or the other liberal democracies. A centralized state dominating a centralized economy inevitably produces a new class (Djilas, 1957) of political rulers, who are largely unchecked in their ability to dominate society at large. Under such a system, the state administration, as distinct from the party, retains a hold upon a portion of the surplus, but the difficulty is primarily a political rather than a bureaucratic one.

Nevertheless, the contrast between capitalist liberal pluralism and socialist centralism should not obscure the fact that most capitalist states are not liberal democracies. Moreover, pluralism itself is not an unmitigated blessing. Dispersed inequalities (Dahl, 1961) are not necessarily preferable to centralized hierarchy and may be harder to regulate. Pluralism is as likely to provide protected enclaves for the provileged as access for the putatively upwardly mobile. The preferability of feudal tyranny to monarchical rule was not clear-cut for the mass of people in the past; neither is the preferability of capitalist pluralist to state domination today.

Such a Hobson's Choice, however, is hardly a defense of the socialist position, and the political difficulty of creating a democratic socialism remains. Marx's evasive prophecy that the government of men will give way to the administration of things does not suffice as even a serious counterargument. There remain two other often proposed strategies, which in their bluntest statement are equally naive, but must be incorporated into any democratic solution of the bureaucratic problem.

The first of these is the anarchist-syndicalist argument, which requires the breakdown of large institutions, including both government and the corporations. Whether social order and a productive economy can be maintained under conditions of radical democracy and small-scale production is unclear (although not obvious). The assertions of some Marxists (Braverman, 1974; Bowles and Gintis, 1976) that the large production unit is designed for labor discipline rather than efficiency ducks the issue of whether efficient production is not directly dependent upon some form of coercion. To put this question another way, how much of the repression involved in modern production is surplus, in Marcuse's (1955) sense,[5] and how much is necessary for everyone's standard of living? Necessary repression must be administered by someone. In addition, while small-scale production and governance reduce the size of the bureaucratic stratum at the level of the productive or governing unit, they give rise to the need of an elaborate bureaucracy to plan and coordinate relationships among the units. Unregulated operation of a small-scale political economy means that there is nothing to prevent the resurgence of corporate domination, and nothing to create the level of environmental protection and individual welfare achievable only through national planning and taxation.

The capitalist public choice solution, as distinct from socialist anarchism, gives no protection to those social groups who lack market power. It is Social Darwinism in new clothes. Even theoretically, it can only work in an economy where monopoly and oligopoly have been eliminated, though it offers no explanation as to how this situation can be achieved in the absence of government regulation. The market, however, does present a decisional mode which avoids the intrusion of a communal body, whether bureaucratic or democratic, into every collective choice. The challenge for a socialist political theory is to incorporate arenas of market freedom into a system governed overall by communal and egalitarian principles, controlled by the votes of citizens rather than the dollars of owners and investors.

DEMOCRATIZATION

Is it possible to have a more democratic bureaucracy within the United States? Several considerations are in order, involving the nature of the present bureaucratic problem, the lessons of recent political history, and, more speculatively, the likelihood of future events. With regard to the bureaucratic problem, certain things are clear. The reduction of state power—debureaucratization—can only lead to greater influence for market rationality and the capitalist class. Short of some monumental negation of the capitalist economic system, the only possible counter to the unmitigated social domination of business necessarily lies in a strong state, though as we have argued, not in the state as presently constituted. The democratization of the state administration must involve its reorientation, the incorporation of lower- and working-class interests into institutional arrangements and into the reference groups of state officials. Large bureaucracies, however, can only be made more democratically accountable through administrative and political decentralization, that is, by a vastly greater role for the lower classes in the governance of bureaucracies at their output ends. The incorporation of new political interests among elected officials must be combined with sufficient administrative reorganization to provide the additional check of client empowerment on administrative behavior. Such changes are radical because they are defined by major shifts in power between classes, and they cannot be achieved without the mobilization of lower- and working-class forces.

Democratization cannot be permanently implemented from the top, nor can it be free from conflict. During the 1960s, progressive reformers initiated two federal programs aimed more or less explicitly at increasing the political power of lower- and working-class populations over urban bureaucracies, as well as at incorporating their interest in new federal agencies. These were the Community Action Programs sponsored by OEO and the Model Cities agencies established by HUD. In many cities, the programs were used as vehicles for further popular mobilizations and constituted centeres of power in opposition to local governments, especially to their accumulation and social control activities. Thus, CAP legal services initiated class-action suits against local police departments and renewal agencies, and frequently represented clients in their dealings with health and welfare bureaucracies. Model Cities agencies advanced explicitly redistributive service programs and plans for community redevelopment in opposition to downtown business interests. The further these programs moved toward effecting democratization, however, the more they came under attack, were defined as divisive, irresponsible, and corrupt. The two were rather quickly vitiated, and then dismantled, as their potential class character and danger to state accumulation activities became apparent, not just to their conservative detractors, but to their liberal sponsors as well. Community Action and Model Cities became defined as "failures" and were maintained for several years only because of mobilized local constituencies.

Urban political movements pushing for bureaucratic enfranchisement produced even more severe conflict because of their lower-class character. Here mobilization genrally preceded programs, and movements were attacked for their tactics of direct action, as well as their objectives, and latter defined by critics as the "politization" of administrative agencies. Moreover, their social base in urban minority groups antagonized white elements within the working class who feared that urban political movements threatened their own interests. Thus, the movements rooted in lower-class communities were not much more effective or long-lasting than the new administrative agencies sponsored directly by progressive government officials. Indeed, it appears that the more mobilized the force for change from the bottom, the greater the political conflict and political reaction.

This lesson of the 1960s does not suggest that democratization can be effected from inside the state, but rather that it requires a base broader than urban minority communities, and that it must be structured through the organizational vehicle of a political party able to capture elected offices. Such a party should be capable of redefining the dominant ideology and its definitions of lower-class action if it is to have a chance of obtaining democratic objectives; it can do so, however, only if it already has sufficient strength. This is the dilemma of a democratic movement in the United States: how to overcome the hegemony of liberal ideology and thereby create a base of popular support.[6] Without the emergence of a class-based party, the American mass will continue to rebel against government; it will remain alienated. But it will continue to be manipulated into the misplaced diagnosis of its troubles as stemming from big government and bureaucracy as such. Its solutions will be tax cuts rather than reform, small government instead of democracy.

At the present moment, the likelihood of either a transformation in the character of the Democratic Party or the formation of a new mass party is small. The American left is in disarray. Its traditional trade union constituency has largely disintegrated; neither race nor client status offers a consistent basis for organization. The "neighborhood movement" has evoked considerable comment, but its existence is more significant in the press releases of its publicists than in the activity of its reputed following. To the extent that neighborhood does provide the basis for political organization, its grasp is limited and its ideology pragmatic.

Without a social force pressing for major change, and in the absence of acute economic crisis, there will be no democratic transformation. Instead, there will be political stalemate and limitations on the power of the public bureaucracies. But limitations on government mean that checks on private power will diminish. The more visible despotism of public authority will be replaced by the disguised control of corporate power legitimized as public choice. Because inadequate resources give most people few alternatives, a nominal pluralism will continue to be the ideological screen which obfuscates the imperviousness of private organizations to democratic control.

NOTES

1. The term "state" encompasses both bureaucratic and political roles within the public sector. Our concern here, however, and the scapegoat for most declarations of governmental failure, is with the state bureaucracy (or more correctly within the United States, bureaucracies).

2. The description "conservative" used throughout this article refers to arguments pressed by a variety of bureaucratic critics, who do not necessarily share the same basic

social values. Thus, some liberals share conservative doubts concerning the responsiveness of the state sector and press for reduction of the bureaucratic role, even though they may place a higher weight on equality as a social goal.

3. Crozier's (1964) explanation of the bureaucratic phenomenon traces it to psychological defenses arising from status incongruities.

4. Marcuse (1955) uses the term "surplus repression" to distinguish between the amounts of constraint necessary and unnecesary for social functioning. George Sternlieb in a personal communication, suggests that the criterion for determining the extent of bureaucratic domination is the amount of surplus captured by the bureaucracy itself. Within a capitalist society, the calculation of bureaucratic impact must assess whether the portion of the surplus taken by bureaucracy is withdrawn from what would be the normal share of capital or labor.

5. See note 4 above.

6. Michels's (1962) problem of goal displacement and elitism within the party need not be faced until this happens.

REFERENCES

BOWLES, S. and H. GINTIS (1976) Schooling in Capitalist America. New York: Basic.

BRAVERMAN, H. (1974) Labor and Monopoly Capital. New York: Monthly Review Press.

CROZIER, M. (1964) The Bureaucratic Phenomenon. Chicago: Univ. of Chicago Press.

DAHL, R. (1961) Who Governs? New Haven, CT: Yale Univ. Press.

DAHRENDORF, R. (1959) Class and Class Conflict in Industrial Societies. Palo Alto, CA: Stanford Univ. Press.

DJILAS, M. (1957) The New Class. New York: Praeger.

FAINSTEIN, S. and N. FAINSTEIN (1978) "National policy and urban development." Social Problems 28: 125-146.

FRIEDLAND, R., F. F. PIVEN, and R. R. ALFORD (1977) "Political conflict, urban structure, and the fiscal crisis." Int. J. of Urban and Regional Research 1: 447-473.

GERTH, H. H. and C. W. MILLS [eds.] (1958) From Max Weber. New York: Oxford Univ. Press.

HARTMAN, C. (1974) Yerba Buena-Land Grab and Community Resistance in San Francisco. San Francisco: Glide Publications.

HIRSCHMAN, A. O. (1970) Exit, Voice, and Loyalty. Cambridge, MA: Harvard Univ. Press.

MARCUSE, H. (1955) Eros and Civilization. Boston: Beacon.

MERTON, R. K. (1957) Social Theory and Social Structure. New York: Macmillan.

MICHELS, R. (1962) Political Parties. New York: Macmillan.

MILIBAND, R. (1969) The State in Capitalist Society. New York: Basic.

O'CONNOR, J. (1973) The Fiscal Crisis of the State. New York: St. Martin's.

OFFE, K. (1975) "The theory of the capitalist state and the problem of policy formation,' in L. N. Lindberg et al. (eds.) Stress and Contradiction in Modern Capitalism. Lexington, MA: D. C. Heath.

INDEX

ABOUT THE AUTHORS

JOEL D. ABERBACH is a Senior Fellow in the Governmental Studies Program of the Brookings Institution, Washington, D.C., and Professor of Political Science and Research Scientist in the Institute of Public Policy Studies at the University of Michigan. His research includes work on alienation and voting behavior, race relations, and the political ideologies of American congressmen and administrators. He is now conducting a study of congressional oversight for the Brookings Institution and recently served as consultant on oversight to the Commission of the Operation of the Senate. He is the author (with Jack S. Walker) of *Race in the City* (Little, Brown, 1973) and of numerous articles in scholarly journals.

ALLEN H. BARTON is Professor of Sociology at Columbia University and specializes in political sociology, research on elites, and methodology. He has written on opinion-making elites in Yugoslavia, decentralizing city government, and communities in disaster, and for fifteen years was Director of the Bureau of Applied Social Research at Columbia.

ALAN K. "SCOTTY" CAMPBELL is the Director of the Office of Personnel Management, the central personnel agency of the U.S. government. He was named to the post in 1979 by President Carter after serving as Chairman of the U.S. Civil Service Commission. Dr. Campbell played a major role in developing the Civil Service Reform Act of 1978 and in guiding the legislation through the Congress. Before coming to Washington, Dr. Campbell served as the Dean of the LBJ School of Public Affairs at the University of Texas and Dean of the Maxwell School of Citizenship and Public Affairs at Syracuse University.

DAVID K. COHEN is Professor of Education and Social Policy at the Harvard University Graduate School of Education. Previously, he was a visiting professor at the Institution for Social and Policy Studies at Yale University.

YEHEZHEL DROR is Professor of Political Science at the Hebrew University of Jerusalem. He has worked for the Rand Corporation. His publications include *Public Policymaking Re-Examined, Design for Policy Sciences, Ventures in Policy Science,* and *Crazy States.*

NORMAN I. FAINSTEIN teaches in the Department of Urban Affairs and Policy Analysis, New School for Social Research. With Susan S. Fainstein, he has written a number of articles on American social policy as well as the book, *Urban Political Movements.*

SUSAN S. FAINSTEIN teaches in the Department of Urban Planning and Policy Development, Livingston College, Rutgers University. She has written a number of articles and the book, *Urban Political Movements,* with Norman I. Fainstein.

DONALD L. HOROWITZ is a Senior Fellow at the Smithsonian Institution's Research Institute on Immigration and Ethnic Studies. He received law degrees at Syracuse and Harvard and a Ph.D. from Harvard. He has served in the Department of Justice and at the Harvard University Center for International Affairs, has been a Fellow of the Woodrow Wilson International Center for Scholars and a staff member of the Brookings Institution. Mr. Horowitz is the author of *The Jurocracy,* a book about government lawyers, and *The Courts and Social Policy,* which won the Louis Brownlow Prize of the National Academy of Public Administration. In the fall, he will deliver the McDonald-Currie Memorial Lectures at McGill University.

CHARLES E. LINDBLOM is Sterling Professor of Economics and Political Science at Yale University and Director of Yale's Institution for Social and Policy Studies. His most recent publications are *Politics and Markets* and, with David K. Cohen, *Usable Knowledge,* from which the present analysis is taken.

GIANDOMENICO MAJONE is currently Professor of Statistics at the Faculty of Economic and Social Sciences of the Universita della Calabria. After receiving his Ph.D. from the University of California, Berkeley, he taught at the Universities of Rome, Bologna, and British Columbia, was a visiting scholar at the Russell Sage Foundation and Philip R. Allen Visiting Professor at Yale. He has published extensively in the fields of applied statistics, decision-making, and policy analysis.

NANCY A. MATHIOWETZ began research on the article in this volume while she was an undergraduate in the Department of Sociology at the University of Wisconsin, Madison. She is currently in the Public Health program at the University of Michigan, Ann Arbor. She is specializing in studies of the validity and reliability of survey methods of data collection.

STEPHAN MICHELSON is a principal in Econometrics Research, Inc., a Washington, D.C. research and consulting firm. He was formerly Senior Fellow at the Urban Institute and, before that, Research Director at the Center for Community Economic Development in Cambridge, Massachusetts. He has a Ph.D. (economics) from Stanford, and has taught at Reed College, Stanford, Harvard, and the University of California at Irvine.

WILLIAM C. MITCHELL has been Professor of Political Science at the University of Oregon since 1965. He has been a visiting professor at Northwestern University, UCLA, the University of California, Berkeley, and Cornell University. He has been a Fellow of the Center for Advanced Study in the Behavioral Sciences and a member of the Social Science Research Council Committee on the Comparative Study of Public Policy. His several books and monographs include *The American Polity* (1962), *Sociological Analysis and Politics* (1967), *Political Analysis and Public Policy* (with Joyce M. Mitchell, 1969), *Public Choice in America* (1971), *Why Vote?* (1971), *The Popularity of Social Security: A Paradox in Public Choice* (1977), and *The Anatomy of Public Failure: A Public Choice Perspective* (1978).

DOROTHY NELKIN is a Professor in the Cornell University Program on Science, Technology, and Society. She is President of the Society for the Social Studies of Science and a Fellow of the Hastings Center for Society, Ethics, and the Life Sciences. Her research focuses on the political issues associated with science and technology in the United States and Western Europe. Among her books are *Controversy: The Politics of Technical Decisions; Science Textbook Controversies and the Politics of Equal Time,* and *Technological Decisions and Democracy.* With Michael Pollak, she is now writing a book on the nuclear energy controversies in France and Germany, *The Atom Besieged Extra-Parliamentary Dissent in France and Germany,* forthcoming from MIT Press.

WILLIAM A. NISKANEN is the Director, Economics of the Ford Motor Company. He previously served as Professor, Graduate School of Public Policy, Berkeley, and in various positions at OMB, IDA, the Department of Defense, and at Rand Corporation. He is the author of *Bureaucracy and Representative Government* and numerous articles.

MICHAEL POLLAK is a research associate in the Program on Science, Technology, and Society at Cornell University. He studied sociology in Austria and France and has a Ph.D. from the Sorbonne. He worked at the OECD's Directorate for Science, Technology, and Industry and as a consultant for the French Ministry of Planning. He has published books on social science policy and on French sociology. With Dorothy Nelkin, he is presently writing a book on the nuclear energy controversies in France and Germany, *The Atom Besieged: Extra-parliamentary Dissent in France and Germany.*

FRANCIS E. ROURKE is a Professor of Political Science at Johns Hopkins University. He has also taught at Yale University and the University of California at Berkeley. Among the books he has authored are *Secrecy and Publicity: Dilemmas of Democracy; Bureaucracy, Politics and Public Policy;* and *Bureaucracy and Foreign Policy.*

TOM W. SMITH is the Associate Study Director of the General Social Survey at the National Opinion Research Center. He specializes in nineteenth-century social history and trend and cohort analysis.

D. GARTH TAYLOR is currently an Assistant Professor in the Department of Political Science at the University of Chicago and a senior study director at the National Opinion Research Center. His main area of interest is in the theory and methods of public opinion research.

CAROL H. WEISS is at the Harvard University Graduate School of Education where she is doing research on the usefulness of social science research for government decision makers. Recognition of the uncertain effects of research on decisions led to her interest in the processes of bureaucratic decision-making. She is the author of *Evaluation Research: Methods of Assessing Program Effectiveness, Evaluating Action Programs: Readings in Social Action and Education, Using Social Research in Public Policy Making,* and the forthcoming *Social Science Research and Decision-Making.*

AARON WILDAVSKY is Professor of Political Science at the University of California, Berkeley. He is the author of *Speaking Truth to Power: The Art and Craft of Policy Analysis* (Little, Brown, 1979) and other works on politics and public policy.

ROBERT K. YIN is a Visiting Associate Professor at the Department of Urban Studies and Planning, M.I.T. He divides his time between Cambridge and Washington, D.C., where he maintains an independent consulting practice. Previously, Dr. Yin worked for nine years at the Rand Corporation. He has authored several books, including *Street-Level Governments* and *Changing Urban Bureaucracies,* and published numerous articles in such journals as the *Journal of Experimental Psychology, Administrative Science Quarterly, Policy Sciences,* and *Sociological Methods and Research.*